Democracy and Defiance

Let your life be a counter-friction to stop the machine.
Henry David Thoreau, *Civil Disobedience*

Democracy and Defiance

Rancière, Lefort, Abensour and the Antinomies of Politics

BRYAN NELSON

EDINBURGH
University Press

Edinburgh University Press is one of the leading university presses in the UK. We publish academic books and journals in our selected subject areas across the humanities and social sciences, combining cutting-edge scholarship with high editorial and production values to produce academic works of lasting importance. For more information visit our website: edinburghuniversitypress.com

© Bryan Nelson, 2024

Edinburgh University Press Ltd
13 Infirmary Street
Edinburgh EH1 1LT

Typeset in 11/13 Adobe Sabon by
IDSUK (DataConnection) Ltd, and
printed and bound in Great Britain

A CIP record for this book is available from the British Library

ISBN 978-1-4744-7722-2 (hardback)
ISBN 978-1-4744-7724-6 (webready PDF)
ISBN 978-1-4744-7725-3 (epub)

The right of Bryan Nelson to be identified as the author of this work has been asserted in accordance with the Copyright, Designs and Patents Act 1988, and the Copyright and Related Rights Regulations 2003 (SI No. 2498).

Contents

Acknowledgements	viii
Introduction: The Antinomies of Politics	1
1. Towards Democracy's Anarchic Condition	19
Democracy as Critique	19
Plato Discovers the Political: Rancière's Reading of the Allegory of the Ship	22
Philosophy's Sovereignty over Politics: Abensour's Reading of the Allegory of the Cave	29
The Polemics of the Polis: The Greek Invention of Politics	33
Democracy's Anarchic Condition: A New Political Ontology	38
Making Politics Thinkable	39
2. Dissolution of the Archê	45
In the Name of Democracy: The *Kratos* of the Demos	45
On the Universality of the Problem of the Archê	48
The Nature of Rule: An Interpretation of Plato's *Laws*	50
Commandment and *Commencement*: The Strange Logic of the Archê Principle	54
In Summary: Archic Government	59

    Enter Democracy: What Does It Mean to be against
        the Archê?   60
    Understanding Democracy's 'Anarchic Title'   61
    Democracy as 'Political' or 'Anarchic' Government   66
    Anarchy: The Infinite Opening   70

3. To Think Democracy Otherwise: Claude Lefort and
   Savage Democracy   77
    On the Status of Political Philosophy   77
    Pierre Clastres and the Logic of Being-Against   81
    The Essence of Democracy: A Question of
        Interpretation   84
    Democratic Revolution: Tocqueville and Lefort   90
    The 'Principle of Anarchy' and the Emancipatory
        Act of Politics   96
    Permanent Contestation: Savage Democracy and
        Human Rights   99
    Thinking Democracy Savage: A Philosophical Exercise   103

4. Democratisation of the Sensible: Democracy against
   the Police   114
    On the Many Forms of Being-Against   114
    Politics and the Police: A Radical Dichotomy   117
    Foucault, the Police and *Governmentality*   119
    The Government of *the Sensible* and the Symbolic
        Constitution of Society: Rancière's Concept of
        the Police   124
    'Logical Revolt': Towards a Theory of the Political
        Subject   130
    On Political Names   136
    The 'History' or 'Tradition' of Emancipation   140

5. The Politics of Emancipation: Democracy against the State   149
    Social Domination and Political Emancipation:
        An Introduction to Abensour's General Approach
        to Democracy   149

From the Frankfurt School to Lefort and Machiavelli:
    Abensour's Critical Political Philosophy　　　　　152
Utopia and Democracy　　　　　　　　　　　　　　156
Against the State: Clastres contra Hobbes　　　　　　160
Marx's 'Machiavellian Moment': Hegel, Sovereignty
    and Political Alienation　　　　　　　　　　　　164
'True' Democracy and the *Reduction* of the State　　172
Insurgent Democracy　　　　　　　　　　　　　　　179
In Summary: Rancière's Democracy against the Police
    and Abensour's Democracy against the State　　　183

Conclusion: '*Hic et nunc*' – the Use of Philosophy and the
Critique of the Present　　　　　　　　　　　　　　194

Bibliography　　　　　　　　　　　　　　　　　　207
Index　　　　　　　　　　　　　　　　　　　　　　219

Acknowledgements

A project such as this cannot be completed in isolation. As Cornelius Castoriadis would remind us, the lesson of democracy is that *one cannot be wise alone*. I would like to therefore take this opportunity to express my sincere gratitude to all those who played a role in its realisation.

I am sincerely grateful to my editor, Andrew Schaap, for his advice, patience and thoughtful reviews of multiple drafts of this book. In addition, I would like to thank Sarah Foyle and Ersev Ersoy at the University of Edinburgh Press for their ongoing support and indispensable expertise in the preparation of this volume.

I am also indebted to James Ingram for his encouragement, advice and assistance in helping bring this volume to press.

Much of the research for this volume was conducted during my doctoral studies in Social and Political Thought at York University, Toronto. My deepest thanks and admiration to Martin Breaugh, Brian Singer and Terry Maley, whose invaluable insights, guidance and scrutiny helped shape and enhance this project from its infancy.

Finally, I would like to express my appreciation to my colleagues and friends for their many discussions and dialogues on the meaning of democracy. Your thoughts, questions and criticisms no doubt helped challenge my assumptions and clarify my ideas.

An abbreviated version of Chapter 3 originally appeared as 'Lefort, Abensour and the Question: What is "Savage" Democracy?', *Philosophy and Social Criticism* vol. 45, no. 7 (2019), 844–61. Copyright © 2019 (Sage Publishing). DOI: 10.1177/0191453719828035.

Introduction: The Antinomies of Politics

Thunder on! Stride on, Democracy! Strike with vengeful stroke!
  Walt Whitman, *Leaves of Grass*

Aristotle's *Constitution of Athens* is often read as a sustained, undeviating chronicle tracing the punctuated democratisation of Athens by a succession of prominent reformers and benevolent political leaders from Solon to Cleisthenes to Pericles. This reading lends itself to the view that the formal institution of Athenian democracy may largely be attributed to a few exceptional aristocratic visionaries whose status and influence facilitated the dramatic transformation of the Athenian political landscape *from above*. And yet, interwoven with this familiar narrative, fragments of another may be extracted and assembled from Aristotle's text. This is the narrative of a vibrant, vocal demos, the class distinguished only by its absence of wealth and rank, whose defiance and clamour played a decisive role both in the creation and preservation of the democratic institutions of their city. Let us consider a single example. While the profound achievements of the Cleisthenian reforms rightly occupy a pivotal place in Aristotle's account of the constitutional evolution of Athens, the unique series of events that would come to place Cleisthenes in the position to realise such reforms is far from overlooked in the text. As Aristotle recounts, following the demise of the tyranny of Hippias (510 BCE), a bitter contest for the control of the city would quickly unfold between Isagoras, a notorious Athenian aristocrat, and his rival Cleisthenes of the Alcmaeonid house. Although Cleisthenes had won great support from the demos, vowing to transfer the seat of government to them,

Isagoras' alliance with Cleomenes soon brought the Spartan king to Athens to help secure his uncompromised rule. With the backing of Cleomenes and his armed entourage, Isagoras successfully forced Cleisthenes into exile, proceeded to dispossess hundreds of prominent Athenian families of their homes, and, poised to install himself as tyrant, moved to dissolve the citizens' administrative council (*boule*) established by Solon himself. However, according to Aristotle, in a moment of remarkable fortitude, the council resisted the assault, and the people of Athens, despite a lack of leadership and direction, assembled nevertheless in opposition to Isagoras, declaring their unwavering support for the council. The spontaneous revolt forced Isagoras, Cleomenes and his band of Spartan forces to retreat to the Acropolis where they were besieged for two days by the insurgency. On the third day, a truce was negotiated, Isagoras and Cleomenes were permanently expelled, and Cleisthenes was summoned to return to the city. Only then did Cleisthenes, remaining true to his commitment to the demos, proceed to introduce his historic reforms that would come to mark a new era of Athenian democracy. As Aristotle remarks: 'The people had taken control of their affairs, and Cleisthenes was their leader and champion of the people [. . .].'[1] In the Athenian polis or far beyond its walls, in ancient times or in the present day, it is this narrative of ordinary men and women 'taking control of their affairs' that interests us here.

While the significance of Cleisthenes' monumental reforms remains undisputed both historically and politically, the question of how to incorporate such emancipatory acts of the demos in a broader theoretical construction of democracy often receives far less consideration. Are examples of such opposition and defiance merely illustrative of the revolutionary prelude or 'democratic excess' of a properly instituted democratic constitution from which we must ultimately derive its concept or do such events remain indicative of something essential to the meaning of democracy itself? Echoing this somewhat alternative reading of Aristotle's *Constitution*, in a series of writings that aim to re-evaluate the legacy of both democracy's genesis and survival, Sheldon Wolin will often remind us that, beyond the accomplishments of the great reformers, Athenian democracy was considerably shaped by the regular disruptions and interventions of the demos. From recurring class conflicts to disputes over exclusion to campaigns against those with extraordinary influence in the assembly (*ecclesia*), Wolin maintains that the democratisation of Athens was in no small part the result of a succession of public challenges that would repeatedly call into question the limits and conventions of existing institutions and relations. Rather than the fixed or settled constitutional form we often find in political philosophy, Wolin sees Athenian democracy as the story of a dynamic and ever-evolving political culture, one that not only values public participation in the formal institutions of government, but at the same time recognises the necessity of those more 'fugitive' moments of rebellion and revolt as well. It is in these moments, however ephemeral or episodic, that *the political* itself is collectively renewed and regenerated. It is in these moments that democracy will most unequivocally refuse its confinement to a constitution. For this reason, Wolin is reluctant to classify democracy as a system of administration, institutional procedure or legal system. Rather, he accepts the charges of the Old Oligarch, Polybius and other ancient detractors who find it profoundly revolutionary, unstable and invariably inclined towards anarchy. To Wolin, beyond a mere form of government, democracy represents the birth of a project that concerns nothing less than the bold discovery of the political agency of ordinary people: it is a response to a grievance, the taking back of one's power, a shared moment of collective political activity that 'protests actualities and reveals possibilities'. Turbulent, at times destructive, repeatedly testing the boundaries of its own relative limits, if we follow Wolin, perhaps democracy must indeed be understood not as a constitution, but as something that *happens* to it.[2]

It is precisely this democracy that 'protests actualities and reveals possibilities' that Claude Lefort's extraordinary allusions to 'savage' democracy invite us to consider. Although at times Lefort is presented as merely contributing a formal theory of the democratic society, his work will prove invaluable in the task of tracing or mapping democracy's more creative and transformative dimensions and capacities. Scattered across his later writings, from the French Revolution to May '68, these curious references to savage democracy, although never defined, appear to call attention to those moments in which democracy presents a profound challenge to oppressive, hierarchical and exclusionary arrangements and practices in society. And while this compelling theme in his work has received little attention from scholars, other readers of Lefort, such as Miguel Abensour, will take savage democracy as something of an invitation to revisit the very question of democracy itself. This will prove a rather productive philosophical exercise. For whatever may be inferred from this perplexing term, what is more certain is that each of these 'savage' democratic moments identified and chronicled by Lefort may be put forward to cast doubt on the limits of our understanding of democracy and what it can mean in modern society. As Abensour demonstrates in his own analysis, savage democracy not only opens up the concept of democracy so it may be considered in new ways, but also subsequently orients that concept according to its most uncompromised and resilient incarnation: its political acts of emancipation, its endless capacity for conflict and contestation, its enduring momentum towards a more participatory and egalitarian society. To approach democracy in this way is to distance its concept from those mitigated, domesticated representations of democracy so pervasive today, allowing us to explore and rediscover everything that the *power of the people* can mean. It challenges us to conceive democracy in terms of what it can do, what it can become and what it can transform. Accordingly, if we are receptive to the more radical facets of Lefort's work, savage democracy can have a profound effect on the way in which we think about democracy and organise its concept philosophically.

It is for this reason that savage democracy provides an ideal vehicle through which we may pursue a conception of democracy formulated according to those moments of contestation and dissensus, according to what it counters and disputes, what it renders irreducibly politically problematic or, in short, what democracy could be said to be *against*. If democracy can be understood to represent an unprecedented political challenge to unrestricted and arbitrary rule, concentrations of authority, strategies of inequality and elaborate exclusionary practices, it is because democracy embodies a defiant orientation against: an against which is never simply a consequence of its politics, but forms the very basis of its emancipatory project. Despite its neglect by many of even the most exhaustive studies of its history and institutions, this 'being-against' remains integral to democracy's formation, orientation and institutional expression. It is what propels democracy forward, what informs its targets and objectives, what galvanises its resolve towards a more democratic society.

It is specifically in this context that we can speak of the antinomies of politics. Perhaps first encountered in Plutarch, I here appeal to the term 'antinomy' not with respect to its modern legal framework (the contradiction or mutual incompatibility of two laws), nor according to the logic of Immanuel Kant (who employs the term to demonstrate the paradoxical limits of pure reason), but rather taken in the most straightforward and derivative sense of the Greek word which conjoins the prefix *anti-* ('against, in opposition to') and *nomos* ('custom, law, that which governs human conduct'), itself derived etymologically from the verb *nemó* ('to distribute, assign or parcel out'). I therefore utilise the term 'antinomies of politics' quite literally to identify the logic and process in which conventions and practices, laws and institutions, distributions and allocations come to be opposed and rendered problematic by the initiation of a very specific challenge of the demos. This challenge will prove to reveal something important about politics in itself. We should resist the temptation to frame the political according to generic power, public administration or the tactics of sly, manipulative politicians. Rather, as Hannah Arendt demonstrates, as discovered in the Greek polis, the meaning of politics is far more particular and will often be found to be conspicuously absent in regimes, ancient and modern, from autocracy to oligarchy to totalitarianism. Indeed, as we encounter both in the work of Cornelius Castoriadis and Jacques Rancière, keeping with its Greek inception, politics must always be understood in close proximity with democracy itself. It is a general property neither of cities, nations nor tribes. Politics is not intrinsic to the social; it is what renders the social problematic. It is not indicative of power relations; it is what renders those relations visible, intelligible and contestable. As we will discover with the historian Christian Meier, to *politicise* something is to make it controversial, to identify it an object worthy of public deliberation and debate. In a word, politics means to challenge what is often simply presumed as a given in society: a rule, arrangement, tradition or command. The agent of this process is democracy. Democracy, it could be said, makes the political actual. When democracy contests the authority of nobles or the wealthy classes, when it opposes rigid hierarchies or concentrations of power, it systematically introduces politics to the scene, calling into question the obviousness, naturalism and inherent legitimacy of a given order, convention or law. It destabilises the very foundations of rule, it reveals the sheer contingency of the organisation of the social, its laws and institutions. Quite simply, the antinomies of politics is the politics of a democracy against. It has no other meaning. Democracy is not a system, society, government or procedure primarily. It is the invention of a strategy to transform *what is*. This begins with a defiant position against.

Why is it that democracy invariably appears in the form of an against? Contrary to Alexis de Tocqueville, who discovers the epitome of the natural conditions for democracy in the open and unobstructed plains of the uncultivated American landscape,[3] historically, democracy is never constituted in a void, but manifests in a dense social field in which various orders of rule, modes of domination and hierarchies of all kinds are already very much established. Democracy appears as an emancipatory act, a transformative agent in society. For this reason, its precise form can be understood according to the context of its emergence, according to the given social order which it comes into being to confront and dispute. This is why it is possible to identify, in different places, at different times, the manifestation of a democracy against oligarchy, a democracy against monarchy, a democracy against patriarchy, a democracy against colonialism, a democracy against capitalism. If democracy cannot be isolated from the objects it appears against, it is because these objects form the basis of its particular incarnation, its particular mode of *being-against*. What democracy is against is never extrinsic or secondary to democracy itself. What it is against remains immanent to its very form.

This book considers democracy according to what it is against: its objects, logic, and broader social and political implications. Moreover, given that the sources which shed light on this question remain quite limited, this is a theme that will naturally draw our research to a very particular body of literature. And yet, this study is not a monograph of any single author, nor does it locate its theses within the conceptual framework of any single theory or work. Instead, it is organised as a series of immanent critiques, extracting, developing and evaluating a range of concepts, arguments and terminologies from a selection of authors whose work will serve to illuminate various facets of what I call the 'antinomies of politics'. While the larger question of democracy will be situated in the broader context of the history of political thought from Plato to Thomas Hobbes to Karl Marx to Hannah Arendt, I will primarily draw from the writings of three figures in continental philosophy whose work has only recently begun to be considered by a more rigorous Anglo-American scholarship: Jacques Rancière, Claude Lefort and Miguel Abensour. Fashioning something of a unique triangulation, this study endeavours to both document and evaluate a productive, yet often neglected, current in contemporary French political thought that, however disjointed and at times discordant, challenges the limits of the concept of democracy and how we think about it. Although we will encounter many parallels, crossings and points of intersection, my aim is not chiefly one of comparison, charting out affinities and points of disagreements between the three. Nor is it a straightforward survey of their arguments in an additive fashion. Rather, my goal is ultimately to put these authors to work, to utilise their theoretical resources in order to navigate and evaluate a particular problem or set of problems so worthy of our consideration today.

While their projects differ considerably and adhere to no single tradition, perhaps what their respective theories of democracy all have in common is something of a shared heritage. The mature work of Rancière, Lefort and Abensour would emerge from a quintessentially French, anti-totalitarian, post-Marxist, post-May '68 environment in which a generation of young philosophers, political thinkers and student activists would come to re-evaluate their entire inherited tradition of the Left (from the PCF to Trotskyism to Louis Althusser to Karl Marx himself). One of the many consequences of this experience would be a renewed interest in democracy. And yet, perhaps what makes the projects of Rancière, Lefort and Abensour unique, in many ways setting them apart from their contemporaries, is an unmistakable refusal to engage with democracy according to its current, often compromised status. On first encountering their work, one will immediately detect a certain commitment to an understanding of democracy that denies it may be reduced to a system of government or set of institutions. Although the scope and objectives of their projects differ considerably, in each case what these authors help us to think is a notion of democracy as something strangely adversarial, defiant. In a Brechtian spirit, their writings function to estrange the concept of democracy from those ubiquitous discourses that perpetuate a domesticated representation of democracy officially sanctioned by the interests of capital and rules of the State so that something that perhaps once appeared so familiar and unequivocal and prosaic may be encountered and engaged in entirely new ways. This is a strategy that unabashedly rejects the kind of sentiment espoused by Slavoj Žižek, which finds the term democracy 'so discredited by its predominant use that, perhaps, one should take the risk of abandoning it to the enemy'.[4] However misused, however corrupted or compromised our political language has become, Abensour would likely respond with caution: 'we know only too well that if we begin by giving up words we will end by giving up things.'[5] Refusing such a risk, refusing the capitulatory gesture of surrendering democracy 'to the enemy', Rancière, Lefort and Abensour can each be read to propose something far more challenging: the rediscovery of the radical imperative at the root of democracy itself, so we may reappropriate the term, give it new life and destabilise a prevailing discourse that limits and confines what democracy can be and what it can mean. If nothing else, what such a strategy makes abundantly clear is that particularly in the modern age, part of what democracy means is the inevitable conflict over its meaning. As Rancière will attest most explicitly, among its many struggles, democracy necessarily entails a struggle over language itself, a struggle for the very word 'democracy'.[6]

Indeed, reading Rancière, Lefort and Abensour, each individually or all together, an entire discourse on democracy appears to be called into question. No longer will its analysis be restricted to topics surrounding the separation of powers, periodic elections, rule of law and the rights of man. In this regard, perhaps what their work serves to demonstrate is that democracy is a question that necessitates a very different approach. Carefully navigating both history and the history of philosophy, their writings provide us the tools to effectively disentangle its concept, so it may be radically reconstructed and placed against a dominant discourse that functions to moderate and pacify its political project. My general approach to these thinkers, therefore, is less as a coherent tradition of democratic theory than as parallel incarnations of a highly productive *counter-tradition*, one that challenges us to rethink the question of democracy and its profound implications for society. Rather than limit its investigation to the customary institutional analysis, rather than confine democracy to an ancient constitution or modern system of government, what this experimental intersection will illuminate with great clarity and nuance is, from ancient times to the present day, democracy can be thought a project of emancipation, one that is born and advanced through conflict. By way of an extended analysis of Rancière, Lefort and Abensour organised as a distinct grouping, the principal aim of this book is to establish and demonstrate precisely that: the vital link between democracy, conflict and emancipation. Against prevailing interpretations of democracy, reading Rancière, Lefort and Abensour through this lens will not only enhance our grasp of these pivotal figures and their larger contribution to political thought, but also serve to elucidate this important postulate of democracy itself.

While their authorships touch upon a wide range of topics and themes, from the intellectual culture of the working class, to pedagogy and aesthetics (Rancière), to bureaucracy and the totalitarian society (Lefort), to fascist architecture and utopian literature (Abensour), by bringing together some of their most important writings on democracy, we converge upon a compelling assembly of ideas that help us theorise the spirit of resistance, popular struggle and social transformation in productive new ways. I will therefore frame their work not as a series of descriptive interpretations of modern society, its institutions and power relations, but as a theoretical toolbox to elaborate, strengthen and encourage arguments for democratisation and social change. By combining their collective insights and observations, by reconstructing some of their most important political and philosophical positions, a rather extraordinary and provocative impression of democracy begins to emerge that remains far less prominent in the literature on political thought: democracy as *defiance*. It is this defiance, this propensity of democracy for being-against, that will be situated and explored according to the antinomies of politics. For this reason, I am particularly interested in those passages in their work that concern the political logics of opposition, contestation, dissensus and dispute. For, in this perspective, the question of democracy becomes immediately recast in terms of how those in society who lack political agency (the demos, the poor, the excluded, the exploited) come to have it. I will argue that Rancière, Lefort and Abensour can help us to conceptualise this process in terms of social conflict, in terms of a unique political challenge from below, from the margins of society. To what extent can we approach these authors as contributors to a new theory of democracy understood as a democracy against? This represents the organising question of this book.

Although more radical interpretations of democracy have been circulated and explored at least since the ground-breaking work of Ernesto Laclau and Chantal Mouffe in the 1980s,[7] what makes the antinomies of politics particularly intriguing is the manner in which it tends to entirely reframe our general approach to democracy: when democracy is considered according to what it is against, we are far more inclined to arrive at a notion of democracy not as a government or institution primarily, but as a transformative instrument of the demos. When presented as a challenge or opposition to various hierarchies, to oligarchy, the State or king, a very different perspective of democracy begins to come into focus. Democracy is no longer perceived as a system, structure or procedure, but appears as an active agent in society. It becomes identified with the bodies and forces that seek to dismantle oppressive and exclusionary arrangements and practices in society and replace them with more participatory and non-hierarchical models of social interaction. Democracy becomes a question of democratisation; the government, the family, the means of production: *what in society can be democratised and to what extent?* The writings of Rancière, Lefort and Abensour supply us with a range of strategies to effectively navigate precisely these kinds of questions. By revisiting and re-evaluating their theses, concepts and critiques in this context, important new insights into democracy become possible: what it is, what it does and what it is against.

Implicit to my approach to Rancière, Lefort and Abensour, therefore, is the view that each of these figures may be read not only as theorists of democracy, but as democrats themselves. One of the advantages of this approach is that it refuses to restrict the form of political theory they are engaged in to mere abstraction, speculation, academic argument. Very consistent across their writings is the insistence that integral to their work is an important critical dimension. Rather than a succession of commentaries on the history of political thought, their projects are organised as a pointed and sustained critique of the social: its forms, relations, distributions, representations and transformations. It is imperative to read their work accordingly. Perhaps this is most apparent in what Abensour will formulate as a critical political philosophy, a theoretical approach designed to intersect the most productive aspects of critical and political theory in order to implement a systematic and open-ended critique of both the modes of domination and possibilities of emancipation in society today.[8] One of the underlying questions considered throughout this book is under what conditions can philosophy itself be understood to be *political*? How do we qualify a political philosophy and on what terms? Do classical works like the *Republic* and the *Leviathan* constitute genuine theories of the political or as Rancière insists most emphatically, do they represent its concealment, its systematic displacement for preferred models of rule, the State, the well-ordered society? The writings of Rancière, Lefort and Abensour may themselves be approached and evaluated according to this theme. What is the critical function of their work, what do they help us to think and, perhaps more importantly, what do they help us to think against?

As Lefort submits in his monumental study of Niccolò Machiavelli,[9] the point of departure for any substantive work of political criticism must always be the problems and dilemmas particular to the '*here and now*' (*hic et nunc*). Similarly, Abensour will repeatedly stress the importance of fastening the work of political philosophy firmly in the present, in the social and political matters of today. But how do we represent the present to ourselves (which of the competing narratives do we accept and endorse)? Which forms of social domination are most prevalent and pressing? And what are the specific challenges facing democracy at this time? While it is obviously not possible here to even begin to diagnosis the immense scope and complexity of the many social issues confronting us today, it is important to remember that, in this context, part of what democratic activity means is to bring those issues to light: to draw them out of the shadows, to name them, to make them visible and intelligible, to render them *political*, a matter of public controversy and dispute. Democracy demonstrates that political affairs do not become so by nature. Oppression, exploitation, injustice, the absence of rights or their outright denial – to these social realities politics must be introduced, often precisely by those who have no status and no voice: the disenfranchised, the minority, the excluded (those Rancière sometimes calls the 'part without part'). Moreover, as societies evolve and change, so do the subjects, conflicts and spaces that democracy compels us to recognise and represent, perceive or perceive differently. This is why many of the democratic struggles of today are often quite different from those of the ancient world, even if the logic of being-against remains the same. Democracy can therefore be understood to have an important phenomenal dimension: it forces us to see things in society that we could not see before. It brings social conflicts into the open, calling attention to a grievance, objection or dispute in a distinct political way. In ancient times or in the present day, these are processes that political thought can help us frame, navigate and articulate in more formal and systematic ways. So while political theory may often appear to occupy itself with a comprehensive range of more abstract social and political questions at the expense of the particularities of current affairs, as Lefort convincingly demonstrates in his work on Machiavelli, critical interpretations of even centuries-old texts like *The Prince* may be executed in such a way that they inform and enhance the parameters of the critique of our own experience today. Perhaps in this respect, Lefort provides us the pathway towards a specifically 'political' hermeneutics, one which involves reading what could be quite distant historical texts according to the conditions and circumstances of the *here and now*.

The political philosophy of Rancière, Lefort and Abensour has never before been considered together in a single volume. This provides an opportunity for new encounters and new interpretations. Their meeting will not only produce new ways of engaging with democracy, but engender new perspectives through which their own work may be engaged. And while their projects should not be merged or conflated, the benefit of reading their work in tandem is that it provides us a rich body of literature from which we may draw and a wide range of critical tools which may be employed to carry out our own investigation into the antinomies of politics here. Against the backdrop of a discussion of the foundations of democracy – or lack thereof – we will begin our analysis by charting out the inherent tension between politics and rule as observed in the Platonic origin of what Arendt understands as the 'tradition of political philosophy' while re-establishing democracy's unique proximity to the political as uncovered in the Greek polis (Chapter 1). Having distanced politics from the rather narrow framework of government, sovereignty and the affairs of the State, reading Rancière, we will then encounter our first example of the antinomies of politics in what will be found to be its most universal or general form: a democracy against the archê, or underlying foundation of rule (Chapter 2). Following this, with the assistance of Abensour, we will then attempt to construct a general concept of democracy consistent with the antinomies of politics through a detailed analysis of what Lefort considers examples of 'savage' democracy since the French Revolution (Chapter 3). Finally, in the remaining two chapters, we will investigate two critical models of democracy's being-against in order to grasp the antinomies of politics in further detail: with Rancière we will explore a democracy against the police considering the role and identity of the political subject (Chapter 4) and with Abensour we will explore a democracy against the State considering the meaning of emancipation and what he identifies as 'insurgent' democracy (Chapter 5). One of the recurring themes that will be encountered across this study is the precise relationship between democracy, politics and philosophy, in ancient Greece and the present day. Although philosophy and democracy obviously share a common origin in the Greek polis, when exactly is philosophy an ally to the democratic project and when is it an adversary? This is a question that will be revisited multiple times, in a number of contexts.

In many respects, this book is motivated by a series of very basic questions, albeit questions that are only rarely posed directly: *How should democracy be thought? How do we go about organising its concept? On what basis? And to what end?* Consequently, if this study offers something of a contribution to the field of political philosophy as opposed to political science, it is because it is primarily concerned with democracy at the level of the concept. Throughout,

I shall largely adhere to a notion of philosophy elaborated by Gilles Deleuze. Following Deleuze, if philosophy does not correspond to some vague notion of contemplation, reflection or communication, it is because philosophy is primarily a practical exercise in concept construction.[10] Deleuze understands philosophy as an encounter or confrontation with a problem. The history of philosophy, it could be said, is the history of such encounters. A problem always originates from the outside, from a place external to philosophy itself. Contrary to René Descartes, thinking never happens in a void. Thought requires provocation – *something in the world forces us to think* – it is compelled, drawn out by an encounter, a problem.[11] Philosophy is a way of rendering problems intelligible. Philosophy navigates and evaluates problems by engineering concepts and relations of concepts through which the contours and complexities of these problems may be thought in coherent and productive ways. For this reason, although concepts may be adopted and developed by later philosophers, they will always bear a trace of the original problem that initially provoked them. This is why philosophical problems are always historical in nature: they are always provoked by something of our own historical milieu. We discover one of the earliest surviving examples of such a provocation in the works of Plato. Interestingly, what Plato's epistemology and political philosophy share in common is that they are both provoked by the very same problem, the prevailing problem that presented itself to Plato in Classical Athens: the problem of *democracy*. Just as his concept of the Forms (abstract essences or pure ideas) represents a particular navigation and evaluation of the problem of democratic *doxa*, the condition that appears to circulate opinion infinitely without standard or measure, his concept of justice (that of the properly ordered city) likewise represents a particular navigation and evaluation of the problem of democracy's radical claim of *equality*, an 'anarchic' equality applicable to both 'equals and unequals alike'. Therefore, according to Deleuze, whether it be Plato's *Forms*, G. W. Leibniz's *monads* or Henri Bergson's *duration*, concepts are not structured to reference external objects or states of affairs and cannot be evaluated in terms of true and false. Rather, as the basic tools of philosophy, concepts are constructions that help us map, formulate and think through problems posed to us by our own historical milieu. And yet, for Deleuze, it is not Plato, as something of a reactionary, who grasps the true political potential of philosophy's practice of concept construction, but Friedrich Nietzsche. Reading Nietzsche, Deleuze explains that, if philosophy does not strive to represent the world in thought, it is because its first task is to organise concepts that act upon the world, that counter the world in its present form and help us to *think against* it. This is precisely what Nietzsche understands as philosophy's critical or 'untimely' vocation. In the foreword to the second essay of his own *Untimely Meditations*, Nietzsche distinguishes the untimely as 'acting counter to our time, and thereby acting on our time, and let us hope, for the benefit of a time to come'.[12] In Nietzsche's view, it is not enough for philosophy to merely represent the present in thought; it must *resist* it. As Deleuze reiterates: 'This is why philosophy has an essential relation to time: it is always against its time, critique of the present world.'[13] An untimely philosophy is one that realises its capacity to resist, to think against, to critique the present world as we find it and as we have inherited it. *This is when philosophy becomes political.* Strictly speaking, political philosophy is not a genre or category of philosophy; it is not the philosophy that simply reflects on the abstract topics of what is vaguely understood to be 'political'. Rather, in the spirit of Nietzsche, philosophy only becomes political when it renders itself *untimely*, when the concepts it generates are created to counter, to challenge the conditions of the present time in the hopes of changing them, of participating in shaping a new and better world than the one we have today.[14] In his *Theses on Feuerbach*, Marx himself appears to espouse a similar view. In this respect, as a mode of critical thought devised not only to interpret, but to engage and critique the conditions of the present, perhaps Deleuze's general interpretation of philosophy will not be found dissimilar from what Abensour, drawing not from Nietzsche, but from Arendt and Lefort, develops as a critical political philosophy. Perhaps in our own time, such a critical political philosophy begins with a new concept of democracy.

Therefore, building a concept of democracy need not be concerned with devising a blueprint for the 'perfect' democratic society, a democracy only suitable, as Jean-Jacques Rousseau has it, for a 'nation of Gods'.[15] Nor should we concern ourselves with deconstruction's messianic promise of a transcendent 'democracy to come', a pure, untarnished democracy posited in an ideal horizon and perpetually projected into a future that never arrives.[16] Rather, a critical, untimely or *political* philosophy is the one that creates its concepts in the present time, for its time, and following Nietzsche, *against* its time. It is the object of political philosophy to critique the conditions of the present, to supply critical concepts that help us challenge and transform *what is*. Undoubtedly, such a model of political philosophy will prove invaluable to our study of democracy here. For what I will postulate as the antinomies of politics is neither arbitrary nor an end in itself: democracy makes no promises, projects nothing into the future, but is concerned only with the democratisation of the present, the ongoing battle for more participatory and egalitarian institutions and relations. If we follow Abensour, philosophical critique represents an important dimension of this larger political project.

Accordingly, this study ventures to construct a concept of democracy as a means to *think against*, to navigate and evaluate perhaps one of the most glaring political problems of our times (a problem quite different, interestingly, than the one that posed itself to Plato in Classical Athens): namely, the claim of the 'universality' of democracy itself, its global consensus, the unquestionable legitimacy of the existing state of affairs. At least since the collapse of totalitarianism, our time is one of the hegemony of a proclaimed democracy without conflict or division, one entirely consistent with capital and the State and the most egregious monopolisation of wealth, power and resources. At the same time, this hegemony signifies the domestication of democracy, the neutralisation of its politics. In a sense, not without irony, this book is an attempt to restore to the concept of democracy precisely what it meant to Plato so long ago: the scandal of an anarchic equality that so indiscriminately overturns so many relations of authority at once. The work of Rancière, Lefort and Abensour will prove critical in this task.

This book represents an inquiry into the antinomies of politics, a meditation on democracy according to what it is against. For this reason, it cannot claim to offer a 'complete' theory of democracy. Important questions regarding the nature of democracy's own institutions have largely been placed aside and postponed. This does not intend to disregard the significance of these institutional problems, but simply attempts to initiate and frame the question of democracy in a different way, from a different starting place. For example, what Aristotle's *Constitution of Athens* appears to demonstrate, as we have seen, is not so much that democracy simply resides in a particular set of institutions, but that it is something that plays a decisive role in shaping them. Accordingly, although I will make the claim that democracy remains irreducible to its institutions, this does not imply that democracy is by definition contrary to them. A concept of democracy that remains incompatible with an institutional framework is really quite futile and counterproductive from the start (at times Rancière has been interpreted in this manner).[17] And yet, if there is something of democracy that cannot be reduced to its institutions, however assembled or arranged, this suggests that the problem of its institutions does not logically come first, but second. Here, we are interested in those questions that *precede* the problem of democracy's institutions, questions that, if addressed beforehand, will undoubtedly recast those institutional problems in a very different light.

In all likelihood, this book will be approached as a theory of radical democracy.[18] But as Abensour reminds us, what terms like 'radical' democracy, 'savage' democracy and 'insurgent' democracy all share in common is, rather than narrow or specify the meaning of democracy, they call on us to resist its ideological appropriation and prevent its confusion with very different matters, however important in their own right (such as political representation or the rule of law).[19] Therefore, as adjectives, as qualifiers, the *radical*, the *savage*, the *insurgent* have a very specific purpose: unlike 'liberal' democracy or 'social' democracy, they do not modify or redirect our concept of democracy in any particular way, but intend only to gesture towards democracy *in itself*, what it can do and what it can create. Radical democracy is democracy. It is not a structure, system or strategy for governing another. At its root, it is a living thing: the demos *acting*. Interestingly, the poetry of Walt Whitman famously associates democracy with images of weeds and grass. It sprouts from below and has the capacity to spread rapidly. Organic, wild, difficult to stamp out, Whitman likens democracy to a force of nature: difficult to control and a marvel to behold. His poems remind us that democracy is not an inert, static entity, established once and for all. It germinates and propagates, like an invasive species, perpetually testing the limits of what in society can be made democratic or more democratic. Resilient, defiant, incessantly pushing forward, always forward, this is the vision of democracy Whitman venerates with an almost spiritual fidelity in *Leaves of Grass*: 'Thunder on! Stride on, Democracy! Strike with vengeful stroke!'[20]

Notes

1. Aristotle, *The Politics and The Constitution of Athens* (Cambridge: Cambridge University Press, 1996), 225. Also see Josiah Ober, *The Athenian Revolution: Essays on Ancient Greek Democracy and Political Theory* (Princeton: Princeton University Press, 1996), chapter 4.

2. Many of these themes cut across Wolin's writings on democracy. See Sheldon S. Wolin, 'Norm and Form: The Constitutionalizing of Democracy', in *Athenian Political Thought and the Reconstruction of American Democracy*, ed. J. Peter Euben, John R. Wallach and Josiah Ober (Ithaca: Cornell University Press, 1994); Sheldon S. Wolin, 'Fugitive Democracy', in *Democracy and Difference: Contesting the Boundaries of the Political*, ed. Seyla Benhabib (Princeton: Princeton University Press, 1996), and Sheldon S. Wolin, *Politics and Vision: Continuity and Innovation in Western Political Thought* (Princeton: Princeton University Press, 2004), chapter 17.
3. Alexis de Tocqueville, *Democracy in America*, vol. I (New York: Vintage Books, 1990), chapter 1.
4. Slavoj Žižek, *On Belief* (New York: Routledge, 2001), 123.
5. Miguel Abensour, 'The History of Utopia and the Destiny of Its Critique', in *Political Uses of Utopia: New Marxist, Anarchist, and Radical Democratic Perspectives*, ed. S. D. Chrostowska and James D. Ingram (New York: Columbia University Press, 2016), 14.
6. Jacques Rancière and Eric Hazan, 'Democracies Against Democracy', in Giorgio Agamben et al., *Democracy in What State?* (New York: Columbia University Press, 2001), 78.
7. See Ernesto Laclau and Chantal Mouffe, *Hegemony and Socialist Strategy: Towards a Radical Democratic Politics* (London: Verso, 2001).
8. See Miguel Abensour, 'Pour une philosophie politique critique?', *Pour une philosophie politique critique* (Paris: Sens & Tonka, 2009).
9. Claude Lefort, *Machiavelli in the Making* (Evanston: Northwestern University Press, 2012).
10. See Gilles Deleuze and Félix Guattari, *What is Philosophy?* (New York: Columbia University Press, 1994), chapter 1.
11. Gilles Deleuze, *Difference and Repetition* (London: Continuum, 2001), 139.
12. Friedrich Nietzsche, *Untimely Meditations* (Cambridge: Cambridge University Press, 2011), 60.
13. Gilles Deleuze, *Nietzsche and Philosophy* (New York: Columbia University Press, 2006), 107.
14. Bryan Nelson, 'New Earth, New People: Deleuze, Democracy and the Politics of the Future', in *Movements in Time: Revolution, Social Justice and Times of Change*, ed. Cecile Lawrence and Natalie Churn (Cambridge: Cambridge Scholars Publishing, 2012), 79–81.
15. Jean-Jacques Rousseau, *The Social Contract* (London: Penguin Books, 1968), 114.
16. See Jacques Derrida, *Specters of Marx: The State of the Debt, The Work of Mourning, and the New International* (New York: Routledge, 2006), 81.

17. Rancière will respond to this criticism most directly in Jacques Rancière, *The Method of Equality: Interviews with Laurent Jeanpierre and Dork Zabunyan* (Malden: Polity Press, 2016).
18. Consider Lummis's helpful clarification of this term in C. Douglas Lummis, *Radical Democracy* (Ithaca: Cornell University Press, 1996), 24–5.
19. Consider Abensour's comments in Miguel Abensour, Jean-Luc Nancy and Jacques Rancière, 'Instances démocratiques', *Vacarme* vol. 48, no. 3 (Summer 2009): 9.
20. Walt Whitman, *Leaves of Grass* (Minneapolis: First Avenue Editions, 2015), 332.

Chapter 1

Towards Democracy's Anarchic Condition

> *The whole political project of Platonism can be conceived as an anti-maritime polemic.*
> Jacques Rancière, *On the Shores of Politics*

Democracy as Critique

Perhaps as much as a political form, democracy can be understood to have a critical function. Democracy provides a basis, a model, a language in which our institutions and relations may be appraised, evaluated and ultimately called into question according to a lexicon of equality and inequality, inclusion and exclusion, participation and the denial of the right to participate. This is why democratic theory is never simply an 'abstract' or 'speculative' science. The very idea of democracy not only supplies us a notion of non-hierarchical modes of social interaction, of ways of being-together *in common*, but may also be put forward as a strategy to critique, to *think against* increasingly sophisticated models of domination and systems of authority. As Abensour submits, a sustained critique of domination represents an indispensable facet of social emancipation. It is in this sense that critique can be appreciated to have an important political dimension. However we perceive the markers of democratisation, for Abensour, political criticism will play a vital role in this process. In some respect, democracy only begins when the idea of the *power of the people* (the *kratos* of the demos) is taken seriously. This is actually more rare today than perhaps many of us would like to admit. And yet, as a mode of critique, perhaps democracy has never been so important. In the field of philosophy, this can readily be observed, for example, in the trajectory of continental political thought over the last half century. In France, particularly following the events of May '68, a number of emerging philosophers and political theorists would eventually break with Marxism and come to approach democracy very much in this way: as an instrument of critique. This trend would give rise to a range of valuable insights into the concept of democracy, its history and conflicts. At the same time, it would also form the basis of a new wave of political criticism in no way limited to the traditional subjects and objects of Marxist economics or communist party policy. In particular, it is Rancière, Lefort and Abensour who interest us here. In broad strokes, it could be said that their critical projects take up two problems at once: the social conditions of the present times (from totalitarianism and bureaucracy to what we so boastfully call 'democracy' today) and the history of political philosophy itself (a tradition that begins with Plato). In this chapter, it is the latter that will serve as our point of departure, revisiting Plato's *Republic* as a strategy to introduce a number of preliminary questions and themes regarding the nature of the political, the foundations of democracy and the reasons for its disavowal by a long line of political philosophers since Plato himself. That Plato's infamous rejection of democracy springs from the hallmark democratic society is not the issue. As for Arendt, it is rather his legacy in the history of political thought that concerns us.

Without controversy, Arendt's critique of what she calls the 'tradition of political philosophy' from Plato to Marx could very well be understood to establish something of a precedent for Rancière's, Lefort's and Abensour's subsequent readings of the history of political philosophy itself. The significance of her thought for this generation of French political thinkers cannot be overstated. For this reason, Arendt's work may be positioned as the common background according to which Rancière's, Lefort's and Abensour's respective projects may be situated and explored with greater clarity and precision. She is very much a source for all three. Perhaps Arendt's staggering importance for these figures will be discovered in her simple refusal to identify politics and rule. According to Arendt, this conflation represents perhaps the greatest blunder of western political philosophy. This explains why she frames the entire tradition, beginning with Plato, not as a systematic reflection on political affairs, but as a science of rule, sovereignty, the affairs of the State. Politics, she insists, is an entirely different matter. Indeed, it would appear that politics remains a topic that much of the history of political philosophy tells us virtually nothing about. Accordingly, if we wish to grasp something of its original meaning and significance, so often lost today, following Arendt, rather than survey the great works of political philosophy, we must return to its historical origins in the Greek polis itself. Drawing from the research of Christian Meier, this will form the basis of my general approach to politics in this study.

Therefore, reading Arendt, we not only identify an important critical source for Rancière, Lefort and Abensour alike, but initiate the important work of extracting a notion of politics from its customary restriction to various arrangements and strategies of rule. *Politics is not the foundation upon which one rules another; it is the condition in which the foundation of rule is called into question.* This is what is paramount to our study. By distancing politics from rule, by breaking with tradition and urging us to consider the political in its own right, what Arendt ultimately helps us to grasp is the inherent tension between these two terms. This is something that would not be lost on Rancière, Lefort and Abensour. Perhaps this is one reason why their research offers so much insight into what I call the 'antinomies of politics'. As soon as politics is dislodged from rule and meticulously bound to a concept of democracy organised against it, the theoretical basis for the antinomies of politics is very much established. Democracy does not simply represent yet another model, regime or arrangement of rule. It is rather what challenges the very division between ruler and ruled. This, I argue, is the basis of its politics.

Hence, very much keeping with the general framework of Arendt's critique, this opening chapter will explore the background to this inherent tension between politics and rule as observed in the tradition of political philosophy. Perhaps nowhere is this tension more apparent than in Plato's own indictment of democracy. Reading Plato with Rancière and Abensour, through a series of rather nuanced interpretations of Plato's use of allegory in the *Republic*, we will carefully consider what this enduring tension between politics and rule so cogently reveals: first, rather than a meditation on the matters of politics themselves, in the guise of Plato, political philosophy describes a rational attempt to undermine the political and establish the underlying foundation for a preferred model of rule, either historical or ideal; second, democracy is that which intrinsically lacks any such foundation. It is for this reason that democracy is so often dismissed and discredited by philosophers as 'anarchic'. Democracy offers no foundation, no archê for rule.

Rather, democracy appears as the political force or agent which throws such foundations into question. This can be witnessed in Plato's own society.

Plato Discovers the Political: Rancière's Reading of the Allegory of the Ship

We begin our analysis not with any proponent or ally of democracy, but with perhaps its greatest antagonist in the history of philosophy: Plato himself. Indeed, we often have far more to learn about democracy from its most devout critics than from its tepid supporters who claim to admire it. Although Plato's objections to democracy are well known, often regarded as the archetype of what would prove to be philosophy's rather consistent appraisal of the regime for millennia to come, particularly when expressed in a somewhat veiled allegorical form, his disparaging portrayal of democracy will prove to reveal far more. While often absorbed by its more epistemological, sociological and psychological implications, Plato's denunciation of what he perceives as democracy's anarchic condition will not only inform the basis of my entire approach to democracy, but inadvertently uncover something intrinsic to its very constitution: democracy is that which can provide no foundation for rule. To explore this theme, let us consider Plato's allegory of the ship.

'Imagine, then, that something like the following happens on a ship or on many ships.' With this invitation, Socrates momentarily suspends dialogue with his small, but acquiescent congregation and once again appeals to allegory. In what follows, Socrates proceeds to narrate a short tale set upon the deck of a naval vessel at sea.[1] What he describes is a vulgar scene of ignorance, bickering, deception and brutality. The many sailors on board, none who have any experience with navigation, quarrel among themselves regarding who should take the helm and captain the ship. They boast that navigation is not a teachable skill, that sailing requires no understanding of the seasons, the skies, the stars, the winds, but is a task that anyone can perform. Dismissing the philosopher as a mere stargazer, the sailors clash among themselves, throwing each other overboard and threatening to cut one another into pieces. Socrates continues: 'I don't think that you need to examine the simile in detail to see that the ships resemble cities and their attitude to the true philosophers, but you already understand what I mean.' Indeed, the allegory of the State as a ship would not be unfamiliar to his interlocutors, the trope having already appeared both in the lyric poetry of Alcaeus and in the opening speech of Aeschylus' *Seven Against Thebes*. But in Plato's account in Book VI of the *Republic*, this chaotic scene, described in vivid detail by Socrates, in which the wisdom of the philosopher is undermined by a savage band of drunken sailors who blindly command an aimless vessel in choppy seas, is intended to represent a particular constitution, one which would be well known to his fellow Athenians: a *democracy*.

What is it about democracy that evokes this image of the sea? As Rancière astutely observes, this is not the only occasion in which Plato's political writings make allusions to the maritime experience. Is it a veiled reference to democratic Athens, the coastal city with an unmatched naval fleet whose economic prosperity, imperial rule and glorious victory over the Persians at the Battle of Salamis depended so considerably upon its proximity to the Aegean Sea?[2] Or does the seascape allude to something more ontological: a shifting surface in constant motion, a great depth upon which no foundation can be established, a vast abyss that cannot be mastered or contained, a wild, unpredictable experience of changing winds and turning tides which lacks all the stability and security of dry land?

Perhaps every appraisal of the *Republic*'s objections to democracy will be struck by how little Plato offers in terms of any institutional analysis of the practices and procedures that facilitate public participation in the governance of the city. Rather, according to Rancière, what we discover (much akin to Tocqueville in the nineteenth century) is something which resembles more of a sociological evaluation of the culture and personality that tend to be encountered in the democratic society:

> Plato is the first one to invent that mode of sociological reading we declare to be proper to the modern age, the interpretation that locates underneath the appearances of political democracy an inverse reality: the reality of a state of society where it is the private, egotistical man who governs.[3]

Consequently, it would appear that the object of the ancient philosopher's criticism is less democracy as a set of institutions than as a state of society, a style of life, a psychological orientation. And in this respect, the conduct of the sailors on board Socrates' allegorical ship will in many ways anticipate Plato's more sustained assessment of what he calls 'democratic man' subsequently in the dialogue.[4]

Plato assumes a certain isomorphism between a city's constitution and the dominant psychology of the inhabitants who dwell there. In an oligarchy we find the oligarchic soul, in a timocracy the timocratic soul, in a tyranny the tyrannical soul, each psychological type corresponding to a particular organisation of the soul in which a spectrum of values or desires become subordinate to one: the accumulation of wealth (the oligarch), the pursuit of honour (the timocrat), the aspiration for unrestrained authority (the tyrant).[5] But when the discussion inevitably turns to democracy, which so often remains something of an exception, the problem becomes less straightforward. While Plato regularly cites equality as democracy's most distinguishing attribute, curiously, it is not some underlying egalitarian sensibility that his psychological typology ultimately finds to dominate the democratic soul, but rather something that cannot be so easily specified: a certain *undecidability*. According to Plato, democracy may be isolated from every other regime in that it represents not a single constitution, but a constitution of constitutions, a 'supermarket of constitutions' in which one may consume political ideologies as if commodities on the free market:[6]

> For Plato, democracy is in its essence a system of variety, and this applies equally well to what is on offer politically: democracy, he says, is not a constitution, but a bazaar filled with all possible constitutions, where anyone can choose to perceive whichever variety they please.[7]

In a society in which every citizen may live as they please, each according to their own preferred constitution, it is here where Plato claims to encounter the greatest variety of dispositions and temperaments. Furthermore, emblematic of this system of variety which so typifies the democratic society, it is precisely this rather confused, fragmented experience that for Plato so defines the psychology of each individual democrat. What democratic man lacks, Plato charges, is a certain consistency of character: he is fickle, erratic, temperamental. Just as democracy ascribes a certain equality to the demos, the psychology of the democrat is one inflicted by a corresponding equality of desires.[8] Experiencing his many appetites and inclinations with equal force and urgency, pursuing the satisfaction of his desires as if selected by lot, unlike the oligarch, timocrat and tyrant, the democratic psyche is one distinguished by the marked *absence* of a singular desire or consistent teleological orientation;

like the infant of psychoanalysis, he lacks both the capacity to organise his impulses as well as the insight to evaluate beneficial ends from harmful ones. Infantile, incompetent, wholly unfit for government, democratic man is therefore destined to confuse courage with impudence, excellence with extravagance, liberty with anarchy.[9]

Indeed, according to Plato's moral psychology, the democrat suffers from a chronic *anarchy of the soul*, a condition in which this exaggerated equality typical of a democracy infects, like a contagious disease, all spheres of life and depths of the soul. Conceived as such, this *undecidability*, this *anarchy of the soul*, may be interpreted as the psychological consequence of a society in which equality reigns over all relations and things, extending itself indefinitely to domains where it does not belong. The problem with democracy, Plato contends, is that it is misguided enough to attribute its radical conception of equality to both the 'equal and unequal alike'. This is why Plato's criticism of democracy includes that farcical caricature of the democratic city in which slaves live as free as their masters, sons discipline their fathers, students contradict their teachers, the young openly disrespect their elders, resident aliens feel as entitled as citizens and even domestic animals assert their own savage equality by roaming proudly through public streets.[10] Democracy, quite simply, is the name of the society which, more than any other, expresses the *need* to be governed.

Dismissive of authority, concerned only with the satisfaction of his most immediate desires, 'ungovernable' by nature – although this more extensive treatment of the democrat only appears much later in the *Republic* – is this not a fitting summary of the reprehensible state in which we find the sailors of Socrates' narrative? Are we not presented with the allegorical ship of democracy precisely to bear witness to the wild anarchy symptomatic of a mass democratic hysteria in which the ungovernable govern the ungovernable? The metaphor is quite appropriate in more ways than one. For while the most famous of the Greek philosophers generally emerged from the aristocratic classes, as Moses Finley reminds us, in the Athenian navy, ships were invariably manned by oarsmen composed of the demos.[11] So just as Rancière will appeal to the shoemaker to symbolise the poor,[12] it is equally befitting that the sailor personify the demos of democratic Athens. Furthermore, while the allegory of the ship clearly highlights the deplorable behaviour of the democratic sailors, obviously intended to lay bare their utter incompetence to govern, if we consider the maritime backdrop of the narrative more thoroughly, perhaps it may suggest a more nuanced reading. For beyond the rather superficial assessment of democratic man (who could no doubt be reformed or simply repressed under the proper order of a new regime), is there not a more profound evil to which Plato's allegorical seascape inadvertently alludes? Perhaps it is not so much the chaotic scene of raucous sailors which unfolds on deck, but what lies beneath the hull, which so troubles Plato about democracy: not so much the psychology of democratic man, but the boundless sea of politics through which they sail, that vertigo-inducing experience of radical indeterminacy, a groundless ontological condition particular to democracy and democracy alone.

Insofar as the *Republic* prescribes the erection of an immense hierarchical edifice ruled by an exceptional class of guardian philosophers, the infrastructure of such a regime cannot be established in the murky Mediterranean waters far from shore. The open sea will provide no foundation for the vast architecture of Plato's ideal city. Much like Hobbes, who hulls in his massive leviathan from great depths so to lay down the sovereign ground of his absolutist State, Plato must first secure the infrastructure of his own city far from the 'great beast of the populace' encountered on ships at sea. For the sea represents a certain unpredictability and volatility. The sea represents the place of *politics*. Perhaps it is for this reason that, in his appropriately titled volume *On the Shores of Politics*, Rancière will contend that: 'The whole political project of Platonism can be conceived as an anti-maritime polemic.'[13] According to Rancière, from beginning to end, Plato's entire political philosophy can be summarised as an imperative against politics, as a project to undermine what is so intrinsic to its experience:

> The sea smells bad. This is not because of the mud, however. The sea smells of sailors, it smells of democracy. The task of philosophy is to found a different politics, a politics of conversion which turns its back on the sea.[14]

It thus becomes the first objective of Plato's political philosophy to abandon politics, to refuse its turbulent, unpredictable life at sea so to establish the foundations of government on *terra firma*, on the solid ground or archê principle of philosophy itself.[15] This is the basis of what, in *Disagreement*, Rancière will identify as 'archipolitics' – a philosophical programme designed to eradicate the threat of politics from the start by instituting a community on the stability of the archê, an underlying principle which distributes the proper relations of rule without remainder and without excess.[16] What Plato seeks to neutralise is the antinomies of politics, the polemics of the polis, the exercise of making the city and the organisation of the city a matter of public controversy and dispute. For on the stormy seas of democracy, the problem is not only that the demos, much like sailing a ship, completely lacks the proper tools and insight required to navigate the monumental task of governing a city:

> It is that at the people's assembly, any mere shoemaker or smithie can get up and have his say on how to steer the ships and how to build the fortifications and, more to the point, on the just or unjust ways to use these for the common good.[17]

When Plato disavows democracy for its profound ignorance of justice and the common good, integral to his charge is that, as a social or cultural phenomenon, democracy appears to lay out a plane of equivalence in which anyone can lay claim to anything in a space dictated only by the rule of *doxa* and *agon*. And yet, while the epistemological implications of this experience are vast, for Plato, the problem of democracy goes deeper still. At its core, perhaps Plato's real concern is that with regards to the order of the city, with regards to the very question of its constitution, democracy undermines the authority of the experts at the same time as it undermines the authority of oligarchs and kings. What democracy unapologetically denies is that there exists a proper order of society and indeed, a privileged class of intellectuals, theologians or wise men with knowledge of such a society. Particularly when associated with ancient democracy, this is precisely how the politics of *doxa* and *agon* should be understood: beyond the still-prevailing Platonic interpretation which reduces these terms to mere rhetoric, circulation of opinion and the interminable contest of debate, democracy's formal institution of *doxa* and *agon* remains a testament to its unwavering position against the notion that there somewhere exists an accessible and decipherable truth of society (that gods sanction the divine right of kings, that mystical sages possess an esoteric knowledge of the nature of society).[18] Rather, what democracy's very institutions unmistakeably imply is that the organisation of the polis is a problem destined to remain *political* and thus unresolved in any absolute sense. As Castoriadis reminds us, democracy demands the polis absolve itself of the claim that its limits may be determined in advance. There is no abstract model of society to be provided by nature or revealed by the gods. There is no ultimate closure to the question of what constitutes justice and the common good. Consequently, democracy can be perceived to open up a vast gulf, an infinite depth which annihilates the claim of a final word or ultimate authority. The meaning of politics is intrinsically bound to this condition.

To displace the sea of politics for the ground of wisdom: this is the ambition of the Platonist. Government must be sheltered from politics, from its lack of foundation, from the perils immanent to its condition. Politics can have no place in the just city. And yet, set on the decks of ships far from shore, does not Plato's presentation of democracy inextricably bound to his absurd sociology of democratic man inadvertently conceal the depth of the real scandal at hand, the scandal of *politics* itself? On the contrary. The fact that Plato remains entirely disinterested in any sustained political analysis of democracy only demonstrates that its often comical depiction merely intends to present a problem to be resolved, a sickness to be cured, an inversion to be righted. As Rancière suggests, is there not a certain reassurance to be taken from Plato's portrait of the disordered, upside-down world of democracy in which all relations from governor and governed to father and son have capsized at once? For this appears to attest that all these relations are of the same nature, that all these inversions are indicative of the same corruption of the proper order of society that could therefore be corrected by the installation of the same principle or set of principles.[19] Although democracy is equated to the overstuffed marketplace, what Plato's moral diagnosis unmistakably reveals is that the disease which so afflicts the regime is not one of abundance, but rather one of lack. As demonstrated by the allegory of the ship, it is precisely democracy's *lack* of an archê which provides all the evidence for the archê's necessity and effectiveness in the composition of the well-ordered society. With respect to democracy's anarchic condition, what the *Republic* posits so unequivocally is not so much an argument for the rule of the philosophers, but for the necessity of the principle which dictates that it is the philosophers and the philosophers alone who constitute the proper rulers of the city. And thus, however trivial its presentation, the *Republic*'s very solution to the problem of democracy, namely, the institution of a government of philosophers, the founding of a rational social order grounded upon a new archê principle, will certainly render the substance and magnitude of the problem entirely transparent. As long as Plato formulates politics and philosophy in antithetical terms, the rule of the philosophers will necessarily imply the negation of politics. Plato allows for no reconciliation. Therefore, rather than a philosophy of politics, what Plato's political philosophy more accurately describes is an *anti-politics*, a contempt for the irreducibility or infinite depth intrinsic to its experience. And in this regard, according to Rancière, the very structure of Plato's solution to the problem of democracy will correspond to what the subsequent history of political philosophy will inadvertently reveal:

> The term 'political philosophy' does not designate any genre, any territory or specification of philosophy. Nor does it designate politics' reflection on its immanent rationality. It is the name of an encounter—and a polemical encounter at that—in which the paradox or scandal of politics is exposed: its lack of any proper foundation.[20]

At least in Rancière's view, what is generally called 'political philosophy' is predicated upon the supposition that there is a rational means to order the roles, spaces and functioning parts of a community. This is precisely what animates a theoretical project intent on discovering a set of normative principles that both ground and justify a given order of rule.[21] The proper name for such a principle is 'archê'. When the logic of the archê is operative in the organisation of the city, the condition of politics, its lack of any proper foundation, is effectively obscured.

Philosophy's Sovereignty over Politics: Abensour's Reading of the Allegory of the Cave

Reading the allegory of the ship alongside a second, even more notorious allegory in the *Republic* will render this *anti-politics* all the more apparent. If it is Rancière's contention that Plato is emblematic of a more underlying tendency across the history of philosophy to suppress or evade the condition of politics, he will not be alone in his assessment. In his own evaluation, Castoriadis argues that Plato's very ontology inaugurates a political philosophy that ultimately rests upon the concealment and closure of the foremost political question: the self-institution of society.[22] According to Castoriadis, in stark contrast to the project of autonomy perpetuated by the early sophists and Socrates himself, Plato is the figure who betrays and abandons this important political and philosophical project in order to invent an imagined city outside history governed not by its citizens but by a new class of philosopher-rulers who dictate laws from above. Likewise, while Arendt's entire authorship could be said to be instigated by the problem of totalitarianism,[23] compelling her formulation of a new concept of politics that draws heavily from the Greek democratic experience, she will repeatedly disavow what she understands as the tradition of political philosophy which discovers its origin with Plato. According to Arendt, Plato identifies the public sphere of speech and action – the being-together of citizens in common – as a realm of darkness and deception that the philosopher must transcend in order to discover the clarity of eternal ideas which would otherwise remain corrupted by the unprejudiced circulation of a public *doxa* without standard or measure.[24] Arendt sees Platonism as the birth of a new model of sovereignty specific to the philosophers, one which first dissolves the integral bond between thought and action, theory and praxis, only to reassemble them in a hierarchical relation that imposes a certain governance of philosophy over politics, *bios theorètikos* over *bios politikos*. Far from signalling a productive alliance, Arendt maintains that, as long as political philosophy engenders the subordination of politics by philosophy, the tradition can only be understood according to the deep-seated tension between these two terms.[25]

Let us retain our proximity to Arendt for a moment longer. For the charges she levels against Plato not only anticipate those of Rancière and Castoriadis, but will serve to further enhance our understanding of the nature of the political itself. This predominance of *philosophy* over *politics*, *thought* over *praxis* begins, for Arendt, with another Platonic allegory: the well-known allegory of the cave.[26] Here, I will follow Abensour's interpretation of Arendt's extraordinary commentary.[27] While there is no need to retell the familiar narrative here, Abensour argues that, if we accept Arendt's strategically political reading, what the allegory of the cave describes in mythological terms is the origin of philosophy's representation of itself as diametrically opposed to the politics of the polis. For Arendt, this exercise of situating philosophy against politics would have a profound effect on the destiny of western political philosophy and its ability to grasp the meaning of politics itself. According to Abensour, by not only isolating the allegory of the cave as the centrepiece of Plato's political thought, but by emphasising the heroic figure of the philosopher at the centre of the narrative, Arendt reads the allegory as symbolic for philosophy's withdrawal from the shadowy world of human affairs in order to discover the Forms as means to establish an absolute standard of measure, a transcendent yardstick, according to which the organisation of the social may be appraised and evaluated *from without*.[28] It is this discovery that will ultimately qualify the philosopher as the proper governor of the city. For it is not that the Platonist desires the arbitrary rule of the tyrant who occupies a place beyond the law. What he seeks to establish is a government of wisdom, a new form of legitimacy constituted by a new model of authority: the authority of the philosophers. This is a model that remains entirely distinct from the comparatively crude strategies of violence and hegemony exercised by the oligarch, timocrat and tyrant, respectively.[29] Rather, the authority of the philosopher is derived from his claim to wisdom, a claim which is itself indicative of his own privileged proximity to the Forms, to truth itself (*aletheia*), that which remains structurally impervious to dispute, debate and public challenge.[30] Abensour understands this model of rule as essentially authoritarian in design. And yet, the basis of such a model, Abensour claims, would have been entirely unknown to the Greeks until Plato.[31] While authoritarianism obviously need not be Platonic in character, it is Plato who introduces this novel authoritarian framework to the ideal of the well-ordered polis. This is what is entirely new. While the Greeks certainly possessed an understanding of unrestricted rule under the name of tyranny, the *Republic*'s promotion of a privileged class of rulers who discover the source of their unchallengeable authority in a publicly inaccessible transcendent field would have been entirely foreign to the Greek political imaginary. This is precisely why Arendt maintains that Plato must acquire the blueprint for his model of government in a series of extra-political relationships: the shepherd and his sheep, the physician and his patient, the master and his slave, the captain and his crew.[32]

Insofar as the allegory of the cave recounts the manner in which, through his discovery of the Forms, the philosopher severs himself from the community and locates the proper order of the city in the transcendence of political relations, Arendt understands the narrative as the original statement of philosophy's formal opposition to the political. Moreover, given the *Republic*'s exemplary status in the larger tradition, Arendt appreciates the allegory to produce vast consequences for the subsequent history of political thought. It is here, Abensour contends, that her reading remains entirely unique from other interpretations of the allegory. Not only does Plato provide a model which establishes the essential antagonism between politics and philosophy, *doxa* and *aletheia*, he supplies a philosophical formula for the constitution of the city specifically designed to cancel out the threat of politics from the start. It is for this reason that Arendt insists that the true political implications of the cave are all too often overshadowed by its far more apparent epistemological dimensions, a problem which may be immediately forestalled when placed side by side with the allegory of the ship discussed above. Rancière has already suggested the formal correspondence between the two:

> The cave is the sea transposed beneath the earth, bereft of its sparkling glamour: enclosure instead of open sea, men in chains instead of rows of oarsmen, the dullness of shadows on the wall instead of light reflected on waves.[33]

Although the epistemological problem of the cave is well known, reading the allegory in light of the more transparent political symbolism of the ship, what becomes increasingly clear is that it is just as essential that the philosopher escape from the indeterminable sea of politics (the ship) as it is from the epistemological prison of illusion and *doxa* (the cave). If the allegory of the ship not only represents the psychology of the demos, but as I have suggested, something of the conditions of politics itself – its lack of any proper foundation – the allegory of the cave may represent with far greater clarity the mythological origins of the philosopher's quest to overcome those very conditions in order to discover the philosophical basis of the proper organisation of the city. Just as the cave concerns the problem of *doxa* which discovers its solution with the advent of the Forms (the ultimate basis for the philosopher's claim to wisdom), the ship concerns the problem of politics' anarchic condition which discovers its solution with the advent of the archê principle (the ultimate basis for the proper relations of rule). Both in the cave and on the ship, what is discernibly lacking is a social order governed by a Platonic vision of *aletheia*, a universal as much located at the limit of politics as it is at the limit of *doxa*. In order to establish the rule of the philosophers, which itself forms the basis of the proper order of society, Plato must first establish the philosopher's privileged relationship to *aletheia*. As demonstrated by Arendt, this is the lesson of the allegory of the cave.

And yet, although the philosopher must escape the bonds of the cave to bear witness to the radiant Forms in the sky above, what particularly interests Arendt, if we follow Abensour, is that the philosopher must inevitably return to the cave in order to realise the Forms in application.³⁴ Until that time, the Forms are destined to remain theoretical, purely aesthetic, their practical social function only truly apparent when the philosopher returns to the city and transforms it according to this abstract standard located beyond the realm of politics and public *doxa*.³⁵ As Arendt reminds us, there is nothing inherently political about the Forms in themselves. As often commented, Plato's recourse to the Forms could simply be taken to resolve a purely epistemological problem: in the democratic city where every statement appears equally reducible to the order of *doxa*, how are we to establish the ultimate criteria in which we may evaluate the veracity of each statement, their relative proximity to truth? But as soon as the philosopher returns to the cave and subjects the organisation of the city to an entirely alien set of abstract ideas which serve as the absolute standard to evaluate the basis of its structural model, political philosophy, as Arendt understands the term, is born.³⁶

The Polemics of the Polis: The Greek Invention of Politics

Therefore, reading Arendt, the larger political implications of the allegory of the cave become more apparent. And yet, it would be a mistake to accept Plato's perspectives as somehow indicative of the Greeks themselves. Perhaps one of the great ironies of the Greek civilisation is that the only culture that could have produced Plato's *Republic* was precisely the one that, more than any other, recognised the immense public significance of political affairs themselves. Nevertheless, Arendt determines, as would Castoriadis and Rancière, that while the *Republic* is often considered the archetype of political philosophy, the dialogue's principal concern is not at all the matters of politics, but rather their eclipse and obscuration. Plato can only arrive at the correct form of government via the formal elimination of politics itself, its displacement for a new model of authority. And while this brief sketch above merely intends to illustrate the allegorical origins of what she takes to be philosophy's rather consistent approach to the political across its history, from Arendt's conclusions we may proceed to draw a more general postulate that will not only serve to throw this customary approach to politics into question but at the same time provide an opportunity for its critical and historical reconstruction. Insofar as she grasps the discrepancy between the rule of the philosophers on the one hand and the matters of politics on the other, Arendt's reading of Plato is consistent with one of her most compelling theses: *politics remains irreducible to rule*.[37] Perhaps this simple revelation represents one of her most profound contributions to modern political thought. In Arendt's view, over the course of its long history, it was the cardinal error of the tradition of political philosophy to affix the concept of politics to a general framework dictated by the problem of rulers, governors, sovereigns and kings. Interestingly, in a somewhat obscure reference in *The History of Sexuality*, Michel Foucault seems to share a similar concern, lamenting political philosophy's apparent inability to think beyond the limits of this rather myopic theme: 'In political thought and analysis, we still have not cut off the head of the king.'[38] Whether a consistent strategy or perpetual oversight, Arendt maintains that this preoccupation with rule creates considerable difficulties for thinking the political in its own right. By displacing the matters of politics for countless theoretical models of rulers and ruled, philosophy has not only functioned to obscure its original meaning, but to deny the political any sustained philosophical inquiry. Here recall a passage from *The Human Condition* so pertinent it must be repeated at length:

> Escape from the frailty of human affairs into the solidity of quiet and order has in fact so much to recommend that the greater part of political philosophy since Plato could easily be interpreted as various attempts to find theoretical foundations and practical ways for an escape from politics altogether. The hallmark of all such escapes is the concept of rule, that is, the notion that men can lawfully and politically live together only when some are entitled to command and the others forced to obey.[39]

Beyond the *Republic*'s promotion of a new model of authority bound to the discovery of the Forms, Arendt suggests more generally that political philosophy's long fixation with rule consistently signals its systematic flight from politics altogether. Consequently, the author of *The Human Condition* clearly acknowledges that her own political phenomenology, which relies so heavily on the experience of the Greek public sphere, must inevitably confront and overturn this entire tradition accordingly. For this reason, rather than navigate various theories of government, sovereignty and the affairs of the State from Plato to Thomas Hobbes to Carl Schmitt, Arendt will opt to circumvent political philosophy for a more historical analysis of the Greek polis itself.[40] Therefore, in many respects, it is Arendt's efforts to dislodge politics from its restricted reference to rule that would ultimately incite her appeal to the Greeks. In attempt to recover something of its Classical roots, Arendt demonstrates that political affairs can never be adequately framed according to various models of rulers and ruled, however assembled or arranged. Politics is that which requires a very different approach. Likewise, when compelled to qualify her own understanding of political freedom, Arendt will routinely allude to the Greek *isonomia* or, more broadly, to the 'conditions of no-rule', the explicit absence of the formal division between governor and governed, ruler and ruled.[41] With great interest to the anarchist tradition, according to Arendt, political freedom can have no other meaning.

This strategy is entirely justified. For, in his landmark historical study *The Greek Discovery of Politics*, Christian Meier will recount the Greek invention of politics in a manner which largely supports Arendt's general claim. Often with reference to Athenian democracy, Meier explains that the word 'political' was used specifically to designate what *pertains to the polis*, that is, what is public, what is common in society (*koinos, xynos*) or what concerns the community as a whole.[42] It could be said that politics was perceived as the invention of a field which functions to intersect or cut across what would otherwise be restricted to the privileged or entitled, facilitating a notion of a political community that effectively suspends traditional filiations and alliances (birth, caste and class) in the deliberation of the affairs of the polis. And yet, politics was not understood as something universal, did not simply correspond to power or authority, did not describe the relations between cities (international relations) and was carefully distinguished from examples of unrestricted rule (the Greeks did not consider tyranny political, just as Arendt does not consider totalitarianism political). Politics, rather, in the broadest sense, was a term reserved to signify what constitutes a political community (*politeia*): it was understood as that which identifies or affiliates a political or citizen body with the polis itself, namely its participation in the sphere of society that is public and thus described the citizen's activity in the affairs of the polis accordingly.[43]

Therefore, in contrast to political philosophy, Meier's research certainly provides us the historical basis to reframe the political in a manner that is no longer dominated by references to the dictates of government, state administration or the authority concentrated in a narrow body of rulers or professional politicians. And yet, this does not imply that politics and rule did not collide and intersect in a number of ways (Meier reminds us, for example, that oligarchy would have been understood to become 'more political' precisely when it was increasingly broadened to include more and more public involvement).[44] In this respect, while Meier undoubtedly regards the *question* of government as fundamentally political in nature, rather than rule itself, he will tend to associate politics with its 'politicisation', the making of rule a political problem, the ever widening of the community's inclusion in the affairs of the polis, the emergence of a political body that encounters itself as a political body through its distinct relation to that which is political. Accordingly, for the Greeks, the meaning of politics was equally bound to both subject and city through this unique nexus between the two: politics renders those who were once simply ruled a political body by exposing the matters of the polis (that which concerns the whole community) to a political field so that the polis itself becomes synonymous with the political body by virtue of its participation in the matters of the polis.

Unquestionably, the implications of the Greek discovery of politics were considerable. It meant that, for the first time, the polis could be represented in a manner that was not possible before. As the polis became envisaged as something set out against any natural or inevitable order of society, as the destiny of the polis became appreciated as something to be shaped by the praxis of its citizens as political agents, the very constitution of the community itself could be interpreted as a problem specific to politics. This is the double movement we tend to encounter with politics: as soon as the problems of the polis become political, the very constitution of the polis itself may be appreciated as a political problem. It is in this respect, echoing Wolin, that Plato and Aristotle, who organise an investigation of the polis via a comparative politics of constitutional forms, arrive too late on the scene.[45] For politics is not a question of the respective styles of government observed across various constitutions, but what renders the constitution a problem of politics in the first place. This is precisely what Meier discovers with ancient Greek democracy:

> For the first time in Greek history—and world history—the civil order as a whole was placed at the disposal of the citizens: it had become a matter of controversy, hence a political issue. For the first time in history men were presented with a clear alternative, the starkest alternative that is possible within civic communities [. . .]:

> Should the governed (that is, those who were not professionally engaged in political life) be granted a decisive voice in civic affairs [. . .], or should they not? It was no longer simply a question of whether or not there should be some kind of public order or of who should have the right to govern (either a monarch or an aristocracy); it was not a question of how government should be conducted or what its precise structure should be. The question was now: Given the alternative constitutions that differ fundamentally, which should be chosen? Should government be in the hands of the nobles or of the people?[46]

For Meier, not unlike Castoriadis, what is significant here is the ability to explicitly pose the question, to discern the polis and the government of the polis as something problematic, as something *controversial*, a question no longer simply allocated to the jurisdiction of monarchs, nobles or the rich. Politics declares that the question regarding the order of the city is not prescribed and not settled. Politics is that which not only raises the question, but maintains that the question itself is political in nature. Consequently, for the Greeks, when there was politics, there was no longer simply rule.

Therefore, insofar as we follow the example of Arendt and maintain a certain fidelity to the Greek invention of the term, politics may be approached in a manner that resists a dominant theoretical paradigm that confines its meaning to various orders of rulers and ruled. Politics is not the problem of how an established set of rulers are to exercise their rule over a community. From what is *common* to what is *public* to what constitutes the *political community* itself, politics refers to an entirely different set of problems first expressed institutionally *as political problems* by a small number of cities scattered across the Greek peninsula. In ancient times, such cities were typically known as democracies. Quite distinct from the arrangements and strategies of rule, politics can be understood as that which collides with rule; it is what makes rule problematic, what puts rule into question as a given or unequivocal relation. Politics initiates a *polemics* of the polis.[47] It identifies the polis as an object worthy of controversy and public debate. At the same time, it denies the closure of political problems, the claim of a proper order or a final word, so that the polis, its constitution, and subsequent parts, roles and spaces remain problematic and ultimately irreducible. Politics is the exercise of making the polis political. As such, it does not describe the administration and management of the polis per se, but what engenders the city and the government of the city a political problem in the first place. Perhaps it is for this reason that, when Rancière speaks of politics, he will refer to acts of *dissensus*, the very process whereby the organisation of the community becomes an object of dispute: according to Rancière, the community is constituted a *political* community only when it is divided by a fundamental disagreement (*la mésentente*) regarding the basis of its partition of parts, roles and spaces. For Rancière, such disagreement is the essence of politics. Likewise, when Lefort speaks of politics (*la politique*), he will not simply refer to conflict and division (which is everywhere in society and hardly worthy of the term), but to what makes conflict and division *political*, visible and intelligible: politics is that which brings conflict in society to the fore, institutes it and gives it a political expression. Contrary to totalitarianism which strives to conceal and deny the manifestations of social division, by framing politics according to the inception of an irreducible forum in which conflict and division may be politically expressed, Lefort understands politics as the permanent contestation of the very question of what governs the relations of self and other at every level of social life. For Lefort, such contestation is the essence of politics.

Democracy's Anarchic Condition: A New Political Ontology

Therefore, by encouraging her readers to revisit the historical origins of the term, Arendt helps us to throw political philosophy's entire approach to politics into question. And while this is not the occasion to elaborate her own, more nuanced phenomenological interpretation of the political (which is in no way limited to the ancient understanding of the term), if we accept the general discrepancy between politics and rule as Arendt frames the terms, we may proceed to draw two inferences that will prove imperative to this study. First, after Arendt, a theory of democracy can no longer be initiated by virtue of the question: *When is rule democratic?* Against this familiar account outlined by figures like Joseph Schumpeter and countless others, democracy cannot be degraded to the situation whereby a community selects its rulers through free and periodic competitions.[48] *Democracy is that which challenges the very division between ruler and ruled.* Secondly, after Arendt, political philosophy can no longer organise its theoretical project around a series of problems that ultimately concern the proper foundations for one to rule another, the few to rule the many: the abstract criteria or first principles according to which an authority is rendered legitimate or an order of a society is rendered harmonious. *After Arendt, political philosophy must become something else altogether.* Perhaps it is for this reason that Abensour (who, unlike Rancière, never abandons philosophy's emancipatory potential or utopian promise) will propose that Arendt's very critique of the tradition of political philosophy makes 'another political philosophy' possible.[49] But rather than the endless pursuit of the proper foundations, standards and abstract criteria of rule, the first task of this new political philosophy, one now devised to resist its very tradition, would be exactly the opposite: a decisive attempt to think the political as *the very absence of any foundation of rule*. Politics opens the polis and the representation of the polis to a condition that lacks any such ontological closure. As such, it is the assignment of this new political philosophy to express, to make intelligible this lack of closure and its profound implications for society. As Castoriadis explains in the most accessible terms:

> If the human world were fully ordered [. . .], if human laws were given by God or by nature or by the 'nature of society' or by the 'laws of history,' then there would be no room for political thinking and no field for political action and no sense in asking what the proper law is or what justice is [. . .].[50]

This is the revelation of politics. When the matters of the polis become *political*, that is, when the problems that concern the whole community are exposed to a political field and articulated against a horizon of *doxa* and *agon* – without closure, without finality, without truth – so that the problem of the common *becomes* common, the problem of the public *becomes* public, and the very constitution of the polis itself is rendered an irreducible object of controversy and dispute, politics will reveal what Lefort could describe as a radical indeterminacy: a vast abyss, an infinite depth, a groundless ontological condition without foundation, without principle, without archê. Beyond the psychology of democrats, this is precisely the condition that Plato discovers with the democratic city. This is why democracy can be thought to be analogous to the sea.

Making Politics Thinkable

To posit an absolute foundation of rule signals the unequivocal closure of politics. As we encountered with Plato, there can be no reconciliation. But at the same time, the contrary is also true. The invention of politics exposes the polis and the constitution of the polis to a radical openness without closure, finality or absolution. It denies that there exists a proper order of society and indeed a proper set of rulers to govern that society. Rather, politics presents the polis as something controversial, an object worthy of interminable debate and dispute. For Meier, this discovery inaugurates an entirely new way to regard the city, its spaces, laws and administration. The political society is the one in which the matters of the polis, that which concern the whole community, are subjected to an irreducible political field. What the government should do, what the laws are for, what war is meant to achieve: no longer are these problems simply allocated to a given body of rulers (a certain class, tribe, family or lineage). They are problems that now belong to the domain of public *doxa* and *agon*. Persuasion replaces coercion; debate replaces command. For the first time, the destiny of the polis is placed at the disposal of its citizens as political agents and hence is expressed as a problem of politics. This represents a monumental shift in the evolution of the Greek polis. Politics is the exercise of making the polis political. As such, it can provide no foundation, no solid ground for rule. Instead, it can promise only the precarious experience of the sea. For this reason, beyond the problematisation of rule, beyond the *politicisation* of the polis, the putting into question of the order of the city and its subsequent parts, places and roles, politics may also describe a condition, the very condition that is indicative of the political society itself: *the lack of any proper foundation*. As the name of a city, a regime, a particular constitution, this is the condition which has long been associated with democracy, especially by its many detractors. Even more than the scandal of a government of the demos, the poor, those who have no right to govern, perhaps this is what so often accounts for its denunciation as disordered, unstable, anarchic.

In an intriguing interview with Eric Hazan, Rancière explains that democracy is the very basis of what makes politics *thinkable*.[51] As long as rule is simply allocated to the strong, the rich, the wisest among us, there is no need for politics. Rule is emblematic of the absence of politics and politics only complicates its application and authority. Rather, as we discovered with Arendt, politics is the exception to rule; it is what puts rule into question, what challenges its premises and assumptions. As witnessed with the Greeks, as soon as there is politics, there is no longer simply rule. When the matters of the polis are expressed as the matters of politics, when the very constitution itself is rendered *political*, rule and the relations of rule can no longer be understood as a straightforward and intuitive arrangement, the order of the city no longer perceived as a given, natural or immutable formation. The agent of this process is democracy. Democracy not only appears as an unprecedented political challenge to the rulers of the city but also serves to undermine the very foundations of rule. Plato understood this well. This accounts for why so much of his political philosophy is organised specifically to demonstrate the consequences – epistemological, sociological and psychological – of the democratic city's anarchic condition, its *need* to be governed. Therefore, as one of democracy's most notorious antagonists, the aim of Plato's project in the *Republic* is not difficult to decipher: to circumvent the political, to lay down a new foundation, to establish the archê of the wise. As Arendt perceived so acutely, so much of the history of political philosophy is dedicated to precisely that: the simultaneous discovery of the proper rulers of the city and the underlying basis which accounts for their authority. It is no surprise, therefore, that this tradition would routinely take issue with democracy. Democracy is that which introduces politics to the problem of rule; it is what erodes its foundations, what subverts its archê. This is perhaps its most important critical function. Democracy teaches us to think *politically*. According to Abensour, a new, *critical* political philosophy must learn to think, to critique, precisely in this manner. At least for Abensour, political philosophy need not be abandoned to its tradition.

Notes

1. Plato, *Republic*, VI, 488a–489d. All references are to Plato, *Complete Works*, ed. John M. Cooper and D. S. Hutchinson (Indianapolis: Hackett Publishing Company, 1997).
2. M. I. Finley demonstrates that, in many respects, the success of Athenian democracy depended upon its imperial power which itself relied upon its naval capabilities at sea. See M. I. Finley, *Democracy Ancient and Modern* (New Brunswick: Rutgers University Press, 1985), 87.
3. Jacques Rancière, *Hatred of Democracy* (London: Verso, 2007), 35–6. That Tocqueville offers a 'sociology of democracy' is a position supported by Castoriadis as well. See Cornelius Castoriadis, 'What Democracy?', *Figures of the Thinkable* (Stanford: Stanford University Press, 2007), 120–1. For a more substantial analysis of the sociological basis for Plato's rejection of democracy, see Thanassis Samaras, *Plato on Democracy* (New York: P. Lang, 2002), chapter 2.

4. Particularly in Book VIII.
5. Gerasimos Santas, 'Plato's Criticism of the Democratic Man in the *Republic*', *The Journal of Ethics* vol. 5, no. 1 (2001): 67. For a more general account of this connection between constitution and psychology in Plato's *Republic*, see G. R. F. Ferrari, *City and Soul in Plato's Republic* (Chicago: University of Chicago Press, 2005), chapter 3.
6. Plato, *Republic*, VIII, 557d.
7. Jacques Rancière, 'The Uses of Democracy', *On the Shores of Politics* (London: Verso, 2007), 42.
8. Santas, 'Plato's Criticism of the Democratic Man in the *Republic*', 62.
9. Plato, *Republic*, VIII, 560d–e. Also see Dick Howard, *The Primacy of the Political: A History of Political Thought from the Greeks to the French and American Revolutions* (New York: Columbia University Press, 2010), 55.
10. Plato, *Republic*, VIII, 562d–563d.
11. Finley, *Democracy Ancient and Modern*, 87.
12. In Jacques Rancière, *The Philosopher and His Poor* (Durham, NC: Duke University Press, 2003).
13. Jacques Rancière, 'Introduction', *On the Shores of Politics*, 1.
14. Ibid., 2.
15. Ibid., 1–2. Also see John McSweeney, 'Giving Politics an Edge: Rancière and the Anarchic Principle of Democracy', *Sofia Philosophical Review* vol. 3, no. 1 (2009): 129–30.
16. Rancière outlines archipolitics in Jacques Rancière, *Disagreement: Politics and Philosophy* (Minneapolis: University of Minnesota Press, 1999), 65–70.
17. Ibid., 16.
18. According to Castoriadis, democracy is the regime explicitly founded on *doxa*. See Cornelius Castoriadis, 'Intellectuals and History', *Philosophy, Politics, Autonomy* (New York: Oxford University Press, 1991), 7. Likewise, Chantal Mouffe will repeatedly emphasise the role of the *agon* in the democratic city. See Chantal Mouffe, 'For an Agonistic Model of Democracy', *The Democratic Paradox* (London: Verso, 2000).
19. Rancière, *Hatred of Democracy*, 38.
20. Rancière, *Disagreement*, 61.
21. See Jean-Philippe Deranty, 'Rancière and Contemporary Political Ontology', *Theory and Event* vol. 6, no. 4 (2003).
22. Cornelius Castoriadis, *Ce qui fait la Grèce. 1 D'Homère à Héraclite* (Paris: Seuil, 2004), 288.
23. Claude Lefort, 'Hannah Arendt and the Question of the Political', *Democracy and Political Theory* (Minneapolis: University of Minnesota Press, 1988), 46.
24. See Arendt's remarks in Hannah Arendt, 'Tradition and the Modern Age', in *Between Past and Future* (London: Penguin, 2006).

25. This remains a predominant theme in her posthumous volume Hannah Arendt, *The Promise of Politics* (New York: Schocken Books, 2005).
26. Plato, *Republic*, VII, 514a–520a.
27. Miguel Abensour, 'Against the Sovereignty of Philosophy over Politics: Arendt's Reading of Plato's Cave Allegory', *Social Research* vol. 74, no. 4 (Winter 2007). Also see Miguel Abensour, *Hannah Arendt contre la philosophie politique?* (Paris: Sens & Tonka, 2006).
28. Hannah Arendt, 'What is Authority?', *Between Past and Future*, 109. Also see Abensour, 'Against the Sovereignty of Philosophy over Politics', 970.
29. Arendt employs the term 'authority' with a great precision. According to Arendt, authority refers to a relationship of obedience organised through a hierarchical structure which locates its legitimacy in a realm beyond the political itself.
30. See Hannah Arendt, 'Truth and Politics', *Between Past and Future*.
31. Abensour, 'Against the Sovereignty of Philosophy over Politics', 960.
32. Arendt, 'What is Authority?', 108. Also see Abensour, 'Against the Sovereignty of Philosophy over Politics', 960–1.
33. Rancière, 'Introduction', 2.
34. Abensour, 'Against the Sovereignty of Philosophy over Politics', 964–5.
35. Hannah Arendt, *The Human Condition* (Chicago: University of Chicago Press, 1998), 226.
36. See Arendt, 'What is Authority?', 11–13. Also see Abensour, 'Against the Sovereignty of Philosophy over Politics', 971–2.
37. Parchen Markell, 'The Rule of the People: Arendt, Archê and Democracy', *The American Political Science Review* vol. 100, no. 1 (Feb. 2006): 3.
38. Michel Foucault, *The History of Sexuality; Volume I: An Introduction* (New York: Vintage Books, 1990), 88–9.
39. Arendt, *The Human Condition*, 222.
40. Although *The Human Condition* offers no systematic analysis of democracy, outlining her concept of politics without explicitly employing the term, Arendt's later work, particularly *On Revolution* and *The Promise of Politics*, will offer a more direct engagement with democracy, now binding it to her notion of *praxis* in a more explicit manner.
41. Hannah Arendt, *On Revolution* (London: Penguin Books, 2006), 20. Also see Arendt, 'Tradition and the Modern Age', 18–19, where she cites Athens as the exemplary model of the city without division between ruler and ruled.
42. Christian Meier, *The Greek Discovery of Politics* (Cambridge, MA: Harvard University Press, 1990), 13.
43. Ibid., 20–1.

44. Ibid., 13.
45. Sheldon Wolin argues that Plato's and Aristotle's political philosophy is more a philosophy of the constitution than a philosophy of politics. See Sheldon S. Wolin, 'Norm and Form: The Constitutionalizing of Democracy', in *Athenian Political Thought and the Reconstruction of American Democracy*, ed. J. Peter Euben, John R. Wallach and Josiah Ober (Ithaca: Cornell University Press, 1994).
46. Meier, *The Greek Discovery of Politics*, 84.
47. Here I draw both from the modern French polémique ('disputatious, argumentative') and from the Greek polemikós ('hostile, warlike').
48. See Joseph Schumpeter, *Capitalism, Socialism, and Democracy* (New York: Harper, 1950).
49. Abensour, 'Against the Sovereignty of Philosophy over Politics', 979–80. Also see Patrice Vermeren, 'Equality and Democracy', *Diogenes* vol. 55, no. 4 (2008).
50. Cornelius Castoriadis, 'The Greek *Polis* and the Creation of Democracy', *Philosophy, Politics, Autonomy* (New York: Oxford University Press, 1991), 104.
51. Jacques Rancière and Eric Hazan, 'Democracies against Democracy', in Giorgio Agamben et al., *Democracy in What State?* (New York: Columbia University Press, 2001), 78–9.

Chapter 2

Dissolution of the Archê

The democratic kratein, the power of the people, is first of all the power to foil the archê and then to take responsibility, all together and each individually, for the infinite opening that is thereby brought to light.
                                       Jean-Luc Nancy, *The Truth of Democracy*

In the Name of Democracy: The *Kratos* of the Demos

Having established the general distinction between politics and rule, keeping with our analysis of Plato, in this chapter we will encounter our first substantive example of the antinomies of politics in what will be determined to be its most universal or general form: a democracy against the archê. As Arendt and Rancière both develop through close readings of Plato's *Laws*, the archê may be introduced as the underlying theoretical principle that functions to both establish and justify the essential divide that separates governor from governed, ruler from ruled. Whether it installs the rule of the king (*monarchy*), the rule of an opulent minority (*oligarchy*) or the hypothetical rule of the wisest among us (Plato's own ideal city), the logic of the archê is the same. In all its forms, it is this very logic that I argue democracy renders problematic wherever and whenever it appears. As Plato clearly observed, democracy's defiant claim of an 'anarchic' equality functions to undermine those very hierarchies so carefully assembled upon the foundation of the archê itself. Therefore, remaining something of an anomaly in political philosophy's rather monotonous exercise of classifying constitutional forms, unlike monarchy, oligarchy and Plato's own utopian city, democracy will refuse to simply be conflated with other models of rule. Rather, democracy is the name of that which frustrates the very division between ruler and ruled. This is the basis of its politics.

Democracy has always meant the *power of the people*, but this power (*kratos*) does not found a new principle of rule in society. As often remarked, unlike 'monarchy' and 'oligarchy', the word 'democracy' makes no reference to an archê principle and, indeed, never testifies to an archê of the demos. The *kratos* of the demos is not the power of a particular body, class or number, but the power of all those who have no archê to which they may appeal, all those who fall short of every standard or criterion which would entitle them to participate in the deliberation of the affairs of the polis. Consequently, as the power of those who by every definition lack an archê to govern, democracy may be interpreted as an extraordinary challenge to the archê itself, the very principle that references a special qualification or entitlement in the rule of the community. Democracy is unique in that it posits itself *against* the archê, against any underlying principle from which a proper set of rulers may be determined or a proper order of society may be established. Accordingly, the precise meaning of the *power of the people* should not be understood as the rule of the people as opposed to the rule of the oligarchs or the rule of a monarch. This is a common misconception. Rather, before anything else, democracy's *power of the people* means this: the power to sabotage the archê presupposed by every other order. It means the destabilisation of the very foundations upon which oligarchs and kings isolate themselves from the rest of the community and claim a certain privilege in the distribution of the relations of rule. Democracy rejects any principle from which a special entitlement to rule may be established. Democracy not only lacks any such principle itself, but it is according to this lack that the *kratos* of the demos must ultimately be understood.

In many respects, Rancière, Lefort and Abensour can each be read to put forward a notion of democracy that may be appreciated, implicitly or explicitly, as *anarchic*. But of the three, it is arguably Rancière who develops this theme most directly and in the greatest detail. It is for this reason that I will centre his various discussions of the topic in my more formal delineation of what I will frame as a democracy against the archê. To what extent can Rancière be interpreted in this way? This is the question I wish to consider. Although Arendt takes us quite far, identifying the first appearance of the archê as an abstract principle of rule in the political philosophy of Plato, Rancière's analysis will be found particularly valuable as he situates the problem in the specific context of democracy itself. Indeed, Rancière understands the anarchy which Plato ascribes to democracy quite literally: not only does democracy invent a notion of government that appeals to no archê, but its strategic fabrication of an 'anarchic title', a title for all those without title, also serves to compromise the very logic of the archê itself. It is in this context that the profound implications of a democracy against the archê become most apparent. When democracy ruptures the logic that functions to isolate the proper rulers of the city, it effectively displaces the order of the archê for the order of politics, that which we already found to offer no solid ground, no foundation, for rule. What Rancière on occasion calls 'political' or 'anarchic' government is therefore the government that offers no apolitical solution to the problem of the organisation of the social. In the absence of an archê, government can simply provide no unequivocal basis to justify its relations, institutional models or design. Rather, government can claim to rest only upon its own contingency and nothing more. Democracy can very much be understood in this way. Contrary to the government that establishes itself on an archic foundation, democracy is political all the way down. It exposes the radical contingency of the social at the root of every regime. To acknowledge and, indeed, to institute this contingency is an important facet of what politics means.

Accordingly, following a detailed analysis of the logic of the archê as uncovered in Plato's *Laws*, reading Rancière, we will carefully formulate and develop democracy's unique strategy to throw this very logic into jeopardy with the 'anarchic title'. My approach to Rancière does not merely extend Arendt's original critique of the archê to democracy in a more explicit manner, but aims to consider the broader consequences (social and institutional) of a democracy understood to be universally organised against the archê itself. Democracy not only lacks an archê, but is also *against* it. Even in a purely theoretical treatment, this *against* will be found to reveal much about democracy's political objectives and claims of equality. At the same time, it will also clarify why historically the archê has remained so attractive to rule. The archê shelters government from the contingency of the social and supplies it a logic, a rationale, an account for why it is this particular class or body of rulers who govern and no one else. Democracy represents a significant challenge to this logic and obliges us to think about the social, institutions, government and its foundations in an entirely different way. To government, democracy introduces the complications of politics. This signifies the dissolution of the archê. It is in this technical sense that democracy can be understood as *anarchic*.

On the Universality of the Problem of the Archê

Let us begin with the problem of government itself. What is the basis for one to rule another, the few to rule the many? Democracy's reply is as uncompromising as it is scandalous: there is no basis. Consequently, democracy regards every initiative to establish such a basis, to discover and secure some underlying principle which functions to ground the division between ruler and ruled and supply an account of that division, to be a priori false. Democracy assumes a sceptical attitude towards any claim of an inherent right to rule, any regime which draws its legitimacy from a metaphysical first principle, whether it be God, nature, history, truth, the party, leader or nation.[1] Perhaps this is why in the preface to his monumental history *The Life and Death of Democracy*, John Keane will introduce the theme of democracy in terms of the *denaturing* of power:

> Democracy required that people see through talk of gods and nature and claims to privilege based on superiority of brain and blood. [. . .] It implied that the most important political problem is how to prevent rule by the few, or by the rich or powerful who claim to be supermen.[2]

Since its earliest institutional experiments in the cities of ancient Greece, democracy has offered a profound rejection of the rule of the nobles, the rich, the virtuous (the aristocrats) and the wisest among us (Plato's philosopher-kings). What it rejects is the bedrock upon which any such privileged status or entitlement to rule may be ultimately established and, in so doing, functions to expose the sheer contingency of every social order. 'The exceptional thing about the type of government called democracy is that it demanded people see that nothing that is human is carved in stone, that everything is built on shifting sands of time and place [. . .].'[3] Whether it be the rule of the prophets or the rule of a party, democracy is that which undermines the very claim of a fixed or immutable foundation of rule. And while Keane may prefer the metaphor of shifting sands to Plato's stormy seas, the connotations of the trope are very much the same: from the beginning, what democracy reveals so convincingly is that every form of government, every order of rule, is essentially artificial, historical, *human* and never carved in stone. Regardless of birth, wealth, seniority or expertise, democracy makes the claim of a special criterion, qualification or entitlement to rule inherently problematic. Of this claim, we may assign the name 'archê'.

On the rather under-theorised problem of the archê (*arkhê*), which we may now delineate with greater precision and detail, it is arguably Arendt and Rancière who, across a number of their writings, will most successfully penetrate both its logic and function in the rule of the community. Look for it and you will find it. In every claim of a natural order, in every claim of birth right or heredity, of divine sanction, of privilege or priority, of the proper order of society, the proper allocation of parts and roles, it is there: the archê principle. As soon as the rulers of the city are identified with birth, wealth, expertise or any other requirement to govern, as soon as the exercise of rule appeals to a principle that distributes the community according to a predetermined set of criteria, the logic of the archê is established. Those in possession of the archê are those who possess the power to elevate themselves over the rest of society. The archê is precisely the power to deny the ordinary voice.[4]

Although Rancière offers no single, integrated or systematic theory of the archê, the problem reappears again and again in his most important writings on democracy. Rancière observes that governments often appear to require an account of themselves, of what grounds and justifies why some occupy the position of rulers and others the position of those who are ruled. Therefore, although rarely articulated by governors themselves, it would seem that, alongside the exercise of rule, government also requires a framework, a rationality for how one comes to rule another. In many respects, we will encounter a somewhat analogous perspective with anarchism, the tradition which adopts a position against the archê in its very name. According to Noam Chomsky, it is anarchism's most basic presupposition that, unless justification can be given, any hierarchy or structure of authority in society (including government, ownership and management, relations between men and women, parents and children, etc.) must ultimately be deemed illegitimate and systematically dismantled.[5] 'That is what I have always understood to be the essence of anarchism: the conviction that the burden of proof has to be placed on authority, and that it should be dismantled if that burden cannot be met.'[6] Interestingly, what both views appear to imply (Rancière's and anarchism's) is that government is never self-authorising or self-legitimating; in every case, something else is required, something which, however valid or invalid, claims to provide an account of that government and the configuration of its relations.[7] The justification of rule is always *supplemental* to the material exercise of rule itself. The diagram of rule is never one dimensional.

The issue at hand is not the cultivation of a practical strategy in which we may determine which authority can be considered legitimate and which cannot (although Chomsky certainly maintains there are examples of legitimate authority, however rare). Nor is it the quintessentially modern question concerning the precise relationship between right and power (theorised so meticulously by figures like Baruch Spinoza).[8] Rather, the issue at hand is that every system and strategy of rule appears to require a supplement, a justification or account of itself which is never immanent to rule in its most immediate or material manifestation. Once rule is distinguished from mere coercion and brute force, it will be found to organise a logic which binds the empirical organisation of a community to an imperceptible principle that determines the basis of its relations. The archê is the principle that at once identifies, selects and allocates so that a classification of rulers may be distinguished from that of the ruled while at the same time providing a consistent frame of reference which justifies the distinction of these roles and the distribution among them. Therefore, establishing the underlying basis of rule is essential to the meaning of the archê: it is for this reason that Rancière will uncover an archê in every order of the police and Abensour in every State-form.[9] The logic of the archê serves to transform the multiplicity and contingency of the social into a means by which a special class of rulers (those who exercise the archê) may be isolated from the rest of the community (those who must submit to its authority). It operates by selecting a particular aspect from the social (such as birth or wealth) and renders this aspect the decisive grounds for the justification of some to govern others.[10] In short, the archê offers a solution to the problem of qualification, of who is entitled to rule.

The Nature of Rule: An Interpretation of Plato's *Laws*

To demonstrate this logic in the most succinct manner possible, Rancière will regularly refer his readers to Plato's *Laws* where the ancient philosopher will most methodically put forward his own enumeration of viable titles or qualifications (*axiomata*) to rule another.[11] Here, in the voice of an unnamed Athenian, Plato lists seven in number (although his catalogue is far from exhaustive), but for the moment let us consider only the first six, the seventh remaining something of an exception. Without hesitation, Plato will draw no distinction between the administration of a city and the authority devised in entirely different institutions (such as the family). That cities, much like families, elevate those with authority over those who must yield to that authority is simply assumed and completely naturalised. Accordingly, the first of the titles to be listed are those purportedly closest to nature: those positions that are determined directly by birth (those who are 'born before' or 'born otherwise'). The census begins with the control that parents exercise over their children. This is followed by the entitlement of those who are highborn (the aristocrats) to govern those of no account. Next is the authority that elders maintain over the young (seniority). The fourth concerns the dominion of masters over their slaves. But then our criteria are modified slightly. Although Plato insists that the following two qualifications remain every bit as agreeable with nature, they can arguably no longer be said to be directly related to birth as the preceding four. These consist of the rule of the strong over the weak (which the Athenian also finds predominant throughout the animal kingdom) and the only title that Plato himself ultimately holds to be valid: 'But it looks as if the most important claim will be the sixth, that the ignorant man should follow the leadership of the wise and obey his orders.' Hence, buried deep within the *Laws*, we finally appear to discover the principle that the *Republic* so desperately requires: the principle that dictates that the wise shall rule the ignorant. And while the cogency of declaring wisdom a 'natural' quality akin to birth or strength could certainly be questioned, Plato's Athenian, perhaps anticipating opposition, will allow for no objections: 'I'm certainly not prepared to say that it is *un*natural.' Regardless, while the essentially unchecked philosopher-kings of the *Republic* make no appearance in the *Laws* (which concerns itself with an impressive range of more practical constitutional matters), it is nevertheless with this sixth qualification that the principle which accounts for their rule will be most explicitly articulated. As with any other title, this too is simply posited as given and axiomatic. Even in the *Laws*, the Platonic text which perhaps more than any other gestures towards the rule of law, that the wise should rule the ignorant requires no more explanation than that of a parent's authority over their own children.

Again, let us suspend the question of the validity of each of these titles. Whether seniority actually represents a legitimate criterion to govern those who are younger and what exactly it means to be the 'stronger' is certainly subject to debate, but it brings us no closer to understanding the logic of the archê itself. Rather than evaluate the specific content of each qualification, what interests us here is the general structure of the archê as it appears in Plato's thought. By virtue of kinship, age or some other quality, with each of the catalogued qualifications we encounter a familiar binary relation (parent/child, nobleman/commoner, elder/young, master/slave, wise/ignorant) organised into a carefully coordinated hierarchy of roles. More importantly, it is clear that Plato understands the distribution of these roles to be determined entirely by *disposition*, that is, according to some inherent or natural difference which informs one's place within a given hierarchical relation. Indeed, what each of these familiar binaries so unambiguously reveal to Plato is that just as there is a natural disposition to rule, there is a natural disposition to be ruled, just as there is a natural disposition to act, there is a natural disposition to be acted upon. As Rancière demonstrates, such determinate superiorities and inferiorities are simply presupposed and, in many cases, can be readily observed across society: 'All these qualifications relate to objective differences and forms of power already operative in society and can all be put forward as an *arkhê* for ruling.'[12] The archê's reference to disposition is precisely an attempt to identify and exploit such 'objective differences'. To simply divide the categories of ruler and ruled is not enough. The archê must simultaneously devise a practical strategy in which real existing bodies may be identified, distinguished and distributed across these categories according to clearly observable and preferably immutable traits and characteristics. Therefore, despite their obvious manifestation in a social field, insofar as Plato's six initial qualifications to rule remain contingent upon one's inherent disposition, the archê may ultimately be understood to appeal to nature (*phusis*): each determinate superiority and its complementary counterpart compose a particular hierarchical arrangement which claims a certain continuity with a purported natural law:

> Each of these titles fulfils two prerequisites. First, each defines a hierarchy of positions. Secondly, each defines this hierarchy in continuity with nature: continuity by the intermediary of familial and social relations for the first four; direct continuity for the last two.

The former titles base the order of the city on the law of kinship. The latter assert that this order has a superior principle: those who govern are not at all those who are born first or highborn, but those who are best.[13]

Hence, it is not with tradition or convention, *nomos* or *mythos*, but with nature that Plato discovers the normative principles that function to determine and regulate these various hierarchical relations across society. Within each natural hierarchy, Plato attributes a latent archê principle which governs the dynamics of that relation and accounts for the harmony of its natural order in a manner that cannot be easily challenged. So just as the criticism of our infamous democratic man of the *Republic* dwells so stubbornly on his psychological disposition – a disposition which may now, in light of the *Laws*, simply be appreciated as the *natural disposition to be ruled* – Plato likewise understands the philosophers of the city to embody the appropriate characteristics indicative of their own natural proclivity to rule. This is a logic which remains very consistent with Plato's perception of democracy as the upside-down world described in the *Republic*: for Plato, democracy represents the society in which those with the natural disposition to be ruled, rule collectively, a scenario played out symbolically on the allegorical ship of democracy. Quite simply, democracy is the agent that effectively inverts the natural order of the proper relations of the social. As I have demonstrated, the allegory of the ship not only intends to demonstrate the ignorance and savagery of the demos but, more to the point, invites us to bear witness to the regime in which no operative archê is in place. For Plato, democracy is that which systematically overturns every archê at once.

Furthermore, this appeal to nature, to the disposition of the philosopher, also explains why so much of the *Republic* is devoted to the topic of education.[14] For if only the wise, those with the natural disposition of the philosopher (the rational soul), are entitled to govern, it is imperative that Plato's city establish an institutional strategy to ascertain *who* in society possesses such a disposition naturally fit to rule. And yet, while it is no doubt his intimacy with the Forms that ultimately establishes the philosopher's wisdom and, hence, his exceptional nature compared to those who are ignorant, Plato recognises that, in terms of assuming his proper place in government, wisdom alone is not sufficient. To establish his position as governor, to be entitled to rule, Plato also requires a principle which dictates that it is the wise who shall rule the ignorant and not the reverse or some other arrangement altogether. Such a principle cannot be said to be provided by the Forms themselves. This is an important detail that Arendt's critique of Plato's allegory of the cave appears to overlook. The Forms may certainly account for the nature of the philosopher's disposition as the wisest among us, but such a disposition only becomes a basis to rule when it is stipulated by the appropriate archê principle. Although essential to his political philosophy, the archê remains supplemental to the Forms and, if we follow Plato, is discovered in nature, not in the heavens above. Therefore, just as Plato thematically associates the *Forms*, *wisdom* and the *sky*, he will likewise relate the *archê*, *entitlement* and *nature*. Whereas the Forms provide an absolute standard or measure to evaluate the organisation of the proper order of the city under the name of justice, the archê provides the basis for the proper relations of rule under the name of natural law. Both in substance and in function, the logic of the archê remains quite distinct from that of the Forms in Plato's thought: as the Forms represent transcendent ideas of eternal essences which intend to resolve the problem of *doxa*, the archê represents a principle attributed to nature which intends to resolve the problem of *politics*. The Forms may provide the theoretical grounds for the philosopher's claim to wisdom, but it is only the archê principle, rather than the Forms themselves, that renders wisdom a qualification and grants the wise his proper place as governor of the city.

Commandment and *Commencement*: The Strange Logic of the Archê Principle

How then are we ultimately to grasp the logic of the archê? As we have seen, the archê attributes the ruler's particular entitlement to rule not to any social or historical institution, but to nature itself, a strategy clearly designed to circumvent the complications of politics from the start. What Plato attempts to coordinate is a *nomos* that coincides with *phusis*.[15] When this is achieved, the possibility for a distinctively political society is effectively foreclosed. And yet, the predictable charge that Plato's six initial titles to govern in actuality represent sociological relations opposed to natural ones is not the point. We can certainly doubt that Plato's qualifications may be drawn from nature as he claims, but that they may function *as* qualifications is something that cannot be so easily disputed. Rather, what can be garnered from Plato's appeal to nature is something far more crucial to the logic of the archê itself: the archê not only represents a principle of rule (*commandment*) but, at the same time, a theory of verification which organises a rationality that understands the legitimacy of rule according to its origin, its temporal beginning or anticipation of itself (*commencement*). As Rancière explains in *Hatred of Democracy*:

> *Arkhê* is the commandment of he who commences, of what comes first. It is the anticipation of the right to command in the act of commencing and the verifying of the power of commencing in the exercise of commanding. The ideal is thus defined of a government which consists in realising the principle by which the power of governing commences, of a government which consists in exhibiting *en acte* the legitimacy of its principle. Those who are capable of governing are those who have the dispositions that make them appropriate for the role, those who are capable of being governed are those who have dispositions complementary to the former.[16]

Insofar as it binds rule to disposition and disposition to destination, the archê contains within it a logic of *priority*. When the archê distributes the social according to a predetermined or predefined set of qualities and attributes, what it ultimately seeks to demonstrate is only those who rule possess the inherent capacity to do so. By qualifying that rule is anticipated by the disposition that is essential to what it means to be a ruler, by placing the exercise of rule in direct relation with its beginnings or the conditions of its beginnings, the archê functions to justify that order of rule in advance. For example, when oligarchy declares that the wealthy represent the appropriate rulers of the city, it claims that only the wealthy possess the capacity to govern and that it is precisely the conditions of wealth which give rise to such a capacity. Likewise, in modern times, when capital declares that only the capitalist class is capable of managing our financial institutions and means of production, it claims that only this particular class embodies the integrity, ingenuity and insight necessary to manage a productive, stable economy and that it is precisely the conditions that make this class what it is that instil it with these essential attributes. Hence, according to the logic of the archê, what the exercise of rule actually reveals is the infinite process of discovering its own legitimacy in the origins of what it is that constitutes the proper ruler of the community in the first place. When rule references the archê, it references the past of itself. Rule always anticipates itself in a time that comes before. It is precisely this anticipation of rule that government calls forth and rehearses in the present act of ruling another. This is indicative of the rather circular logic the archê appears to set in motion: just as the exercise of rule enacts or recalls the source of its origins, these origins claim to verify and confirm that rule in advance by virtue of its very rule. This circularity forms the basis of Rancière's most concise definition of the term:

> An *arkhê* is two things: it is a theoretical principle entailing a clear distribution of positions and capacities, grounding the distribution of power between rulers and ruled; and it is a temporal beginning entailing that the fact of ruling is anticipated in the disposition to rule and, conversely, that the evidence of this disposition is given by the fact of its empirical operation.[17]

Plato's appeal to nature clearly corresponds to this second dimension of the archê, but that he formally intersects these two ostensibly unrelated terms ('commandment' and 'commencement', 'ruling' and 'beginning') would in fact have remained generally consistent with the ancient understanding of the concept.[18] As Rancière acknowledges, this is something that does not escape Arendt. In *The Human Condition* and a number of other texts, Arendt is perhaps the first political theorist to recognise that our conventional translations of *arkhê* and *archein* as 'rule' and 'to rule' in English and *herrschaft* and *herrschen* in German often serve to eclipse the significance of this second dimension of the Greek term (which, according to Arendt, may have actually been its primary meaning).[19] Consequently, Arendt will repeatedly demonstrate that, in addition to its allusions to rule, the archê may also signify 'to begin', 'to initiate', 'to lead' and even 'to set in motion' and it is for this reason that she tends to associate the term with her own theory of political activity in the public sphere (*praxis*): for Arendt, politics is the order of equals who possess the power to initiate action in the polis, to set the polis in motion.[20] To participate in the polis is therefore to take part in the archê, to take initiative in governing and to lead the polis collectively. It is in this context, quite opposed to Rancière, that she will tend to characterise the political in terms of the public distribution of the archê, a collective sharing of the task of governing the city as equals.[21] Likewise, when Arendt speaks of revolution in terms of a 'new beginning' or 'beginning again' (opposed to its more customary associations of insurrection and social upheaval), it is likely she is alluding to this often forgotten dimension of archê as commencement once again. For essential to Arendt's understanding of revolution in the modern age is a notion of freedom bound to the experience of a new beginning, the establishment of a new order or foundation.[22] And while her own discussions of the archê may admittedly at times be found to accentuate these 'new beginnings' or 'initiations of action' at the expense of its reference to rule, this will only sharpen her grasp of Plato's particular organisation of the concept for his own strategic purposes:

> it is decisive for Plato, as he says expressly at the end of the *Laws*, that only the beginning (*archê*) is entitled to rule (*archein*). In the tradition of Platonic thought, this original, linguistically predetermined identity of ruling and beginning had the consequence that all beginning was understood as the legitimation for rulership, until, finally, the element of beginning disappeared altogether from the concept of rulership.[23]

Although Plato's archê indeed represents the formal conjunction of 'commandment' and 'commencement', 'ruling' and 'beginning', in keeping with the Greek term, Arendt warns that our general understanding of the archê should in no way be determined by Plato's particular arrangement of the concept as it comes down to us in political philosophy. In contrast to her own theory of praxis, which she clearly associates with the public 'distribution of the archê' across the polis, Arendt insists that it is Plato, once again establishing something of a precedent for the tradition of political philosophy, who rather discovers in the archê a first principle for rule. This is what is entirely new. And if Arendt is correct, Plato's theoretical manoeuvre here will not be difficult to retrace. In his own research, Rancière locates a very early illustration of the archê in Homer: Odysseus, publicly affirming Agamemnon as the sole commander of the Greek army, declares Agamemnon the one in possession of the archê, implying that Agamemnon takes the lead, while everyone else walks behind.[24] But at least since Anaximander, ancient philosophy consistently employs the term *arkhê* to identify a metaphysical first principle, the substance, source and immutable nature of an existing thing which preserves the essence of its origin in all subsequent transformations and expressions.[25] Therefore, we may hypothesise that, when Plato indiscriminately applies this distinctively Presocratic conception of the archê to a theory of government, what he is able to extract from the archê is precisely a first principle in which the legitimation of rule is located at the beginning of rule itself, at its source or origin. As we have seen, as the commandment of what commences, of what comes first, the archê organises a logic in which rule anticipates itself in that which comes before, the disposition to rule that is both demonstrated and confirmed by the very exercise of rule itself. Therefore, insofar as the concept appears in the tradition of political philosophy under the guidance of Plato, the archê can be said to locate the justification of rule in an immemorial past: it organises a theory of legitimation which privileges a time past, a time which perpetually precedes politics, anticipates its disruptions and seeks to hinder them from the start.

Accordingly, this explains why Rancière's approach to the problem of the archê deviates so drastically from that of Arendt's.[26] As Arendt presumably endeavours to re-establish what she purports to be the archê's original political relationship to the polis, Rancière's analysis suggests the predominance of the relatively unchallenged Platonic interpretation of the concept has so eclipsed its meaning throughout the history of political thought that it must simply be appraised and evaluated on this basis, any residual pre-Platonic connotations seemingly futile to salvage. This disparity will likewise account for the divergence between Arendt's and Rancière's respective positions on the archê's political significance. While Arendt understands politics as the collective possession of the archê equally distributed across the polis, Rancière insists that politics involves nothing less than the archê's uncompromised dissolution. There is indeed some validity to Rancière's concerns. For whatever its original political formulation in the Greek polis, the general problem that Plato seeks to resolve with his appeal to the archê remains as relevant as ever. As long as government implies the formal division between governor and governed, ruler and ruled, it will likewise require a general framework in which the legitimation of this division may be readily verified. As we have seen, this is precisely what Plato attributes to the archê. In many respects, this is what anarchism appears to associate with the archê as well. Therefore, if the tradition of political philosophy since Plato has long been enchanted by the archê principle (or its general logic), this only confirms once again its enduring commitment not to democracy and equality, but to the establishment and preservation of its preferred rulers over the ages. Wealth, blood, class or brain: whenever it is declared only the exceptional among us possess the inherent capacity to govern, the logic of the archê has been initiated. Whenever the justification for that government is referred to the anticipatory origins of what makes that government what it is, the function of the archê has been achieved.

In Summary: Archic Government

Therefore, in the broadest strokes, what can be taken from Plato's model of the archê? The archê fosters a representation of society in which its primary task is to become identical with itself, to establish an order of government that corresponds with its underlying principle. A monarchy is not simply the city ruled by a king, but the city in which its underlying principle stipulates that it is the king who represents its proper ruler and no one else. Once the archê is posited theoretically, the organisation of the community may be interpreted as a rational problem as opposed to a political one. This explains its long appeal to philosophy. The archê inaugurates a project of discovering the grounds, the underlying principles, which claim to justify various social hierarchies and relations of rule, some already established in society, some remaining purely hypothetical (Plato's philosopher-rulers). Predicated upon the postulate that there is a nature of the social, the archê identifies the basis for the proper order of rule in the proper relations of the social. This intends to obstruct politics or the potential for politics, by claiming that the regulation of society remains consistent with natural rules. Under the guise of nature, of natural disposition, the archê introduces a principle of the social in order to dictate its basic relations of rule. Accordingly, as Rancière demonstrates, the archê allocates particular bodies to particular roles, functions and spaces by virtue of their inherent capacities purported to be self-evident. Some are destined to exercise the archê, others destined to submit to its authority. Hence, once the logic of the archê is established, the complications of governing a city become substantially simplified to one of how to institute the community according to the principle which dictates these basic relations.

One of the consequences of such a representation of society is that it denies the ability of the polis to be appreciated as something to be shaped by its citizens as political agents. As an appeal to the archê intends to lay out an absolute foundation of rule, as soon as the logic of the archê is operative in the community, the field of politics is effectively dissolved, its condition covered over. The political is reduced to the social, and, in turn, the social is reduced to an imperceptible principle that claims to perpetually anticipate it. The archê therefore offers to government the gift of rule without politics and community without political subjects. To posit an archê is to posit the potential of the polis to achieve harmony with itself, to realise its proper order so that its model of rule reproduces or repeats its underlying principle. The ideal realisation of the archê is therefore the government that perfectly coincides with its principle in institutional form.

Enter Democracy: What Does It Mean to be against the Archê?

But when democracy appears, the entire logic of the archê is compromised. Democracy not only calls into question the grounds upon which governors distinguish themselves from those they govern, it renders problematic the very division between ruler and ruled in itself. What is it that makes democracy's challenge to the archê so compelling? Democracy represents the exception to every other regime in that it does not reproduce the logic of the archê by founding a new criterion for which a new form of government may be established. It does not institute a principle of the demos to combat those competing principles which facilitate the rule of oligarchs and kings. Rather, the ingenuity of democracy is that it discovers a way to undermine the logic of the archê altogether. By disrupting the foundations upon which the rulers of the community elevate themselves, democracy reveals the intrinsic artificiality and arbitrariness of every hierarchical relation. By exposing the essential groundlessness upon which the organisation of the social is ultimately constructed, democracy reveals the sheer contingency of every social order. When this occurs, the edifice of rule begins to crack and crumble, its justification rendered untenable. In the modern world, this is something perhaps first articulated by Tocqueville who observes, somewhat disconcertingly, that what democracy appears to dismantle is precisely the conventions of aristocracy (democracy exposes aristocracy's conventions for what they are: conventions and nothing more).[27] As Keane develops with broader connotations:

> Democracy skewered talk of stern necessity through the heart. It highlighted the contingency of things, events, institutions, people and their beliefs. The originality of democracy lay in its challenge to habitual ways of seeing the world, to thoughtless regard for power and ways of governing people, to living life as if everything was inevitable, or 'natural'.[28]

Perhaps this is why Lefort can claim that, as soon as notions of natural inequality and fixed, transhistorical hierarchies are eliminated, society is already in some manner *democratic*.[29] What democracy introduces to the city is the problem of politics. By rendering the polis a political problem, by frustrating the foundations which dictate its social relations, the archê of government is sabotaged, its hierarchies effectively denaturalised. Democracy means confronting the archê with a notion of society in which the order of the community lacks any such foundation. It means denouncing a representation of the polis in which the legitimacy of rule may be expressed in terms of its formal correspondence with an underlying principle. If we follow Rancière, this is integral to the meaning of politics itself:

> politics is not the enactment of the principle, the law, or the self of a community. Put in other words, politics has no archê, it is anarchical. The very name *democracy* supports this point. As Plato noted, democracy has no archê, no measure.[30]

It is for this reason that democracy cannot simply be appreciated as a constitution like any other. Democracy possesses no archê itself and always appears in the form of a *democracy against the archê*. Therefore, just as the *Republic* may be read in its entirety as one long argument against democracy and its lack of foundation, as a critical strategy, the topic of democracy may likewise be initiated according to its own *being-against* what the *Republic* so unabashedly promotes: in the most general sense, what democracy is against is the archê of society. By undermining the foundations of a given social order, by disrupting the logic which distributes rule to a select few, democracy locates the radical indeterminacy at the root of every regime of government. It demonstrates that even our most established and most sacred institutions are not given by nature or sanctioned by the gods, but are rather founded upon nothing but their own contingency. Likewise, when democracy fashions its own institutions, it can only do so according to this underlying anarchic condition it so boldly uncovers. Thus, 'democratic' government, insofar as we may employ the term, can never claim to achieve identity with itself as its very foundations are destined to remain irreducible, a condition expressed formally in the institution of *doxa* and *agon*. If democracy has a foundation at all, it is the condition of anarchy itself: the foundation of rule that lacks a foundation. This is the very condition that I have called 'politics'.

Understanding Democracy's 'Anarchic Title'

Let us return to Rancière in attempt to appreciate democracy's unprecedented strategy to undermine the archê principle. Rancière's fourth thesis on politics establishes democracy not as a proper regime, but as a rupture in the logic of the archê.[31] Here Rancière introduces a problem that will be developed in greater detail in *Hatred of Democracy*: if the demos is the body that possesses no archê, if the demos by definition does not count and has no right to take part, how is democracy, as the reputed government of the demos, to be understood? How are we to resolve the paradox of the government of those who by every account have no right to govern? Certainly, this is the very problem that so troubled Plato about democracy. But, as Rancière explains, this paradox that appears to encapsulate the very essence of democracy is not a problem to be resolved, but the very solution to understanding democracy itself. Without question, throughout history the two predominant criteria to govern are persistently birth and wealth, the former bound to a superiority of kinship, the latter to a privileged position in the organisation of production and distribution: 'Societies are usually governed by a combination of these two powers to which, in varying degrees, force and science lend their support.'[32] To these long-standing entitlements, Plato desperately seeks to throw wisdom into contention. But to govern the highborn, the rich and the wise alike, democracy must devise something of a supplementary title specific to all those with no qualification whatsoever, all those with no status or position, entitlement or claim: 'Now, the only remaining title is the anarchic title, the title specific to those who have no more title for governing than they have for being governed.'[33] For Rancière, this *anarchic title* is key to grasping the meaning of democracy itself. Democracy is neither a predetermined distribution of roles nor a particular claim to exercise the archê: 'Democracy first of all means this: anarchic "government", one based on nothing other than the absence of every title to govern.'[34] This anarchic title, the title based on nothing other than the absence of title, is precisely Plato's mysterious seventh title included in the *Laws*: 'And we persuade a man to cast lots, by explaining that this, the seventh title of authority, enjoys the favour of the gods and is blessed by fortune.'[35] So after the careful delineation of his six initial qualifications to rule, each positing a particular archê principle, Plato curiously ventures to include a seventh which appears rather incongruous from the rest: a claim to rule based on no principle at all. For what grounds this title is not a proper archê but, if we follow Plato, something which remains indeterminate: the casting of lots, the arbitrariness of *chance* itself. If the archê functions both to divide ruler and ruled and distribute the right to rule to those with the inherent capacities of the ruler, this seventh title certainly fails to perform either of these two functions. The casting of lots, the practice that remains indifferent to title and specifies no formal qualification to govern, represents a definitive break with the logic of the archê, replacing the specificity of birth and wealth with the sheer randomness of chance. This is precisely what Plato appears to associate with the casting of lots. Lot or sortition is that peculiar institution engineered with the greatest degree of precision and calculation for the sole purpose of injecting the element of unpredictability into government.[36] By blindly selecting members of the community to fill temporary positions in various offices and the administrative council (*boule*), it functions to *select out* the entitlement of those few who enjoy wealth, status and privilege. As the archê attempts to isolate those with a special capacity to govern, lot, by its very nature, appears to propose that participation in the affairs of the city requires no special qualification whatsoever, that the disposition to govern is no different from the disposition to be governed. It implies that government is not the discipline of experts or professional politicians, but that the task of governing the community rightly belongs to the community itself. Lot is therefore the ancient institution designed specifically to facilitate this elusive anarchic title. And it is for this reason that Rancière considers lot the very symbol of what is so scandalous about democracy itself:

The scandal of democracy, and of the drawing of lots which is its essence, is to reveal that this title can be nothing but the absence of title, that the government of societies cannot but rest in the last resort on its own contingency.[37]

To declare that government ultimately rests upon its own contingency is in part, to affirm a radical negation. It implies that there is no ultimate basis for one to rule another, the few to rule the many. It implies that there is no necessity to the manner in which social arrangements are organised and coordinated. To affirm the contingency of the social is to reject that there is a nature of society that transcends the bounds of history, custom and convention. It is to refuse the postulate that social relations are intuitive, straightforward, unequivocal. Therefore, perhaps one of the more profound implications of the democratic project is that as a general category 'the social' must necessarily be appreciated according to an indefinite series of contingencies that constitute its relations.

Against Plato, the social is in no way indicative of an organic and stable set of natural bonds. There is no formula or foundation for government to be discovered in a series of extra-institutional relations of the social thought to be *simply there*. To Arendt's point, the proper order of the city cannot be deduced from examples of the shepherd and his sheep, the master and his slave, or the captain and his crew. There is no nature of the social which dictates one's proper place in a given hierarchy or relation of rule. There is no static social space to be uncovered beyond the artifice of institutions themselves. However established and ingrained our various social arrangements appear to be, they offer no basis, no blueprint, no model for institutional government. *The social is already instituted from the start.* While Rancière is rarely considered a thinker of institutions, this is something that his concept of politics never allows us to forget. Divided, episodic, segmentary, discordant, if the social can be articulated in general terms at all, for Rancière, it is only as a domain dominated by the universality of its perpetually conflicting forces.[38]

Therefore, if politics may be conceived as the absence of foundation, it is only because the social itself lacks any stable or immutable basis upon which the organisation of the community may ultimately ground itself. Indeed, in Rancière's view, politics only takes place when the distribution of the social is thrown back on its own inherent contingency. Politics, it could be said, involves a radical exorcism of the natural from the social, so that for the first time the social appears *as* the social and *irreducibly* social, as something entirely onto itself. This is not to suggest that 'the social' and 'the political' remain indistinguishable, but that part of what politics involves is the demonstration that the social is always particular, instituted, historical. The social is the *object* of politics, and politics is something that *happens* to the social. Politics is the name of that which prevents the few, the rich, the highborn from transforming the contingencies of the social into various titles for ruling. It reveals the immeasurable gulf which separates these contingencies from any inherent right to rule.[39] Politics may not be an exercise as modest as simply juxtaposing nature with convention or as hubristic as claiming to represent 'the truth' of the social, but what it does is render problematic the assertion that from the nature of the social an archê which determines the proper governors of the city may be ascertained and put forward as a foundation for rule. If we follow Rancière, the very lack of such a nature of the social is precisely what makes politics possible:

> Politics exists simply because no social order is based on nature, no divine law regulates human society. [. . .] [A]nyone who wants to cure politics of its ills has only one available solution: the lie that invents some kind of social nature in order to provide the community with an *arkhê*.⁴⁰

As we have seen, the reinstallation of the archê is Plato's only solution to the scandal of democracy, the regime perceived to be grounded by the indeterminacy epitomised by the casting of lots. In order to combat this anarchic condition, Plato can only attempt to conceal it once again by claiming to establish a new foundation of rule via the discovery of a new archê principle. Anticipating his later studies on democracy, this procedure is precisely what Rancière, in *The Philosopher and His Poor*, will encapsulate as 'Plato's lie'.⁴¹ The principal theme of the *Republic* may very well be what constitutes the justice of the city, but insofar as its conclusions ultimately rely upon little more than the whim of the city's architect, the basis for the proper order of the just city remains entirely arbitrary. Plato's lie is that his ideal city, complete with its partitioned classes affixed to particular roles and functions, is founded upon nothing more than that which remains contingent still. Plato may claim that his city's design is thoroughly rational, but rational design in no way cancels out those very contingencies bound up with the ancient philosopher's own preferences. Plato may put forward a model of the city governed by the wise, but he in no way escapes the underlying contingency of the social so dramatically exposed by democracy itself. By creating a new entitlement to govern from a fraudulent premise of the social, he merely succeeds in theoretically obscuring this condition once again. Therefore, just as Rancière deciphers an essential equality concealed beneath every form of inequality (expressed in terms of even the lowest slave's acknowledged membership to the linguistic community), he likewise identifies an underlying anarchy beneath every model of hierarchy (expressed in terms of the contingency of the social).⁴² Obviously, such a view does not deny the existence of hierarchies of all kinds everywhere in society, but what it demonstrates is that immanent to every hierarchical relation is the always possible means to dismantle it. If democracy has proven successful in this task, it is because it discovers a way to undermine those hierarchical relations at their very foundation, namely, by demonstrating that their foundation is not a foundation at all.

Democracy as 'Political' or 'Anarchic' Government

Accordingly, this curious 'anarchic title' may be understood as the cornerstone of democracy's strategy to topple those very hierarchies so meticulously assembled upon an archic foundation. In this regard, why exactly Plato considers the anarchic title among his list of legitimate titles in the *Laws* admittedly remains unclear. Plato will elaborate upon this seventh title and the reasons for its inclusion no further. Perhaps we should assume that, by including it, his intentions are simply to expose that the dominant title of his day – the baseless title which facilitates a government of the demos – is the only title founded upon nothing at all: merely chance, accident, 'the fortune of the gods', the throw of the dice. Perhaps the incontestable artificiality of the seventh title is only exhibited to substantiate, by way of contrast, the inherent validity of his six initial titles drawn from nature, the institution of lot only referenced to reaffirm the natural order of rule spanning from parent and child to wise and ignorant. If this is so, then, just as we found with the allegory of the ship, Plato's only aim is to once again subvert the government of the demos by demonstrating that, compared to other examples of the archê, the archê of democracy is the only archê that is not an archê at all. Regardless, by including the seventh qualification only to discredit it, Plato actually does a great service to the theory of democracy: by identifying the radical indeterminacy upon which democracy must so precariously position itself, he reveals that democratic government is the only government to be installed upon the *absence* of any proper entitlement to govern. Against every other qualification, every other title, democracy fabricates an anarchic title for all those who possess no title at all, the only title, therefore, that may be understood to be *political*. It undermines a given distribution of the social that binds governors and governed to particular qualities and attributes. It cuts across the rigid filiations and alliances of birth, caste and class and opens up a field in which traditional identities, roles and relations are broken down – or at least suspended – with respect to the deliberation of the polis, its legislation and occupation of civic offices and juridical posts. Perhaps it is specifically in this context that Cleisthenes' historic reforms must be understood. What is it that makes Cleisthenes' reforms so indisputably monumental for the systematic institution of Athenian democracy? By at once configuring a new model of 'tribal' association (*phulai*) and distributing this model across an entirely reorganised regional division of

Attica, Cleisthenes discovered a way to formally disrupt the traditional bonds which dictate age-old familial, economic and spatial relations in the rule of the community, fostering the unprecedented emergence of a uniquely political identity intersected by an entirely novel representation of civic space.[43] Put another way, borrowing the terminology of Deleuze, by deterritorialising the traditional modalities which govern the spaces and identities of Athens, only to reterritorialise those very spaces and identities according to a purely civic conception of the city, Cleisthenes' reforms functioned to obstruct the distribution of rule to a particular title, lineage or class. What Cleisthenes' reforms can be said to have achieved, therefore, is the structural bases (both geographic and identitarian) in which the government of Athens is rendered political, that is, in which the claim to govern is drawn exclusively from the anarchic title and nowhere else. The so-called government of the demos, the rule of those who have no more right to govern than to submit, is only possible when the identities, spaces and relations of government are rendered political accordingly. In 508–7 BCE, Cleisthenes' reforms of the Athenian political landscape represent an unprecedented movement in this direction.

Hence, the *power of the people* is not the power to exercise the archê. Quite the contrary, the *power of the people* is the power that has become political. In opposition to the government which claims to rest upon a principle of itself, democracy invents the only notion of government to be founded upon politics itself, upon the explicit institution of the contingency of the social expressed in terms of the very contradiction of the qualification of the unqualified, the title that belongs to no particular class or tribe, that is bound to no capacity or condition, but rather invokes the empty form of *anyone at all*:

> What remains is the extraordinary exception, the power of the people, which is not the power of the population or of the majority, but the power of anyone at all, the equality of capabilities to occupy the positions of governors and of the governed. Political government, then, has a foundation. But this foundation is also in fact a contradiction: politics is the foundation of a power to govern in the absence of foundation.[44]

Far from redundant, what Rancière here calls 'political' government is precisely the government established to facilitate the equality to occupy both the positions of governor and governed. Government becomes political when the foundations which prop up the rule of a particular class of governors fall away, so that the right to participate in the deliberation of political affairs may be generalised to include that generic subject traditionally known as the *demos*: not only the demos as an excluded class or disenfranchised body, but the demos understood with respect to the anarchic title, that is, the demos as *anyone at all*. Therefore, while Rancière remains dismissive of Ernesto Laclau's view of 'the demos' as an empty signifier to be filled with various content, he will nevertheless insist, much like Lefort, that what ultimately constitutes the meaning of 'the people' is destined to remain indeterminate, controversial. The idea of the demos is one always imbued with an essential tension and ambivalence. So it is no contradiction when Rancière declares democracy at once the regime of the *poor*, the excluded, the marginalised (the 'part without part') and the regime of the *people* (the part, we could say, that has become indistinguishable from a representation of the whole via the contentious relation between parts). When expressed in terms of the anarchic title, the demos is the name that simultaneously represents the particular and the universal: the demos is both a part of the community and the part that becomes analogous to the whole. The channel through which it moves from one to the other is the field of politics itself.

And yet, if one of the implications of Rancière's anarchic title is that it may be positively expressed in terms of the 'equality of capabilities', his position could very well be said to echo an argument that would not have been unfamiliar to the Greeks themselves. Insofar as Rancière binds his conception of politics to the equality of capabilities, the structure of his argument remains rather consistent with one of the few ancient philosophical defences of democracy which purportedly survives. If we accept the general account of the position espoused by the sophist as portrayed in the Platonic dialogue which takes his name, Protagoras appears to have argued that, unlike architecture, geometry and navigation, the capacity for 'deliberating on the administration of the city' (*politike techne*) is not a specialised skill such as those possessed by artisans or experts, but a capacity that remains universal to all people, noble and common, wealthy and poor.[45] To illustrate this claim, Plato has Protagoras recount a myth in which, during the creation of humans, Zeus bestows something unique to this rather defenceless species that other animals do not possess: to each individual Zeus imparts an equal share of political judgement (*politike techne*) so that, simply by virtue of living in a city and without any training whatsoever, all people may be capable of political deliberation and, hence, of participating in the affairs of city. Therefore, much like Rancière's celebrated ignorant schoolmaster whose pedagogical strategies are predicated upon the axiom that simply assumes the equality of intelligence (the equal capacity to learn), according to Protagoras, as a professional sophist, the only reason that it is possible to instruct in the art of politics at all is because *politike techne* is already a capacity presumed to be equally possessed by all people from the start.[46] For Protagoras, it is this inherent capacity – and not the social contract of the moderns – that makes living together in a political community possible, an argument that historians will routinely put forward as one of the more compelling ancient defences of democracy.[47] If democracy indeed posits that the capacity to occupy the position of governor is nothing beyond the capacity to occupy the position of the governed, then it must be concluded that equality cannot simply be considered an institutional consequence of democracy, but something a priori and presupposed from the beginning: just as we discover in the work of Rancière, equality is not the goal but the very *axiom* of democracy itself.

At the same time, to occupy both the roles of governor and governed is something quite different from reciprocity. Whereas reciprocity still implies to rule and be ruled *in turn* and could very well be construed as the circulation or exchange of the archê, the notion of 'anarchic' government appears to commit us to the government founded solely upon this paradoxical status of the qualification of the unqualified.[48] And while this distinction may appear rather subtle, for Rancière, it is paramount for grasping what isolates democracy from every other regime:

> Democracy is the specific situation in which it is the absence of entitlement that entitles one to exercise the *arkhê*. [. . .] In this logic the specificity of the *arkhê* – its redoubling, that is, the fact that it always precedes itself in the circle of its own disposition and exercise – is destroyed. But this situation of exception is identical with the very condition that more generally makes politics in its specificity possible.[49]

Democracy is not a regenerated process to circulate or distribute the archê in a manner in which its logic remains intact. This is precisely where Rancière disagrees with Arendt. Rather, it is the specific situation in which the logic of the archê is made to undermine itself through its very form. If the archê may be described as the logic which binds an imperceptible principle to the empirical organisation of the community by grounding the right to rule in a capacity or condition that anticipates that rule in a time that comes before, then democracy describes the operation in which the archê, put through the indeterminacy that constitutes the anarchic title, loses its specificity and returns to itself as an empty form, without referent, without specification, so that the circle which binds rule to disposition and disposition to rule is ruptured. In other words, democracy represents a radical break with the archê principle, not simply by virtue of its outright rejection of its logic, but by inundating its form with an indecipherable reference to *anyone at all*. What distinguishes Plato's seventh title from his preceding six is that, formally incapable of isolating the appropriate set of rulers of the community, the indeterminacy that permeates the so-called archê of the demos is forcibly externalised, thereby functioning to disrupt the various criteria of every other archê. When this occurs, the justification for the rule of the highborn, the rich and the wise is rendered illegitimate, leaving only one title remaining: the only title based upon politics itself.

Consequently, the outstanding question regarding democracy's own legitimacy is one impossible to appraise and evaluate within the given framework stipulated by the archê. This is because, beyond the order of politics itself, democracy can appeal to no underlying foundation which serves to justify its institutional models or claims of equality. Thus, if we wish to remain consistent with the general formulation of democracy as 'political' or 'anarchic' government, government that claims only to rest upon the condition of its own contingency, democracy must be said to be the government that at once *legitimises* and *de-legitimises* itself in a single gesture. As Abensour acutely observes, anarchy is that which cannot reign, cannot be sovereign, cannot be expressed as a principle without contradiction.[50] Democracy can therefore provide no absolution, no proof and no guarantee. It has recourse to no principle or external frame of reference from which its justification may be verified in any unequivocal or absolute manner. Its foundation is inextricably bound with its absence of foundation, its ground with its absence of ground. It is precisely for this reason that, from the beginning, we likened its condition to the sea.

Anarchy: The Infinite Opening

The challenge which democracy poses to archic government not only exemplifies the antithetical nature of democracy and the archê but also, perhaps more importantly, reveals something of the nature of politics itself. Politics, it could be said, is *anarchic* by definition and only appears in government when the archê is nullified and no longer operative in the organisation of the community. This is the lesson of democracy. As we have seen, democracy not only lacks an archê but also appears in society as a formal opposition to it, allowing us to think about government, people and their capacities to participate in the affairs of the polis in an altogether different way. Before the name of a regime, before a set of institutions, Rancière understands democracy as just that: a transforming force that opens a space for polemics and dissensus so that the social and the organisation of the social may be subjected to public debate and dispute.[51] When approached and considered according to its universal form, its being-against the archê, it is precisely this transforming force that will appear with the greatest clarity and salience. Expressed in terms of the anarchic title, the equality of *anyone at all*, democracy can be understood to offer an unprecedented objection to an order of society that categorically divides governor and governed according to an abstract principle of rule. In this context, equality itself must be appreciated not as the consequence of a particular institutional arrangement, but as the political basis for democracy's invalidation of the archê. Consistent with the myth of Protagoras found in Plato's eponymous dialogue, equality here implies the equality of capabilities, the assumed competence of people without any qualification to occupy both the roles of governor and governed alike. This is the notion of equality that remains eternally in contradiction with the logic of the archê. This is the meaning of the 'anarchic' equality that Plato so intimately associates with democracy.

In all its forms, democracy is against the archê as the apolitical solution to the problem of rule, of *who* is entitled to govern. However the Greeks may have understood the archê and its relation to the polis prior to the philosophy of Plato, without question, it is the predominant Platonic interpretation which binds ruling and beginning (*commandment* and *commencement*) that would cast a long shadow over the concept in the subsequent history of political thought. Both Arendt and Rancière understand this well. In particular, Rancière's writings on democracy provide an excellent source for grasping its logic as it appears under the guidance of Plato. In his careful analysis of the *Laws*, Rancière is able to decipher that, in its attempt to circumvent the political – or prevent its appearance altogether – the archê is designed to fasten the rule of the community to nature, to the natural disposition of the ruler, the natural superiority of the few. We therefore do not need to look very far to identify the logic of the archê at work throughout history: in monarchy, in oligarchy, in patriarchy and colonial rule. The allure of the archê principle is its ability to conceal and deny the intrinsic artificiality and arbitrariness of every hierarchical relation, of one ruling another. This is the revelation of democracy. Democracy exposes the contingency of governments, hierarchies, *the social* itself. It demands we collectively recognise this contingency, incorporate it into our very institutions and govern our societies accordingly. For Castoriadis, this is an important dimension of the meaning of autonomy.

If an appeal to the archê intends to establish a solid foundation for rule, what democracy introduces to this strategy are the complications of politics. As Plato recognised, democracy's subjection of the polis to politics serves to undermine the logic of the archê and subsequently expose the order of government to an underlying anarchic condition, the sheer contingency of every social order. As the *power of the people*, democracy is not only committed to the annihilation of the archê as such, but also to the task of keeping this condition open. As Jean-Luc Nancy eloquently conveys in *The Truth of Democracy*:

> In this sense, democracy equals anarchy. But anarchy commits one to certain actions, operations, and struggles, to certain forms that allow one rigorously to maintain the absence of any posited, deposited, or imposed *archê*. The democratic *kratein*, the power of the people, is first of all the power to foil the *archê* and then to take responsibility, all together and each individually, for the infinite opening that is thereby brought to light.[52]

The notion that anarchy commits us, both individually and collectively, to a certain responsibility, to a certain fidelity to the radical openness made bare by the dissolution of the archê is indeed a compelling one. For as we have seen, the implications are quite vast: for government, for institutions, for the legitimacy of authority itself. This is a theme that cuts across much of the later work of Rancière, Lefort and Abensour alike. Anarchy, indeterminacy, the contingency of the social: in this context, these are terms which amount to the same. Regardless of the terminology, I have tried to demonstrate that democracy, the nature of politics itself, can really be understood in no other context. Both in theory and in practice, the condition of democracy is anarchic. To Nancy's point, democracy itself therefore obliges us to acknowledge and ceaselessly think through the social, moral and epistemological significance of this anarchy with which it remains so inextricably intertwined. And yet, beyond this political commitment to which Nancy refers, some could object that this anarchy, this 'infinite opening' that appears to underpin the whole of the democratic experience, could be taken to produce some rather significant challenges for the study of democracy itself. For on what basis are we to ground a consistent theoretical formulation of democracy when democracy itself appears to lack any such stable ground? This was indeed the larger ontological problem which so baffled Plato about democracy. This is one of the reasons he refused to accept democracy as a genuine constitution. To navigate the contours of this more philosophical problem, we will turn to Lefort, who unlike Plato, remains unfazed by a conception of democracy formulated according to the very condition of its radical indeterminacy. Indeed, for Lefort, it is precisely from this indeterminacy that democracy gathers its conviction and strength.

Notes

1. John Keane, *The Life and Death of Democracy* (London: Simon & Schuster, 2009), 852.
2. Ibid., xii.
3. Ibid.
4. Nick Hewlett, *Badiou, Balibar, Rancière: Rethinking Emancipation* (London: Continuum International Publishing Group, 2007), 99.
5. Noam Chomsky, 'Anarchism, Marxism and Hope for the Future', *Chomsky on Anarchism* (Oakland: AK Press, 2005), 178.
6. Ibid.
7. On the question of anarchism, Rancière summarises his position as follows: 'At a fundamental philosophical level my position can be called anarchist *stricto sensu* since I hold that politics exists insofar as the exercise of power does not rest upon any *arkhê*.' See Jacques Rancière, 'Against an Ebbing Tide: An Interview with Jacques Rancière', in *Reading Rancière*, ed. Paul Bowman and Richard Stamp (London: Continuum International Publishing Group, 2011), 238. Also see Jacques Rancière, Todd May, Benjamin Noys and Saul Newman, 'Democracy, Anarchism and Radical Politics Today: An Interview with Jacques Rancière', *Anarchist Studies* vol. 16, no 2 (2008). Much of Todd May's recent work explores this underlying connection between Rancière's political thought and the anarchist

tradition. In particular, see Todd May, *The Political Thought of Jacques Rancière: Creating Equality* (University Park: Pennsylvania State University Press, 2008), especially chapter 3.

8. See, for example, Baruch Spinoza, *Political Treatise* (Indianapolis: Hackett Publishing Company, 2001), chapter 2.
9. See Chapters 4 and 5 below.
10. Joseph J. Tanke, *Jacques Rancière: An Introduction* (London: Continuum International Publishers, 2011), 52–3.
11. Plato, *Laws*, III, 690a–690c. All references are to Plato, *Complete Works*, ed. John M. Cooper and D. S. Hutchinson (Indianapolis: Hackett Publishing Company, 1997).
12. Jacques Rancière, 'Does Democracy Mean Something?', *Dissensus: On Politics and Aesthetics* (London: Continuum, 2010), 51.
13. Jacques Rancière, *Hatred of Democracy* (London: Verso, 2007), 40. Also see John McSweeney, 'Giving Politics an Edge: Rancière and the Anarchic Principle of Democracy', *Sofia Philosophical Review* vol. 3, no. 1 (2009): 119.
14. See Nickolas Pappas's discussion of education in *Plato and the Republic* (London: Routledge, 1995), 47–52.
15. Jacques Rancière, *Disagreement: Politics and Philosophy* (Minneapolis: University of Minnesota Press, 1999), 68–70. Also see McSweeney, 'Giving Politics an Edge', 115. For a more extensive analysis of *nomos* and *phusis* in Plato's political thought, see Robert W. Hall, *Political Thinkers: Plato* (London: G. Allen & Unwin, 1981), chapter 2.
16. Rancière, *Hatred of Democracy*, 38–9.
17. Rancière, 'Does Democracy Mean Something?', 51.
18. Josiah Ober offers a concise introduction to the Greek understanding of arkhê as both 'ruling' and 'beginning'. See Josiah Ober, 'The Original Meaning of "Democracy": Capacity to Do Things, Not Majority Rule', *Constellations* vol. 15, no. 1 (2008): 5–6.
19. Parchen Markell, 'The Rule of the People: Arendt, Archê and Democracy', *The American Political Science Review* vol. 100, no. 1 (February 2006): 4.
20. Hannah Arendt, *The Human Condition* (Chicago: University of Chicago Press, 1998), 177, 189. Also see Hannah Arendt, *The Promise of Politics* (New York: Schocken Books, 2005).
21. There is indeed a historical basis for Arendt's claim. With reference to Cleisthenes' reforms, J. P. Vernant writes: 'The polis was a homogeneous whole, without hierarchy, without rank, without differentiation. *Archê* was no longer concentrated in a single figure at the apex of the social structure, but was distributed equally throughout the entire realm of public life [. . .].' Quoted in Pierre Lévêque and Pierre Vidal-Naquet, *Cleisthenes the Athenian: An Essay on the Representation of Space and Time in Greek Political Thought from the End of the Sixth Century to the Death of Plato* (Atlantic Highlands: Humanities Press, 1996), 52.
22. Hannah Arendt, *On Revolution* (London: Penguin Books, 2006), 19.

23. Arendt, *The Human Condition*, 224–5.
24. Jacques Rancière, 'Ten Theses on Politics', *Dissensus*, 30.
25. See Constantine J. Vamvacas, *The Founders of Western Thought: The Presocratics* (Dordrecht: Springer, 2009), 36, and William Keith Chambers Guthrie, *A History of Greek Philosophy, Vol. 1: The Earlier Presocratics and the Pythagoreans* (Cambridge: Cambridge University Press, 2000), 77.
26. Andrew Schaap offers a helpful discussion of the concept of the archê as it appears in Rancière and Arendt. See Andrew Schaap, 'Hannah Arendt and the Philosophical Repression of Politics', in *Jacques Rancière and the Contemporary Scene: The Philosophy of Radical Equality*, ed. Jean-Philippe Deranty and Alison Ross (London: Continuum International Publishers, 2012), particularly 155–6.
27. Pierre Manent, *Tocqueville and the Nature of Democracy* (Lanham: Rowman & Littlefield, 1996), 71.
28. Keane, *The Life and Death of Democracy*, 51.
29. Claude Lefort, *Complications: Communism and the Dilemmas of Democracy* (New York: Columbia University Press, 2007), 69.
30. Jacques Rancière, 'Politics, Identification, and Subjectivization', *October* vol. 61 (Summer 1992): 59.
31. Rancière, 'Ten Theses on Politics', 31–2.
32. Rancière, *Hatred of Democracy*, 46.
33. Ibid.
34. Ibid., 41. Todd May offers considerable analysis of this statement in Todd May, 'Rancière and Anarchism', in *Jacques Rancière and the Contemporary Scene*, 117–28.
35. Plato, *Laws*, III, 690c.
36. From the drawing of lots to ballot machines to water clocks, John Keane will make this point regarding many of the institutional mechanisms employed by ancient democracy. See Keane, *The Life and Death of Democracy*, 51.
37. Rancière, *Hatred of Democracy*, 47.
38. For an analysis of Rancière's general take on *the social*, see Michael J. Shapiro, 'Radicalizing Democratic Theory: Social Space in Connolly, Deleuze and Rancière', *The New Pluralism: William Connolly and the Contemporary Global Condition*, ed. David Campbell and Morton Schoolman (Durham, NC: Duke University Press, 2008), 198, 202.
39. Tanke, *Jacques Rancière*, 54–5.
40. Rancière, *Disagreement*, 16.
41. See Jacques Rancière, *The Philosopher and His Poor* (Durham, NC: Duke University Press, 2003), chapter 1. Also see Oliver Davis, *Jacques Rancière* (Cambridge: Polity, 2010), 75.
42. Rancière, *Disagreement*, 16–17. Also see Davis, *Jacques Rancière*, 79.
43. For a still-unequalled analysis of Cleisthenes' reforms, see Lévêque and Vidal-Naquet, *Cleisthenes the Athenian*.

44. Rancière, *Hatred of Democracy*, 49.
45. Plato, *Protagoras*, 319a–323a. Castoriadis argues that ancient Greek democracy is predicated upon the notion that there are no experts regarding the affairs of politics, that political wisdom belongs to the community as a whole. Perhaps it is for this reason that Castoriadis asserts, drawing from *Antigone*, that democracy reveals that *one cannot be wise alone*. See Cornelius Castoriadis, 'The Greek *Polis* and the Creation of Democracy', *Philosophy, Politics, Autonomy* (New York: Oxford University Press, 1991), 108, 120.
46. Jacques Rancière, *The Ignorant Schoolmaster: Five Lessons in Intellectual Emancipation* (Stanford: Stanford University Press, 1991). Eric Mechoulan offers an analysis of Rancière in light of Protagoras' claim. See Eric Mechoulan, 'Sophisticated Continuities and Historical Discontinuities, Or, Why Not Protagoras?' *Jacques Rancière: History, Politics, Aesthetics*.
47. See, for example, M. I. Finley, *Democracy Ancient and Modern* (New Brunswick: Rutgers University Press, 1985), 28.
48. Rancière, 'Ten Theses on Politics', 31.
49. Ibid.
50. Miguel Abensour, 'An-archy between Metapolitics and Politics', *Parallax* vol. 8, no. 3 (2002): 16.
51. Hewlett, *Badiou, Balibar, Rancière*, 108.
52. Jean-Luc Nancy, 'The Truth of Democracy', *The Truth of Democracy* (New York: Fordham University Press, 2010), 31.

Chapter 3

To Think Democracy Otherwise: Claude Lefort and 'Savage' Democracy

Democracy has consequently been abandoned to its wild instincts, and it has grown up like those children who have no parental guidance, who receive their education in the public streets . . .
Alexis de Tocqueville, *Democracy in America*

On the Status of Political Philosophy

In this chapter, we turn our attention to some of the larger questions animated and set in motion by what Lefort sometimes calls 'wild' or 'savage' democracy (*démocratie sauvage*).[1] As seductive as it is puzzling, while many readers of Lefort simply ignore his sporadic references to savage democracy, others, such as Abensour, place it at the very centre of their interpretation of his thought. For my own part, I appeal to Lefort here in attempt to organise a general concept of democracy consistent with the antinomies of politics. In many respects, to theorise democracy according to what it is against demands we revisit and reconsider the way we think about democracy altogether. This is an exercise that perhaps Lefort would suggest remains essential to the work of philosophy itself. If we accept Lefort's most elementary position that modern democracy's symbolic displacement of the body of the king opens to a condition of indeterminacy, lacking any fixed or absolute foundation, we must likewise accept that, insofar as democracy remains inextricably bound to this condition, there is no immutable basis from which we may definitively derive its concept. Democracy is a phenomenon that deposits our concepts in a place of radical uncertainty and thus compels a mode of thinking characterised by a persistent and interminable questioning. This no doubt explains why the origin of philosophy itself coincides with ancient Greek democracy. According to Lefort, philosophy concerns that 'unlocalizable and indeterminable question that accompanies all experience of the world', initiating a form of interrogation that must likewise remain just as indefinite and open-ended in scope.[2] This is precisely the test that savage democracy puts to our political thought. From the extraordinary democratic potential of the French Revolution to his own experience of May '68, these pivotal historical moments Lefort tends to associate with savage democracy seem to require we bracket all assumptions about what democracy means and return again and again to those fundamental philosophical questions: *How should democracy be thought? How do we go about organising its concept? On what basis? And to what end?* As Abensour develops in his own analysis, however enigmatic, savage democracy compels us to conceive democracy not as a regime, government or institution primarily but, according to its emancipatory political acts, its capacity to resist, defy and transform. If we follow Abensour, Lefort can therefore be read to provide us with an entirely new strategy in which democracy may be approached and considered philosophically. It is precisely for this reason that his work informs the basis of my general approach to the construction of its concept.

As Deleuze reminds us, concepts never appear ready-made; they are never simply *there*. In his final work, *What is Philosophy?*, Deleuze reflects that central to the practice of philosophy is the creative exercise of concept construction.[3] With reference to particular problems posed to philosophy from without, these concepts help us to think in new ways that were not possible before. Deleuze insists that philosophy is a practical discipline, even suggesting the value of what it creates must be evaluated according to its practical, often non-philosophical uses. What is the use of philosophy? 'Philosophy does not serve the State or the Church, which have other concerns. It serves no established power. [. . .] Philosophy is at its most positive as critique, as an enterprise of demystification.'[4] Drawing from Nietzsche's *Untimely Meditations*, Deleuze understands this enterprise to have a critical relation to time: philosophy is a critique of the present, so that we may counter *what is*, think against it, and discover new possibilities for thought and new possibilities for action. *This is when philosophy becomes political. This is how political philosophy should be understood.* Political philosophy is not a meditation on the topics of governance, sovereignty or the affairs of the State. Rather, in the spirit of Nietzsche, it is a form of resistance, a mode of thinking against. Philosophy hurls its concepts at the world not to grasp it as it is, but to change it, to help modify social forms and ways of being. Interestingly, it is here, on the topic of philosophy's political and emancipatory potential, that Abensour will differ with Rancière.

While Rancière clearly distances his own work from the discipline, finding the general approach of political philosophy to be broadly organised around the discovery of a rational means to account for the structure and functioning of a given social order, if we follow Abensour, philosophy's contribution to the political can in no way be limited to Rancière's rather narrow typology of *archipolitics*, *parapolitics* and *metapolitics*.[5] While Abensour shares much of Rancière's disparaging appraisal of political philosophy in its traditional form, drawing from Arendt and Lefort, his own critical political philosophy demonstrates that the practice of philosophy may be formulated not only to resist the anti-democratic currents that permeate so much of political thought since Plato, but, at the same time, to critique modes of domination particular to the *here and now*.[6] As we have seen, Abensour praises the political writings of Arendt for their decisive opposition to the longstanding tradition of political philosophy which has so often served to obscure the very problems and polemics specific to politics itself. Similarly, Abensour proposes a model of political philosophy, specifically designed for a critical and emancipatory project, that returns not to the abstract topics of political thought but, in accordance with Machiavelli, to the *matters of politics* themselves, that 'burst into the present' demanding renewed interrogation.[7] It is here that Abensour's approach to political philosophy shares a certain consistency with that of Deleuze: political philosophy is not about systems or abstract thought; it is about the present, resistance, critique. As Marx understood all too well, criticism becomes a weapon in its ability – its *willingness* – to challenge social conditions and inspire historical change. And yet, as Marx duly reminds us in typical fashion, while philosophy is no substitute for the material necessity of political action, while the 'weapon of criticism cannot replace the criticism of weapons',[8] what Abensour's political philosophy appears to advocate is twofold: first, that the struggle for emancipation can never be severed from a permanent critique of social domination; and secondly, that such a critique both compels and is enhanced by a constructive reformulation of the concept of democracy itself. In this regard, at a time when the idea of democracy has been so appropriated and domesticated by the interests of capital and the rules of the State, perhaps Abensour could declare the first task of political philosophy to be the cultivation of the ability to *think democracy otherwise*. Despite their many differences on the emancipatory potential of political philosophy itself, this is something that undoubtedly remains just as vital to Rancière. Perhaps now more than ever, we need a concept of democracy organised according to what it can do, what it can become and what it can transform. This is precisely what, in his own writings, Lefort's compelling allusions to savage democracy invite us to consider.

It is for this reason that I take savage democracy to represent an indispensable moment of thinking the antinomies of politics. However ambiguous or obscure, what Lefort calls 'savage' democracy helps us to *think against* what passes for democracy today, urging us to consider its more creative and transformative dimensions and capacities. As Abensour demonstrates, savage democracy not only functions to prevent the closure of the question of democracy, but also challenges us to conceive of democracy according to its most uncompromised and resilient incarnation: its political acts of emancipation, its endless capacity for conflict and contestation, its enduring momentum towards a more participatory and egalitarian society. Therefore, while Lefort's larger theory of modern democracy could very well be presented in the context of a democracy at once against monarchy and against totalitarianism, rather than extract a particular model of the antinomies of politics from his work, we turn to Lefort here in pursuit of a way of thinking about democracy that challenges the conventional limitations of its concept as it is so often circulated today. Calling attention to those spontaneous, at times insurrectionary moments of strife and social turmoil, what Lefort understands to be 'savage' about democracy reveals just how limited and benign our concept of democracy has become, forcing us to confront those moments, however rare, when democracy demonstrates its profound commitment to bringing about sweeping social change through conflict. Although notoriously undefined (or perhaps because of it), Lefort's savage democracy may therefore be taken as an experimental strategy to emancipate democracy *in thought*. It helps us resist a 'domesticated' interpretation of democracy so ubiquitous today and consider a more defiant democracy *against*. If the theory of the antinomies of politics necessitates a way of thinking about democracy that incorporates those more revolutionary moments of confrontation and defiance, Lefort's savage democracy will prove invaluable in the philosophical exercise of organising such a concept.

Accordingly, navigated by Abensour's considerable elaboration of this exceptionally difficult term, I will offer an extended reading of Lefort's savage democracy as a strategy to develop the general concept of democracy consistent with the antinomies of politics. In the context of Lefort's larger political philosophy, savage democracy will first be situated according to Tocqueville's democratic revolution, locating the modern appearance of the antinomies of politics in a revolutionary rejection of the very ontology of the *ancien régime*. Then, following Abensour's vivid interpretation of savage democracy as an emancipatory political act, the term will be further explored in light of what Lefort has described as permanent contestation, orienting our broader understanding of the antinomies of politics according to a more protracted, ongoing democratisation of society. Hence, tracing those instances of savage democracy across his writings and interviews, it is with Lefort that we will bind and intersect what is most imperative to the project of the antinomies of politics itself: the *act* of being-against and the *process* of democratisation. This is what is critical to the concept of democracy we are pursuing here.

Pierre Clastres and the Logic of Being-Against

Before turning to the political philosophy of Lefort, let us begin more generally with an attempt to isolate the logic of the antinomies of politics which I take to be so epitomised by those examples of savage democracy Lefort identifies across modern history. Although we cannot speak of a principle or foundation of democracy, I have suggested that, if we were to isolate its originary or germinal impulse, it would unmistakably take the form of an *against*, an against which does not simply describe an effect or consequence of its politics, but defines a democracy that manifests as a defiant political act *from its very inception*. In this respect, what democracy can be understood to be against is something quite different from what democracy simply contradicts or negates. For the object of its being-against does not merely compose an external relation with democracy itself, but remains immanent to its very form. Perhaps this is explained by the fact that historically democracy is never constituted in a void, but invariably appears in the guise of a counter or objection to an established order of society in which a spectrum of familiar modes of domination are already very much in place: unrestricted or arbitrary rule, concentrations of authority, monopolies of decision, strategies of exclusion and marginalisation, *archic* government. From the beginning, as the initiation of a unique political controversy and dispute, whether a response to oligarchy or theocracy, to the rule of despots or kings, democracy comes into being in the form of an against which at all times remains integral to its composition, orientation and institutional expression. Consequently, it could be said that democracy reveals exactly what it is against by virtue of its very form. For example, democracy is often declared to be organised around a defiant claim of equality (what Plato understands quite literally as an 'anarchic' equality). But what this anarchic equality makes strikingly apparent is that democracy necessarily involves a being-against the archê that must be considered just as essential to its concept as this positive claim of equality itself. As we have seen, democracy does not simply encounter the archê from without, but composes itself in the immanent form of a *democracy against the archê* from the start. This means that democracy does not simply lack an archê, but more accurately describes a distinct political manifestation against it, against both the various orders of the archê it confronts and disputes in society as well as the archê that perhaps always threatens to emerge within the walls of its own institutions. Therefore, what democracy is against – and incorporates and internalises in the form of a *being-against* – is never extrinsic to democracy itself, but represents an inalienable dimension of its very form. As the immanent expression of what it is against, what democracy's 'being-against' can therefore be understood to signify is the inability of democracy to be formally isolated from that which it counters, contests and renders politically problematic.

Perhaps, as a formal theoretical model, we discover something of a parallel of the general structure of democracy's being-against in the political anthropology of Pierre Clastres. In his seminal study *Society against the State*, Clastres ventures to discredit an established anthropological attitude which had long prevailed over the discipline: just as primitive societies were thought to lack architecture, scientific inquiry and a written history, the politics of tribal cultures was likewise understood in terms of a marked *absence*: primitive societies are societies without politics.[9] But as Clastres explains, when anthropologists traditionally went looking for the markers of politics in primitive societies, their very parameters tended to be subject to a modern western ethnocentric bias inclined to locate the political according to what is perceived to be its proper place in civilised societies and hence according to precisely what is lacking in tribal communities, namely *the State*: that coercive, hierarchical 'command–obedience relationship' in which the organs of power are isolated from the whole community and consolidated in the hands of a select few.[10] It is against these parameters that Clastres develops his core theses. Through extensive fieldwork with the Guayaki tribes of Paraguay, Clastres demonstrates that, while primitive societies do indeed lack a State as anthropologists often observe, this is not indicative of the lack of a very meticulous organisation of power in tribal communities, but rather of our own flawed comprehension of how power may be arranged in stateless societies. In this context, Clastres recognises that, if we wish to consider the politics of tribal cultures at all, the concept can no longer be centred around the relations of the State, but according to the extensive institutional strategies specifically intended to *prevent* the State's emergence. What distinguishes primitive societies from State societies is an elaborate institutional model designed to retain the organs of power under the control of the whole community. In this respect, we must take the title of Clastres's volume quite literally. Primitive societies are not simply societies *without* a State, but societies *against* the State, against the very capacity inherent to every society to concentrate the means of authority in the hands of the few. Therefore, contrary to the dominant anthropological perspective of his day, Clastres insists that primitive societies do not represent embryonic cultures momentarily suspended in an inevitable development towards an advanced political society coordinated around the State-form. It is precisely this vague evolutionist paradigm his work seeks to challenge.[11] Rather, what primitive societies represent to Clastres are societies in which an immanent *being-against* the State forms the very basis of their politics: not only do tribal communities lack any semblance of a centralised state administration, but they also reveal a deliberate institutional orientation against the perpetual threat of its appearance. For Clastres, it is precisely according to this immanent being-against that primitive societies must be approached and understood politically.

Hence, although Clastres reveals no intention to exhibit tribal societies as examples of primitive democracies, his research certainly uncovers a social model that encapsulates the formal structure of the being-against that remains so essential to my interpretation of democracy here. Much like Clastres's description of the politics of primitive societies, what democracy is against should not be thought secondary to other qualities or characteristics which customarily define it. Although rarely explored in political and historical studies, a grasp of this being-against is imperative for a more nuanced and multifaceted understanding of its logic, objects and orientation. When a concept of democracy locates the against at its very centre, what is uniquely facilitated is a theoretical inquiry far more disposed to discern democracy as an emancipatory instrument of the demos. Democracy is not a static entity; it is an active agent. It is not so much a type of society as something that happens to it. Democracy is the name of an unprecedented challenge to modes of domination, strategies of inequality and hierarchies of all kinds. It may be identified with the forces that seek to expose, contest and transform oppressive and exclusionary arrangements and practices from below, from the outside, from a *minoritarian* positionality. In the simplest formulation, democracy is the democratisation of society, its institutions and relations. It carves out new spaces for democracy, locates social fields where there is potential for greater democracy and confronts obstructions where democracy is blocked, channelled away or refused altogether. This is an attempt to conceive democracy at its most libertarian, its most revolutionary or, in the language of Lefort, its most *savage*.

The Essence of Democracy: A Question of Interpretation

While Clastres certainly helps us grasp the logic of the being-against so intrinsic to the antinomies of politics, his political anthropology really provides us no concept of the democracy constituted by such a logic. For this, we turn to Lefort. Although Lefort cannot be said to share Clastres's general mistrust of the State itself, his philosophical surveys of modern democracy uncover an unmistakable form of contestation and defiance that appears from its very inception against the order of the king at the dawn of a new historical era. And yet, critical to his theory of democracy, Lefort understands this being-against not to recede and diminish with the demise of the king, but to persist and continue to confront and challenge new forms of social domination in a new form of society. Perhaps this is exhibited most profoundly in those moments he identifies as 'savage' democracy. Abensour suggests we consider these passages in Lefort's work with great care. For they will challenge us to think about democracy in radically new ways.

Perhaps the heuristic power of savage democracy will be discovered in its capacity to revive and reactivate the very question of democracy itself. Lefort's writings are devoted to many facets of modern democracy that often remain only obscure or marginal themes in comparable theoretical studies: its formal abolition of the generative principles of the *ancien régime*, its institutional legitimation of conflict and division, its categorical rejection of the totalitarian solution to the problem of politics. Distancing the question of democracy from the customary topics of government, sovereignty and the affairs of the State, much of his mature work can be approached as a descriptive phenomenological appraisal of how what democracy renders political is both represented symbolically and experienced socially.[12] His project considers the manner in which democracy radically transforms not only the institutions of society, but the very horizon against which questions of authority, legitimacy, law, justice and knowledge are perceived and evaluated. Lefort is often considered a thinker of indeterminacy.[13] This view is hardly unjustified. And yet, what is often forgotten, or hastily overlooked, is that beyond democracy's revelation of the contingency of the social, the absence of a stable ontological ground, part of what indeterminacy implies for Lefort is an unequivocal refusal of *mastery*. This remains an important dimension of his broader approach to democracy itself: 'It is to dream to think that we possess democracy [. . .]. Democracy is but a play of possibilities, one inaugurated in a still recent past and about which we still have everything to explore.'[14] Therefore, as much as Lefort represents a thinker of indeterminacy, he is also a defiant critic of mastery.[15] Perhaps this forms the basis of both his moral and epistemological critique. From his earliest surveys of bureaucracy and totalitarianism, to his ultimate disavowal of Marxism and the seductive image of the 'good society', to his later acclamations of democracy's subversion of everything that is absolute, certain, fixed, this innate suspicion of mastery is a theme which extends across nearly every facet of his oeuvre. It is likewise a theme that will illuminate some of the most challenging passages to appear in his later writings. When Lefort puts forward a notion of democracy as something unmasterable and unrestrained, as something that refuses to be regulated or pacified, he will tend to refer to a 'savage' democracy, a curious phrase ostensibly reserved to distinguish democracy's more unbridled and subversive dimensions and capacities.[16] And while some may find the term to remain rather elusive, it is nevertheless according to this savage democracy that Lefort will identify what is most essential to democracy itself:

> It is true that, in a certain sense, no one holds the formula for democracy and that it is most profoundly itself by being savage democracy. Perhaps this is what constitutes its essence; as soon as

there is no ultimate reference on the basis of which the social order might be conceived and determined, this order is constantly on a quest for foundations, in search of its own legitimacy, and it is precisely the opposition and the demands of those who are excluded from the benefits of democracy that constitute its most effective wellspring.[17]

Lacking any formula or foundation, deriving its forces from the opposition of those who are most excluded, perpetually in search of its own legitimacy, how are we to approach and evaluate this savage democracy that, according to Lefort, constitutes democracy's very essence? And is Abensour, who not only provides the most exhaustive analysis of the term, but who also adopts something of a savage conception of democracy to inspire his own theory of a democracy against the State, justified in his rendering of savage democracy as the centrepiece of Lefort's thought and the key to interpreting his larger oeuvre?

In a short essay on Deleuze's aesthetics, Rancière will preface his remarks stating that: 'Understanding a thinker does not amount to coinciding with his centre. On the contrary, to understand a thinker is to displace him, to lead him on a trajectory where his articulations come undone and leave room for play.'[18] With respect to Lefort, perhaps this holds especially true. While one could hardly locate savage democracy at the 'centre' of Lefort's work, if we follow Abensour, when interpretations of Lefort take his thought to its most radical point, perhaps it is indeed savage democracy that represents its 'necessary outcome'. As Abensour explains in his indispensable essay '"Savage Democracy" and the "Principle of Anarchy"', what the adjective 'savage' first intends to signify – as a qualifier opposed to a demarcation – is the indetermination bound up with the very question of democracy itself; it is what raises the question over and over again, keeping the idea of democracy unsettled and perpetually open.[19] For the savage evokes everything about democracy that challenges the limits of its established concept, urging us to push our thinking of democracy ever further. Unbinding the concept from the constraints that so often circumscribe its limits and determine its reference, what savage democracy will refuse is the authority to definitively master its formula and monopolise its meaning. Thus, in the broadest sense, savage democracy may be introduced as the idea of democracy at its most unshackled, its most *deterritorialised* and therefore may serve as a vehicle to propel our thinking of democracy in unprecedented new directions, exposing it to entirely new possibilities. *Savage democracy demands not only that we reflect upon what is savage about democracy, but also that we think democracy in a savage way.* In this regard, if savage democracy remains one of the more difficult terms to decipher in Lefort's lexicon, perhaps it is because, rather than proposing a proper concept of democracy, it functions to throw the concept into question, challenging our basic attitudes and underlying suppositions. For this reason, Lefort provides an extremely effective strategy to emancipate democracy in thought. By eliciting everything that is revolutionary about democracy, Lefort discovers a way to release the concept from all the snares that so often entrap, limit and confine what democracy can be and what it can mean, allowing us to reimagine it anew according to its most unconventional and provocative incarnations. Therefore, although this rather peculiar phrase appears only at the margins of Lefort's writings, perhaps Abensour is correct to suggest that to understand Lefort we must understand savage democracy and, likewise, to understand savage democracy we must understand something that is essential to democracy itself.

In this respect, at the same time as savage democracy raises a whole series of questions about our interpretation of democracy, it also gives us cause to reflect upon the various interpretations of Lefort himself. Not surprisingly, Lefort's comments on savage democracy often receive little attention across the major surveys of his work. It is largely only Abensour's rather unorthodox reading that grants these passages such prominence in Lefort's thought. But as Lefort illustrates in his own highly original discussions of hermeneutics outlined in his colossal work on Machiavelli, the art of interpretation is not ultimately a question of mastering a text or uncovering some indisputable truth regarding its author, but an attempt to open up a world of thought through a horizon of the work that perhaps the author holds together, but which, given the particularity of the interpretative reading, remains irreducible to the reconstruction of his doctrines and lends itself to ever-renewed possibilities and powers.[20] Thus, it could be said that Lefort elevates interpretation to a political act itself. Following Lefort, the mode of interpretation that escapes the limitations of ideology and rises to the demands of politics is precisely the one that binds the particularities of our own interpretation to the conditions of the 'here and now' (*hic et nunc*), not only so our present experience may inform the critique of the work, but also so the work may inform the critique of our present experience.[21] This is critical to political philosophy itself. Accordingly, perhaps there is something about our own conditions, our own *here and now*, that for Abensour calls for a concept of democracy that rejuvenates everything that is radical about what it can do and what it can become. For when Abensour reads Lefort, he not only locates the most radical democratic moments in Lefort's thought, but he also interprets Lefort's thought as a whole according to those very moments.[22] The result is a picture of Lefort that is, although not unfamiliar or obscure, one in which the possibilities and powers of his thought are taken to their highest point.

Although the phrase rarely appears in his major works, a series of references to savage democracy will be found scattered across a number of Lefort's later essays and interviews, suggesting a notion of democracy that, given its atypical qualification, must be somewhat distinguished from his more characteristic phenomenological rendering of democracy as a symbolic order or form of society. But why *savage*? What is at the source of this curious qualification? We can only speculate. Abensour certainly warns against the temptation to associate the term with either Clastres's ethnological studies of the 'savage' society or with Hobbes's chaotic state of nature that remains perpetually in a state of *war of all against all*.[23] Rather, given that Lefort appears to want to draw attention to democracy's more 'undomesticated' and uncompromised manifestations, it is possible that the adjective is borrowed from (or simply inspired by) an equally difficult term encountered in the late writings of his teacher and mentor Maurice Merleau-Ponty. In his unfinished manuscript *The Visible and the Invisible*, a text that Lefort would himself prepare for publication, Merleau-Ponty appears to re-evaluate his entire phenomenological approach to ontology. In a rather unorthodox move for an author who long endeavoured to break down the sharp distinctions between subject and object, appearance and essence, Merleau-Ponty appears to want to distinguish between a being that is organised according to the conditions of subjective experience and a being that, it can only be postulated, remains external to those very processes of subjective mediation. In attempt to articulate this unintegrated being in a manner that does not reinstate a notion of an absolute Being or an essential *thing-in-itself*, Merleau-Ponty will tend to refer to a 'brute' or 'wild' being (*l'être sauvage*).[24] Although the status of this wild being is difficult to determine, much like Theodor Adorno's negative dialectics, this rather unusual qualification does allow Merleau-Ponty to express something that was not possible before, even if only as a series of negations: wild being is that being which exceeds organisation and resists ontological closure; it is that being which escapes the rules of an established order and refuses to be arranged into an overarching scheme; it is that being which cannot be incorporated into a system and falls outside the realm of facts, figures and predicable patterns. Instead, wild being recalls the 'wildness' of wildflowers that remains irreducible to the cultivated garden.[25] It is that excess of being always in the process of inundating its boundaries and speaks to an ontology without closure, without principle, without essence. Is this not precisely the manner in which Abensour conveys Lefort's savage democracy, a democracy that, 'like an impetuous river that incessantly overflows its bed, cannot "go back home" and submit to the established order'?[26]

It is in this respect that Lefort's savage democracy could be taken to bear a trace or vestige of Merleau-Ponty's wild being. And yet, perhaps this only raises more questions. In his own analysis, Abensour argues that insofar as it resists domestication and is incapable of being domesticated, democracy may be understood to remain faithful to its 'savage essence'.[27] But as he clearly recognises, if the *savage* qualifier intends to release the concept of democracy from the narrow confines of a fixed or preconceived framework, prompting us to think democracy beyond all reference to foundation, principle or archê, can we then even speak of a 'savage essence'? Particularly in light of Merleau-Ponty's wild being, does not the savage attempt to undermine the very notion of an *essence* of democracy? And if so, how do we reconcile this apparent contradiction? This is a problem, however semantic, that appears to be resolved by Bernard Flynn. According to Flynn, Lefort once explained that, if he at times relies on a language of essences, he is not thinking of essence in the sense of Plato, but in the sense of 'gasoline, fuel, which one puts in a car'.[28] If we can extrapolate from this rather intriguing remark, when Lefort refers to savage democracy as the 'essence' of democracy, he does not intend to lay down a new formula or foundation to which democracy must adhere conceptually. Instead, what he intends to express, supporting Abensour's reading, is the *power* of democracy itself, the living source of its transformative agency. When Lefort asks us to think democracy according to its savage essence, he is asking us to draw our basic conception not from a restricted, domesticated representation of democracy, but according to its most revolutionary potential in society. Lefort is interested in what democracy can do and what it can achieve. He is interested in what propels democracy forward, how it transforms our institutions and relations as well as the manner in which those institutions and relations are represented and experienced symbolically. Therefore, contrary to those rather monotonous declarations lamenting democracy's 'fragility', savage democracy invites us to consider its enduring strength and perseverance in modern society. This is something that much of Lefort's work attempts to demonstrate.

Democratic Revolution: Tocqueville and Lefort

Although never properly defined by the author himself, even the most cursory survey of Lefort's employment of the term will discern that savage democracy is often associated with spontaneous revolutionary currents that have tended to unfold throughout some of the most monumental events to punctuate modern European history: from the earliest days of the French Revolution to February 1917 to May '68. Even if all of these events could be declared to have ultimately failed to realise their democratic potential, Lefort nevertheless appears to identify something inside each of them that captures his imagination: a power, an impulse, a radical democratic moment that, however ephemeral its manifestation, refuses to be tempered or restrained:

> This ferment may only be an element of revolutions, but it is extraordinary enough to warrant our interest. For a period of time that can be longer or shorter, it gives form to savage democracy, the trace of which can be lost, or is always lost, yet it reveals certain specific aspirations of the modern world.[29]

Through all the chaos and confusion and contradictions inherent to each of these examples of popular social upheaval, Lefort is able to discern something important, something he considers essential to the meaning of democracy itself. And yet, at the same time, these observations do not imply that, for Lefort, 'savage democracy' and 'revolution' are terms which amount to the same. At least since his early disillusionment with Trotskyism,[30] Lefort cannot be said to be guilty of falling prey to what he sometimes calls the 'myth of revolution', the naive promotion of a certain revolutionary voluntarism most often associated with Vladimir Lenin and firmly ingrained in the popular imagination of the French Revolution itself.[31] Rather, following the example of Tocqueville, Lefort is intent on distinguishing between the *model* of the French

Revolution on the one hand and the *forces* of democratic revolution on the other. It is against this backdrop of Tocqueville's understanding of democratic revolution that savage democracy must be situated and explored.[32] Contrary to that familiar representation of the momentary insurrection that overturns the very conditions of society, Lefort understands democratic revolution as a far more protracted, *irreversible* democratising process, one in which, however uneven and sporadic, democracy perpetually confronts its own relative limits:

> Beyond a historically determined system of political institutions, I wish to call attention to a long-term process, what de Tocqueville called the democratic revolution, which he saw coming to birth in France under the *ancien régime* and which, since his time, has continued to develop.[33]

Therefore, while respecting Tocqueville's careful distinction between the two, perhaps Lefort could be said to understand democratic revolution as something which *passes through* the French Revolution, a tendency or capacity that may survive and reappear long after the culmination of the historical revolution had itself receded and diminished.[34]

Perhaps it is for this reason that Lefort understands the fundamental task of political philosophy today to be a comprehensive grasp of what Tocqueville describes as 'democratic revolution'.[35] Even if the aristocratic surveyor of American democracy regularly expresses certain reservations about its 'savage instincts', Lefort praises Tocqueville for his ability to grasp democracy's profound capacity for creation, innovation and reinvention beyond the limited framework of elected government. In a passage which Lefort particularly admires, Tocqueville writes:

> Democracy does not give the people the most skilful government, but it produces what the ablest governments are frequently unable to create: namely, an all-pervading and restless activity, a superabundant force, and an energy which is inseparable from it and which may, however unfavourable circumstances may be, produce wonders.[36]

Against those countless interpretations of Tocqueville which conclude with the maxim that we should love democracy, but love it 'moderately',[37] what Lefort adopts from Tocqueville is a vision of democracy as an 'uncontrollable adventure', one that unleashes an extraordinary enthusiasm for equality and destroys the very positions of those who traditionally dominate society by virtue of their wealth, status and privilege.[38] What democracy makes possible is a society where hierarchies can no longer be claimed natural, right can no longer appeal to the divine and differences in rank will no longer go unchallenged. These are the forces that Lefort understands to have ultimately undermined the foundations of monarchy during the French Revolution. These are the forces that savage democracy invites us to consider.

It is here where we may establish the link between the *savage* and the *against* with greater precision. Following Tocqueville's general account which locates democracy's revolutionary origins in the waning conditions of premodern Europe, Lefort's writings on democracy can be appreciated to elaborate a detailed theoretical perspective that meticulously positions democracy against the very ontology of the *ancien régime*.[39] Drawing heavily from the research of Ernst Kantorowicz, Lefort understands modern democracy as an unprecedented challenge to the entire order of the monarchical system, not only by displacing the body of the king but, more importantly, by violently breaking down the very basis of monarchy's symbolic representation of right, power and legitimacy.[40] What exactly is it that democracy is against for Lefort?

> At the source of democracy can be found the rejection of a number of things: power detached from the social ensemble, law that governs an immutable order, and a spiritual authority possessing knowledge of the ultimate ends of human conduct and of the community. However, it is not enough to say *at the source of democracy*: this rejection has been democracy's permanent driving energy.[41]

Consequently, what democracy is against is precisely that which renders monarchy a tenable model in the first place, a rejection which does not degrade or dissipate over time but, as Lefort contends, remains democracy's 'permanent driving energy'. Like gasoline in a car, it is this rejection, this *against*, that fuels democracy and propels it forward. For Lefort, much like Tocqueville before him, democracy cannot be reduced to a regime of law, to the limits traditionally ascribed to the *état de droit*.[42] Rather, what emerged against the *ancien régime* is indicative of a savage democracy. Setting up a field in which a unique political conflict may unfold, democracy inaugurates an experience in which the very questions of authority, legitimacy and right are subjected to an incessant controversy and dispute:

> In other words, modern democracy invites us to replace the notion of a regime governed by laws, of a legitimate power, by a notion of a regime founded upon *the legitimacy of a debate of what is legitimate and illegitimate* – a debate which is necessarily without guarantor and without any end.[43]

Democracy exposes society to a new ontology, a radical indeterminacy, so that, in Lefort's view, institutions can never become fixed, knowledge can never become absolute and the quest for unity can never eclipse an underlying conflict and division.[44] Contrary to totalitarianism in the twentieth century, democracy is the regime, following Abensour, that never retreats, never shies away from this inescapable experience of conflict and division:

> Inversely, democracy is seen as constituting itself through the acceptance, or better, the elaboration of the originary division of the social; democracy is the form of society that, unsatisfied with merely recognizing the legitimacy of internal conflict, comprehends conflict instead as the originary source of an ever renewed invention of liberty.[45]

Shattering the representation of a unified body politic, opening up a confrontational space in which social division may be politically expressed, violently displacing the powers embodied in the absolute authority of the crown, what Lefort's writings effectively reveal is that located at the origins of modern democracy is a revolutionary *being-against* monarchy, an against that would not vanish with the death of the king, but would endure and go on to contest new forms of inequality and new modes of domination that appear with a new society. Hence, expounding his larger theory of modern democracy with respect to this historic rejection of the *ancien régime*, it is in this context that Lefort will isolate what is often put forward as the most distinguishing attributes of the society that emerges from the democratic revolution: the disincorporation of power, the spatialisation of power, law and knowledge, the dissolution of the markers of certainty, the indeterminacy of the people.

It could therefore be argued without controversy that what Lefort chronicles here and there as savage democracy may be situated and explored according to Tocqueville's general formulation of democratic revolution. And yet, perhaps even these terms should not be conflated too hastily. Whereas Tocqueville's democratic revolution frames democracy's more protracted democratising trajectory, seemingly touching every facet of social and cultural life, what Lefort's examples of savage democracy appear to isolate, within this larger process, are those more transient and explosive moments of heightened social turmoil and confrontation. When Lefort speaks of savage democracy, he invokes democracy's radical transformative capacities at their most pronounced, decisive and unwavering, those spectacular moments in history, however brief, when democracy demonstrates its utter refusal to be mastered, domesticated or restrained. It is in this respect, for example, that Lefort will repeatedly employ the phrase to describe the waves of civil unrest he witnessed sweep through France during the summer of 1968, an event that would have a profound effect on Lefort, as it would many other French political thinkers of his generation:[46]

> To suddenly see such a liberation of words, powerful words, that was in itself an extraordinary event. It was a new mode of socialisation, a wild socialisation, which could not last. I never had the hope of a revolution in 68; only some idiots ascribed that idea to me. On the other hand, [. . .] [i]n the midst of that savage democracy there was a sort of freedom which, I confess, was extremely precious to me.[47]

Perhaps what Lefort finds so inspiring about the events of May '68 is not only its unpredictable and spontaneous character that effectively disposed of every model of what proper (Marxist) revolutionary action should look like, but also its proliferation of an entirely new language against authority, hierarchy and bureaucracy and its expression of a genuine desire for liberty and equality that unleashed something very powerful, something that, according to Lefort, is almost always restricted, if not repressed outright.[48] Without a leader, without a unified programme or overarching design, May '68 discharged an upsurge of creative, improvised political activity that was able to at once break down partitions that normally isolate diverse groups, occupy spaces that are ordinarily forbidden, challenge existing hierarchies in ways never before seen and articulate demands in a manner that could no longer go unheard.[49] Perhaps it is for this reason that Lefort will identify something of May '68 that is for him consistent with everything that is savage about democracy.

And yet, Lefort is certainly not the first to observe democracy's more savage character. The history of political thought reveals a long line of critics, adversaries and detractors of democracy who observe these tendencies with great clarity, often with far greater clarity, in fact, than those insipid proponents of democracy who claim to advocate it. We have already seen, for example, how Plato portrays democracy as the anarchic disruption of the wild mob, equating democracy allegorically to the aimless ship whose disobedient sailors undermine the authority of the captain and recklessly commandeer the doomed vessel.[50] Similarly, Polybius, the Greek historian, unapologetically catalogues democracy's 'savage rule of violence' as its principal vice which perpetually threatens democracy itself and remains inseparable from it.[51] When considering democracy's case for popular self-government, Jean Bodin questions disparagingly: 'How can a multitude, that is to say, a Beast with many heads, without judgement, or reason, give good council? To ask council of a multitude is to ask for wisdom in a mad house.'[52] On the opposite side of the English channel, penning his *Leviathan* at the height of the civil war, Hobbes casually remarks that, for many, there is nothing to distinguish between 'democracy' on the one hand and 'anarchy' on the other, signifying not a distinct kind of government, but precisely its lack.[53] Moreover, when Adam Ferguson, of the Scottish Enlightenment, compares democracy and despotism as archetypal examples of corrupted, lawless societies, he concludes that: 'Democracy seems to revive in a scene of wild disorder and tumult: but both the extremes are but the transient fits of paroxysm or languor in a distempered state.'[54] In a similar vein, warning his new found nation of the unbridled dangers of democracy, James Madison famously writes:

> Democracies have ever been spectacles of turbulence and contention; have ever been found incompatible with personal security, or the rights of property; and have in general been as short in their lives, as they have been violent in their deaths.[55]

In *The Philosophy of Right*, his major contribution to political thought, G. W. F. Hegel recoils at democracy's very proposition of 'popular sovereignty', insisting that not only does such a confused notion distort the very meaning of sovereignty itself (properly expressed in the embodiment of a monarch), but is likewise predicated on a '*wild* idea of the people'.[56] Finally, in a remarkable passage in the preface which opens his prodigious *Democracy in America*, Tocqueville himself proclaims that democracy, lacking in education, religion and morality:

> has consequently been abandoned to its wild instincts, and it has grown up like those children who have no parental guidance, who receive their education in the public streets, and who are acquainted only with the vices and wretchedness of society.[57]

Violent, unstable, rebellious by nature and provoked by the likes of drunken sailors, wild mobs and orphaned children, a recurring theme throughout the history of political thought is democracy's indictment for offering no viable foundation for government and fostering a political experience that indeed can only be denounced as 'savage'.

The 'Principle of Anarchy' and the Emancipatory Act of Politics

Let us return to Abensour, whose insights will help give shape to Lefort's savage democracy in a manner we have hitherto not yet seen. Whether Lefort cites the events of May '68 or the French Revolution itself, what immediately strikes Abensour about savage democracy is the way in which it tends to emerge self-generated, seemingly bound to no particular rules and subject to no particular conditions. Savage democracy appears to spring up at will, at the most unexpected times, assuming the most unpredictable forms. And while by no means hostile to organisation or institutional engagement, what particularly seems to intrigue Abensour about savage democracy is its propensity to manifest in such a way that it reveals no identifiable formula, no underlying schema, and thus evades all ideological categories and classifications:

> 'Savage democracy' evokes, rather, the idea of the wildcat strike (*grève sauvage*), that is, a strike that arises spontaneously, that begins with itself and unfolds in an 'anarchic' fashion, independent of any principle (*archê*), of any authority – as well as of any established rules and institutions – and that strikes in such a way that it cannot be mastered. It is as if 'savage' connotes the inexhaustible reserve of turmoil that soars above democracy. In a word: to forge a 'libertarian idea' of democracy is to think it as savage.[58]

Perhaps this is as close to a definition as we are likely to come. Spontaneous, governed by no overarching order, subject to no organising principle or archê, Abensour not only situates savage democracy according to an anarchic condition, but at the same time, frames his larger discussion according to Lefort's very consistent morality against mastery. This is a recurring theme in Lefort's work I have tried to underscore here. As we have seen, Lefort regards democracy as *savage* when it resists subordination and pacification; a democracy that cannot be easily possessed, neutralised or restrained. Savage democracy not only manifests in opposition to various logics of mastery in society, but also manifests in such a way that it refuses to be mastered itself: by a leader, party, policy or plan. This is likely the reason why radical democratic movements are so often decried as 'disorganised', 'fractious', 'anarchic'. And yet, perhaps what Abensour finds most compelling about savage democracy's anarchic character in this regard, is the manner in which it appears to challenge the way we typically theorise spontaneous political activity itself. With reference to Lefort's *Un homme en trop*, Abensour routinely presents savage democracy as the 'libertarian idea' of democracy.[59] When Abensour reflects upon this libertarian idea, when he considers what this string of references to savage democracy that cuts across Lefort's writings all share in common, what he ultimately discerns is a form of emancipatory political activity that liberates political activity itself. If we extrapolate from Abensour's compelling exegetical analysis, savage democracy may be interpreted both as action and as form: the political *action* that expresses a resolute desire for emancipation; and the *form* in which this political action is itself liberated from any overarching principle, design or command. Carefully developing this libertarian idea of democracy alongside Reiner Schürmann's 'principle of anarchy',[60] Abensour is able to provide Lefort's savage democracy some much needed theoretical elaboration.

If we follow Abensour's somewhat unconventional reading, even without going into any depth into Schürmann's work, what the principle of anarchy provides Abensour's analysis of savage democracy is a theory of political action released from the confines of a first principle. No longer bound to its origins, the political act can no longer simply be appropriated and understood according to the conditions from which it came. At the same time, nor must the political act be subjected to a *telos*, to an ultimate goal, end or final cause.[61] Rather, with the principle of anarchy, we may think the political act liberated from any imposed order, doctrine or imperative: action becomes an *event*, self-legitimating, an end in itself.[62] For Abensour, this is essential to understanding Lefort's savage democracy. Refusing the limitations of the principle-derivation model, marking a decisive break from a strict rationalism of causality and finality, Abensour understands savage democracy to realise a form of political activity free to unfold in multiple and even contradictory ways, remaining open to the accident, to fortune, to error, to the unforeseen and to the unforeseeable. *Is this not a fitting description of the logic of spontaneity itself?*

Therefore, placing aside the intricacies of those longstanding questions regarding the precise relationship between *theory* and *praxis*, *thinking* and *acting*, Schürmann's principle of anarchy, although not a reference for savage democracy, provides something of a model for the form of political activity that Abensour appears to want to ascribe to it. In the most concrete terms, savage democracy traces a particular political action or form of political action that allows democracy's ongoing struggle against social domination to materialise and unfold in a uniquely spontaneous and anarchic fashion. It may be understood both in terms of the political activity that expresses a desire for emancipation as well as the opening up of a space in which that political activity may transform and evolve in any number of ways. In this respect, when conceived as a political act, what savage democracy first seeks to liberate is the political act itself. This is something that Abensour's analysis of savage democracy will not allow us to forget. Perhaps this represents his most important contribution to Lefort's concept of democracy.

Accordingly, both in substance and in form, what Abensour appears to draw from savage democracy is the emancipatory act of politics. It designates that unprecedented political challenge which, given its spontaneous, anarchic character, breaks with a theory of praxis that finds the only legitimate political activity to be the one that remains sanctioned, preordained, *governed*. Democracy refuses to be restricted to a particular sphere of society, frame of time, subject or object. Lefort certainly allows for a broader conception of democracy than this. It is precisely the emancipatory act that must at times break the silence, disturb the peace and challenge established norms, institutions and conventions. As Lefort appears to confirm in a particularly intriguing remark drawing from Salman Rushdie:

> In democracy itself, the institution of individual and political freedoms couldn't make one forget that freedom is not given; speech always requires an *interruption* of the ordered relations among men, a right that exceeds all definition, a sort of violence.[63]

With this passage, Lefort wishes to remind us that freedom is never something to be given, handed down from above; it must be *taken*. It must be seized, created, affirmed. This can be a violent act. Even in the context of the broader topic of rights, on which he certainly writes a great deal, Lefort rejects the notion that rights and freedoms are simply harboured by institutions, distributed by the State.[64] Rather, what Lefort's writings demonstrate quite convincingly is that freedom, however defined, is something intrinsically bound to a long process of political action, persistent questioning and permanent contestation. To signify this process, Lefort will at times appeal to Tocqueville's democratic revolution, at others, to his own more idiosyncratic savage democracy.

Permanent Contestation: Savage Democracy and Human Rights

Lefort's contribution to the theory of human rights will offer additional insights into his understanding of savage democracy. As early as *Éléments d'une critique de la bureaucratie* (1971), Lefort will frame the struggle for rights so central to the modern political experience in terms of an undomesticated, *savage* democracy:

> Let it once again be said, it is not only the protection of individual liberties that is at issue, but also the nature of our social ties; where there is spreading feeling for rights, democracy is necessarily savage and not domesticated.[65]

In addition to providing a compelling point of departure for an intriguing analysis of Lefort's highly original appraisal of rights in a democratic society, such remarks may be advanced to chart out the relative distinction between what he terms 'savage' democracy on the one hand and what he describes more generally as the democratic form of society on the other. This is an important nuance in Lefort's work that warrants far more attention than it receives. Although the language of rights remains a prominent feature of his formulation of modern democracy in his later work, if Lefort ultimately rejects both Marx's and Arendt's familiar claim that rights must necessarily be situated within the bounds of an established institutional framework, it is because Lefort himself tends to locate the source of those rights, as is well known, in a symbolic field which extends beyond the realm of any such concrete institution.[66] Rights are never simply legal or institutional in character, the State or constitution never simply their proprietor or guarantor. Something of the reality of rights could be said to hang in the symbolic imaginary of the society that understands itself (and experiences itself) as 'democratic'. Therefore, insofar as he binds the language of rights, and indeed the very recognition of rights, to a symbolic field, Lefort's larger concept of democracy will correspond not to a set of institutions, but to a particular form of society distinguished by a particular symbolic mutation, one that distributes an abstract or indeterminate figure of rights across a horizontal social imaginary that organises both meaning and representation in society.[67] As Lefort repeatedly insists, the demand for rights can never be dissociated from a wider social awareness of rights themselves.[68] And yet, although Lefort understands the larger discourse of rights according to this symbolic dimension so constitutive of the modern democratic society, this does not overlook the fact that the *struggle* for rights is never merely symbolic in character. Rather, when Lefort considers that 'spreading feeling for rights', that demand for rights, the actual political battle for rights on the ground, he can no longer be said to be gesturing to the symbolic order which so defines the democratic form of society, but more specifically to that emancipatory political activity that Abensour associates with savage democracy, a struggle played out, if we follow Lefort, against the backdrop of this symbolic horizon which infuses that struggle with its salience and social significance. So perhaps Lefort must ultimately locate rights *between* the symbolic and the real: far from abstract, they play an indisputable role in the concrete objectives of real political struggles of oppressed people.[69] It is in this respect that Lefort's reflections on rights may serve to exemplify the two intrinsically interwoven dimensions of his larger concept of democracy ceaselessly being worked out throughout his later writings. In the context of a society which not only establishes a representation of rights in its social imaginary, but one in which the precise subject or recipient of those rights is destined to remain indeterminate, perhaps savage democracy testifies to that defiant *demand* for rights itself, the struggle to institute new rights, the effort to extend rights to more and more disenfranchised people. So it is not really a matter of isolating a 'liberal' Lefort and a 'radical' Lefort, but a matter of identifying the particular context in which Lefort deploys his concept of democracy: either as a *form of society* or as a *savage* democracy. The 'savage' compels us to consider democracy's striking capacity to create and transform, its inventions as well as its interventions. It invites us to bear witness to the fact that human beings are never simply the subject of rights, but at the same time their authors.[70] Much like equality for Rancière, rights are something to be created, contested and confirmed.[71] They remain inextricably intertwined with their enunciation.[72] As Lefort avows: 'rights are not simply the object of a declaration, it is their essence to be declared.'[73] Therefore, cutting across the many illusions and misattributions which so often obscure the discourse of rights, Lefort may be read to offer an assessment of democracy which succeeds far better than most in identifying the substantive political function of rights in the modern era: they provide a language, a logic, an instrument according to which the protracted democratisation of society may be advanced. For, as Abensour testifies, the demand for new rights is ultimately a demand for new social relations, a new way for society *to be*.

Drawing on Lefort's admiration for the work of historian E. P. Thompson, whose research traces the struggles of an emerging proletarian class under the conditions of early capitalism, Abensour will develop this persistent declaration of rights which so epitomises savage democracy for Lefort according to a larger open-ended process of permanent contestation.[74] It is this permanent contestation that Abensour locates at the very heart of democratic revolution. Insofar as rights can never be fixed, fastened or established absolutely, Lefort will tend to define democracy in terms of an ongoing *theatre of contestation*.[75] Essential to Lefort's understanding of democracy is the installation of a field in which rights and other demands and grievances may be declared and debated, at times in quite combative terms. As we have seen, rights are neither found in nature nor are they granted by the heavens above. They must be articulated, demanded, realised, most often by those who find themselves excluded from the benefits and protections that rights can provide. But just as their realisation cannot be dissociated from their articulation, their articulation cannot be dissociated from their contestation. The very demand for rights itself implies a certain provocation or defiance, a certain '*interruption* of the ordered relations among men'. Accordingly, as the perpetual initiation of a unique political controversy and dispute, the experience that Lefort chronicles as permanent contestation may first be recognised to contain a distinct phenomenal dimension. Democracy is always something demonstrative, something visible, the making apparent what was not apparent before. Perhaps this is one reason why its distinguishing act of contestation may be considered *theatrical*, an account that will feature just as prominently in the writings of Rancière.

To the extent that his own theory of democracy is formulated according to an inherent *disagreement* regarding the very distribution of the sensible, Rancière will often present democracy as a 'staging' of equality.[76] Democracy opens up a space of litigation by that part of the community that has no part (*les sans-part*), a demonstration of equality that, for Rancière, must effectively reconstitute the very sensible of the community itself: those who could not be seen now appear, those who could not be heard now speak. Similarly, what Lefort calls 'permanent contestation' may likewise be appreciated to open up a space in which a unique political conflict may unfold: 'Democracy must be seen as this *milieu* for conflicts, as a *milieu* in which we have to know how to engage in contestation.'[77] Consequently, Lefort's understanding of contestation should not be confined, as we occasionally find in more narrow readings of his work, to the institution of legitimate conflict so that competitions, rivalries and antagonisms may be played out according to procedural rules (thereby excluding all those conflicts already deemed 'illegitimate'). Rather, the act of contestation that remains consistent with a savage democracy is the one that functions to raise the very question of what constitutes *legitimate* and *illegitimate* conflict and refuses the closure of this question in any absolute sense. This is precisely what it means to render conflict *irreducibly* political. Analogous to 'disagreement' in the work of Rancière, 'contestation' remains Lefort's preferred term for the act that we found to be essential to the meaning of politics itself: the making controversial what was not controversial before, the making problematic what was not a problem before. Contestation does not simply imply adopting a resolute position on a particular social problem, or set of problems; it is rather the act which itself renders the social politically problematic. It is what divides the social or recasts an antecedent social division in a renewed political form. Perhaps this is how Abensour should be interpreted when he declared above that democracy is not merely the acceptance but *elaboration* of that originary division of the social. Therefore, what democratic contestation could be said to introduce to the generality of social conflict is the particularity of the antinomies of politics, a *being-against* that is not so much a type of conflict, but as the specific challenge of the demos, the minority, the excluded, one that successfully reconfigures or reconstitutes social conflict as an irreducible problem of politics. In this regard, if permanent contestation inevitably takes the form of an against, it is not simply because it embodies a defiant opposition, but because what it opposes is subjected to the condition of politics, a condition that exposes what it is against to a radical indeterminacy undermining its absolution, certainty and fixity.

Savage democracy's distinguishing practice of contestation and the permanent nature of this contestation is itself indicative of a democracy in perpetual motion, a democracy unsettled and profoundly discontent. Lefort will refuse that modern democracy, even long after the revolutionary era from which it springs, may be presumed a settled form, a stabilising agent, a completed project. As I have argued, democracy does not represent the resolution to the problem of the political society. On the contrary, it is what renders society political in the first place, what makes it problematic, not in a single gesture, however monumental, but repeatedly, over and over again. As a succession of political contests engendered by an increasingly diverse body of actors located at the most divergent corners of society, since the dawn of its modern incarnation against the order of the *ancien régime*, democracy has offered an enduring political challenge to the given relations of the social. However sporadic and discontinuous, it is the very permanence of this challenge – perpetually reborn, regenerated, resumed – that must frame Lefort's concept of democracy according to a protracted process of democratisation, what Tocqueville, in his own analysis, described as 'democratic revolution'. Democracy is not simply the name of that emancipatory political act to which Abensour refers; it is also the name of the society that this act invariably seeks to create: a more democratic society distinguished by more inclusive, participatory and egalitarian institutions and relations. This cannot be achieved in a single moment. It is a project that necessitates a prolonged, sustained effort. Accordingly, contrary to the regimes of monarchy and totalitarianism to which Lefort routinely posits it against, democracy may be understood to open up a representation of time in which its movements and transformations, successes and failures, must be charted and evaluated according to an extended trajectory, a *becoming*. Democracy strives for a future more democratic than the past. To appeal to Nietzsche once again, democracy can be thought to organise an 'untimely' relation to the present: it resists the conditions of the present in the hopes of creating a better future to come. In addition to its constitutive openness to the indeterminate and the indefinite, perhaps this is why Lefort will declare democracy the *historical* society par excellence.

Thinking Democracy Savage: A Philosophical Exercise

If we have appealed to Lefort's admittedly obscure references to savage democracy to organise a working concept of democracy for the purpose of this study, it is because, rather than supply a definitive model or prescriptive formula for democracy, we found it to expose the concept to new possibilities and experimentation. Savage democracy does not simply represent another qualified interpretation of democracy (such as 'liberal' democracy or 'social' democracy). More than a description or explanation, what savage democracy makes possible is a new way to think about democracy. It invites us to revisit and reconsider our most underlying assumptions about democracy, constantly testing the boundaries and limitations of its accepted concept. In this respect, perhaps we could ascribe a certain savage democracy to Rancière, to Abensour and no doubt others as well. Whenever a theory of politics challenges the prevailing representation of democracy, daring us to explore the potential of what the *power of the people* can mean, such a theory could very well be said to elicit a savage conception of democracy. Lefort appears to utilise the savage qualifier to draw attention to democracy's transformative potential, what it can do and what it can create. It is in this sense that Lefort can be appreciated to emancipate democracy in thought. His curious passages on savage democracy demand not only that we reflect upon what is savage about democracy, but also that we think democracy in a savage way. Thinking democracy savage entails distancing its concept from those mitigated, domesticated representations of democracy so prevalent today, allowing us to rediscover its more creative and transformative dimensions and capacities. This is why savage democracy can be taken as an exercise of thought as much as a particular characterisation of democracy itself. It helps us resist what is so readily endorsed as democracy today, rendering the concept something of an instrument to critique the conditions of the *here and now*. This is also why savage democracy provides a fitting conceptual basis through which we may pursue what I have called the 'antinomies of politics'. For if nothing else, those revolutionary moments Lefort tends to associate with savage democracy compel us to consider democracy in terms of what it contests, what it counters and disputes, what it is *against*. It is for this reason that Lefort is so pivotal to our study.

In part, the link between the savage and the against could be established in Lefort's work because his own recurring allusions to savage democracy must always be situated in the context of his broader political project which routinely incorporates a distinct model of democracy's being-against into its core theoretical framework: a democracy theorised at once against the monarchic and totalitarian forms of society. As we encountered, these are the two objects that Lefort often posits his concept of democracy against. Perhaps Abensour would very much endorse reading Lefort in this way. For what particularly interests Abensour about Lefort's political philosophy is that it is organised not as an abstract system or elaborate defence of any particular regime, but as a critique of the realities of social domination. And if Abensour, very much at odds with the majority of the scholarship, elects to centre savage democracy in his interpretation of Lefort's larger project, it is because it is here that he sees Lefort most vividly isolate the manner in which social domination is challenged from below: in the *ancien régime*, in totalitarianism, in our own society today. Accordingly, following the example of Abensour, if we have pursued Lefort's savage democracy to organise our basic conception of democracy here, it is because, beyond releasing the concept from a more compromised representation of democracy, it is precisely what Lefort understands to be savage about democracy that helps us to conceptualise a democracy that cannot be reduced to a form of government or set of institutions, that cannot be confined to rule of law or the *état de droit*, but constitutes a unique political challenge to an order of society permeated by hierarchies, inequalities and modes of exclusion. Such a concept is critical to the project of the antinomies of politics. To theorise democracy according to what it is against is an attempt to think democracy as an emancipatory, transformative agent in society. This is precisely what savage democracy compels us to consider.

I have argued that Lefort represents an important thinker of the antinomies of politics. In *Complications*, his final work, Lefort writes of a radical 'rejection' at the root of modern democracy itself. Without question, this rejection is indicative of a democracy against monarchy, a democracy against the very ontology of the *ancien régime*. And yet, in Lefort's terms, if democracy invariably appears in the form of an against, as I have contended, it is because this rejection is not only located at the revolutionary 'source' of modern democracy but also, as Lefort maintains, constitutes its 'permanent driving energy'. It is precisely the permanence of this against that should not escape our attention. For neither arbitrary nor an end in itself, the antinomies of politics will attest to a very particular political project: the ongoing democratisation of society, its institutions and relations. Situating Lefort's savage democracy according to both Tocqueville's democratic revolution and his own discussions of permanent contestation, it is precisely this more protracted democratisation of society that becomes more apparent.

In Lefort's words, savage democracy constitutes the 'essence' of democracy, a statement that has undoubtedly prompted much speculation among his readers. Indeed, it is a remark that seems to implore interpretation. But if we understand this savage essence of democracy to signify its more unbridled and subversive powers and potentials, its capacity to resist, defy and transform, we can see why figures like Abensour are so captivated by Lefort's use of the term. As Abensour develops, taken as the emancipatory act of politics, savage democracy appears to call into question everything about how political activity is typically theorised and understood, particularly in the tradition of orthodox Marxism. Spontaneous, self-generated, bound to no particular conditions, savage democracy testifies to that unpredictable, incalculable political action that appears to spring up at will and refuse to be mastered or restrained. Drawing from Schürmann's 'principle of anarchy', this is the form of political activity Abensour ascribes to savage democracy. For this reason, Abensour's essay is immensely helpful in providing savage democracy something of the much needed structure that it otherwise lacks in Lefort's own writings. As I suggested, this represents an important contribution to Lefort's concept of democracy.

Following Deleuze, if we ultimately understand the exercise of philosophy as the construction of concepts for practical and critical purposes, the concept of democracy should be no exception. Philosophy is an enterprise of demystification. Its concepts are not representations, but instruments of critique, a resistance to the present. It is imperative that the concept of democracy be organised accordingly. This is the significance of savage democracy. While it can hardly be said that Lefort's brief remarks on savage democracy supply us with a substantive concept of democracy, they present us with an opportunity to reflect upon the larger philosophical task of *thinking* democracy itself, of organising its concept for political use. If a distinctively political philosophy is one that organises its concepts to navigate, evaluative and critique the *here and now*, Lefort certainly provides us with an exemplary model. Perhaps this best encapsulates Abensour's general assessment of Lefort's political philosophy. And when Abensour ventures to construct his own concept of a democracy against the State, he will not fail, like so many, to recognise and incorporate its savage dimension. Savage democracy helps us to think a democracy against. It helps us organise a concept of democracy as a spontaneous, anarchic political act that contests the present relations of the social and strives for a more democratic society to come. Once again, such a concept is critical to the project of the antinomies of politics.

Hence, although often eclipsed by more prominent facets of his work and rarely explored, what may ultimately be extracted from Lefort's studies of democracy are the two indispensable components that must be included in any philosophical construction of its concept: the *act* of being-against and the *process* of democratisation. More than any particular conclusion about democracy, this forms the basis of the concept that we have pursued throughout this study. To think a democracy against is to think a democracy that binds the persistent democratisation of society to that distinct challenge of the demos we have hitherto associated with politics itself. To think a democracy against is to think democracy *savage*.

Notes

1. The term *démocratie sauvage* has been translated as 'savage' democracy, 'wild' democracy and 'untamed' democracy across various English translations of Lefort's work.
2. Claude Lefort, 'Philosopher?', *Writing: The Political Test* (Durham, NC: Duke University Press, 2000), 248–9. Also see Oliver Marchart, *Post-foundational Political Thought: Political Difference in Nancy, Lefort, Badiou and Laclau* (Edinburgh: Edinburgh University Press, 2007), 88.
3. Gilles Deleuze and Félix Guattari, *What is Philosophy?* (New York: Columbia University Press, 1994).
4. Gilles Deleuze, *Nietzsche and Philosophy* (New York: Columbia University Press, 2006), 106.
5. Archipolitics, parapolitics and metapolitics are outlined in Jacques Rancière, *Disagreement: Politics and Philosophy* (Minneapolis: University of Minnesota Press, 1999), chapter 4. For a general introduction to these terms, see Bruno Bosteels, 'Archipolitics, Parapolitics, Metapolitics', in *Jacques Rancière: Key Concepts*, ed. Jean-Philippe Deranty (Durham, NC: Acumen Publishing, 2010.)
6. We will find this approach across Abensour's oeuvre. In particular, see the essays contained in his volume Miguel Abensour, *Pour une philosophie politique critique* (Paris: Sens & Tonka, 2009). For additional analysis of Abensour's critical political philosophy, see Martin Breaugh, 'Critique de la domination, pensée de l'émancipation. Sur la philosophie politique de Miguel Abensour', *Politique et Sociétés* vol. 22, no. 3 (2003) and Gilles Labelle, 'La philosophie politique et le "choix du petit" dans le travail de Miguel Abensour', *Monde Commun* vol. 1, no. 1 (Autumn 2007). Also see Chapter 5 below.

7. Martin Breaugh, 'From a Critique of Totalitarian Domination to the Utopia of Insurgent Democracy: On the "Political Philosophy" of Miguel Abensour', in *Thinking Radical Democracy: The Return to Politics in Postwar France*, ed. Martin Breaugh et al. (Toronto: University of Toronto Press, 2015), 235.
8. Karl Marx, 'Critique of Hegel's "Philosophy of Right": Introduction', *Early Writings* (London: Penguin Books, 1992), 251.
9. Pierre Clastres, *Society against the State: Essays in Political Anthropology* (New York: Zone Books, 1987), 189–90. Both Lefort and Abensour have written on various facets of Clastres's work. Some of their writings appear in Abensour's edited volume, Miguel Abensour, *L'Esprit des lois sauvages: Pierre Clastres ou une nouvelle anthropologie politique* (Paris: Seuil, 1987).
10. Clastres, *Society against the State*, 16, 189–90, 203–4.
11. Gilles Deleuze and Félix Guattari, *A Thousand Plateaus: Capitalism and Schizophrenia* (Minneapolis: University of Minnesota Press, 1987), 357. Deleuze and Guattari offer a nuanced, multifaceted and ultimately critical assessment of Clastres's evolutionist hypothesis. See Marc Abélès, *Thinking beyond the State* (Ithaca: Cornell University Press, 2017), chapter 1.
12. See Bernard Flynn, 'Lefort as Phenomenologist of the Political', in *Claude Lefort: Thinker of the Political*, ed. Martín Plot (Houndmills, Basingstoke, Hampshire: Macmillan, 2013).
13. Salih Emre Gerçek argues that Lefort originally draws his concept of indeterminacy from the work of Merleau-Ponty. See Salih Emre Gerçek, 'From Body to Flesh: Lefort, Merleau-Ponty, and Democratic Indeterminacy', *European Journal of Political Theory* vol. 19, no. 4 (2017).
14. Claude Lefort, *Éléments d'une critique de la bureaucratie* (Paris: Gallimard, 1979), 28, as quoted in Abensour, '"Savage Democracy" and the "Principle of Anarchy"', *Democracy against the State: Marx and the Machiavellian Moment* (Cambridge: Polity, 2011), 109.
15. Alain Caillé, 'Claude Lefort, the Social Sciences and Political Philosophy', *Thesis Eleven* vol. 43, no. 1 (1995): 54. Rancière can also be interpreted as adopting a position against mastery. See Peter Hallward, 'Jacques Rancière and the Subversion of Mastery', *Paragraph* vol. 28, no. 1 (March 2005).
16. Martin Legros offers a helpful introduction to the concept as it appears both in Lefort and Abensour. See Martin Legros, 'Qu'est-ce que la démocratie *sauvage*? De Claude Lefort à Miguel Abensour', in *Critique de la politique. Autour de Miguel Abensour*, ed. Anne Kupiec and Étienne Tassin (Paris: Sens & Tonka, 2006).
17. Claude Lefort and Paul Thibaud, 'La communication démocratique', *Esprit* no. 9–10 (September–October 1979): 34, as quoted in Abensour, '"Savage Democracy" and the "Principle of Anarchy"', 106–7.

Reprinted with minor variations in Claude Lefort, *Le Temps présent: Écrits 1945–2005* (Paris: Belin, 2007), 389–90.
18. Jacques Rancière, 'Is There a Deleuzian Aesthetics?', *Qui Parle* vol. 14, no. 2 (Spring/Summer 2004): 1.
19. Abensour, '"Savage Democracy" and the "Principle of Anarchy"', 102.
20. See Claude Lefort, *Machiavelli in the Making* (Evanston: Northwestern University Press, 2012), Parts 1 and 5. For a general introduction to Lefort's theory of interpretation, see Bernard Flynn, *The Philosophy of Claude Lefort: Interpreting the Political* (Evanston: Northwestern University Press, 2005), chapter 3.
21. Lefort, *Machiavelli in the Making*, 504. Also see Dick Howard, *The Specter of Democracy* (New York: Columbia University Press, 2002), 76.
22. For an analysis of Abensour's 'radical democratic' interpretation of Lefort, see James D. Ingram, 'The Politics of Claude Lefort's Political: Between Liberalism and Radical Democracy', *Thesis Eleven* vol. 87, no. 1 (2006).
23. Abensour, '"Savage Democracy" and the "Principle of Anarchy"', 105.
24. References to 'wild being' will be found throughout the text. See Maurice Merleau-Ponty, *The Visible and the Invisible* (Evanston: Northwestern University Press, 1968).
25. Eleanor M. Godway, 'Wild Being, the Predicative and Expression: How Merleau-Ponty Uses Phenomenology to Develop an Ontology', *Man and World* vol. 26, no. 4 (1993): 389. Interestingly, it is in this sense of 'wildflowers' that Lévi-Strauss will employ the term 'savage' in order to distinguish an 'untamed' human thought from a more methodical or scientific mode of reasoning in *La Pensée sauvage*: 'In this book it is neither the mind of savages nor that of primitive or archaic humanity, but rather mind in its untamed state as distinct from mind cultivated or domesticated for the purpose of yielding a return.' See Claude Lévi-Strauss, *The Savage Mind* (Chicago: University of Chicago Press, 1966), 219.
26. Abensour, '"Savage Democracy" and the "Principle of Anarchy"', 107.
27. Ibid.
28. Flynn, 'Lefort as Phenomenologist of the Political', 31–2.
29. Claude Lefort, 'Relecture sur Mai 68', *Le Temps présent*, 592 (translation by Martin Breaugh).
30. As documented by his essay Claude Lefort, 'The Contradiction of Trotsky', *The Political Forms of Modern Society: Bureaucracy, Democracy, Totalitarianism* (Cambridge, MA: MIT Press, 1986).
31. See, for example, Claude Lefort, *Complications: Communism and the Dilemmas of Democracy* (New York: Columbia University Press, 2007), 50.
32. Antoine Chollet will also make the link between Lefort's savage democracy and Tocqueville's democratic revolution. See Antoine

Chollet, 'L'énigme de la démocratie sauvage', *Esprit* no. 451 (January–February 2019).
33. Claude Lefort, 'The Image of the Body and Totalitarianism', *The Political Forms of Modern Society*, 302.
34. Before Tocqueville and Lefort, Immanuel Kant will articulate this very point, distinguishing between, on the one hand, the actual historical events of the French Revolution and, on the other, a revolutionary spirit or 'enthusiasm' which runs through it and extends beyond it. See Immanuel Kant, 'The Contest of Faculties', *Political Writings* (Cambridge: Cambridge University Press, 1991), 182.
35. Samuel Goldman, 'Beyond the Markers of Certainty: Thoughts on Claude Lefort and Leo Strauss', *Perspectives on Political Science* vol. 40, no. 1 (2011): 31.
36. Alexis de Tocqueville, *Democracy in America*, vol. I (New York: Vintage Books, 1990), 252. Also see Claude Lefort, 'Reversibility', *Democracy and Political Theory* (Minneapolis: University of Minnesota Press, 1988), 169, as well as Steven Bilakovics, *Democracy without Politics* (Cambridge, MA: Harvard University Press, 2012), 150.
37. Perhaps most notably in Pierre Manent, *Tocqueville and the Nature of Democracy* (Lanham: Rowman & Littlefield, 1996), 132.
38. Claude Lefort, 'From Equality to Freedom: Fragments of an Interpretation of "Democracy in America"', *Democracy and Political Theory*, 196.
39. Bernard Flynn, 'Democracy and Ontology', *Research in Phenomenology* vol. 38, no. 2 (2008): 224.
40. Ernst Kantorowicz, *The King's Two Bodies: A Study in Mediaeval Political Theology* (Princeton: Princeton University Press, 1957). For Lefort, democracy institutes a 'society without a body' or one that 'undermines the representation of an organic totality'. See Fred Dallmayr, 'Postmetaphysics and Democracy', *Political Theory* vol. 21, no. 1 (February 1993): 114–15. Also see Daniel Steinmetz-Jenkins, 'Claude Lefort and the Illegitimacy of Modernity', *Journal for Cultural and Religious Theory* vol. 10, no. 1 (Winter 2009).
41. Lefort, *Complications*, 124.
42. Claude Lefort, 'Politics and Human Rights', *The Political Forms of Modern Society: Bureaucracy, Democracy, Totalitarianism*, 258.
43. Claude Lefort, 'Human Rights and the Welfare State', *Democracy and Political Theory*, 39. For discussions of this passage, see Ingram, 'The Politics of Claude Lefort's Political', 42–3, and Steven Hendley, 'Reconsidering the Limits of Democracy with Castoriadis and Lefort', in *Reinterpreting the Political: Continental Philosophy and Political Theory*, ed. Lenore Langsdorf, Stephen H. Watson and Karen A. Smith (Albany: State University of New York Press, 1998), 174–5.
44. Lefort, 'The Image of the Body and Totalitarianism', 305.

45. Abensour, '"Savage Democracy" and the "Principle of Anarchy"', 105.
46. For an analysis of the impact of May '68 on Lefort's political thought, see Wim Weymans, 'Deepening Democracy through Contestation? Lefort and Gauchet on May 1968 and Its Legacy', *The Tocqueville Review* vol. 41, no. 1 (April 2020). For a discussion of the wider significance of May '68 on contemporary French political philosophy, see Julian Bourg, *From Revolution to Ethics: May 1968 and Contemporary French Thought* (Montreal: McGill–Queen's University Press, 2007).
47. Claude Lefort and Pierre Rosanvallon, 'The Test of the Political: A Conversation with Claude Lefort', *Constellations* vol. 19, no. 1 (March 2012): 14. Lefort, in collaboration with Edgar Morin and Jean-Marc Coudray (Cornelius Castoriadis), would write the first full-length volume to consider the events of May '68. See Edgar Morin, Claude Lefort and Jean-Marc Coudray, *Mai 1968: la Brèche* (Paris: Fayard, 1968).
48. Lefort, 'The Image of the Body and Totalitarianism', 309.
49. Claude Lefort and *Anti-mythes*, 'An Interview with Claude Lefort', *Telos* no. 30 (1976): 187.
50. Plato, *Republic*, VI, 488a–489d. All references are to Plato, *Complete Works*, ed. John M. Cooper and D. S. Hutchinson (Indianapolis: Hackett Publishing Company, 1997). This notion of democracy as the rule of the 'wild mob' is also prevalent in Pseudo-Xenophon's 'The Constitution of the Athenians'. See J. M. Moore, *Aristotle and Xenophon on Democracy and Oligarchy: Translations with Introductions and Commentary* (London: Chatto & Windus, 1975).
51. Polybius, *The Histories: Books 5–8* (Cambridge, MA: Harvard University Press, 1972), 291.
52. Jean Bodin, *Six Books of the Commonwealth*, as quoted in Jennifer Tolbert Roberts, *Athens on Trial: The Antidemocratic Tradition in Western Thought* (Princeton: Princeton University Press, 1994), 8, fn. 5.
53. Thomas Hobbes, *Leviathan: Parts One and Two* (Upper Saddle River: Prentice-Hall, 1958), 153. Also see Alan Apperley, 'Hobbes on Democracy', *Politics* vol. 19, no. 3 (September 1999): 166–7.
54. Adam Ferguson, *An Essay on the History of Civil Society* (New York: Cambridge University Press, 1995), 73.
55. Alexander Hamilton, James Madison and John Jay, *The Federalist* (Cambridge: Cambridge University Press, 2003), 44.
56. G. W. F. Hegel, *Elements of the Philosophy of Right* (London: Oxford University Press, 1962), 182–3.
57. Tocqueville, *Democracy in America*, vol. I, 7–8.
58. Abensour, '"Savage Democracy" and the "Principle of Anarchy"', 106. Abensour repeats this general formulation of Lefort's savage

democracy in Miguel Abensour, 'Utopia and Democracy', in *The Weariness of Democracy: Confronting the Failure of Liberal Democracy*, ed. Jason Powell Frausto and Sarah Vitale (Cham, Switzerland: Palgrave Macmillan, 2020), 33–4.
59. As early as 1971, Lefort declares his commitment to a 'libertarian idea of democracy'. See Lefort, *Éléments d'une critique de la bureaucratie*, 15.
60. Reiner Schürmann, *Heidegger on Being and Acting: From Principles to Anarchy* (Bloomington: Indiana University Press, 1987).
61. Abensour, '"Savage Democracy" and the "Principle of Anarchy"', 115. Also see Miguel Abensour, 'An-archy between Metapolitics and Politics', *Parallax* vol. 8, no. 3 (2002): 8–9.
62. Abensour, '"Savage Democracy" and the "Principle of Anarchy"', 115.
63. Claude Lefort, 'Humanism and Anti-Humanism: Homage to Salman Rushdie', *Writing*, 31.
64. See, for example, Lefort, 'Politics and Human Rights', 264, as well as Lefort, 'Human Rights and the Welfare State', 43.
65. Lefort, *Éléments d'une critique de la bureaucratie*, 23, as quoted in Abensour, '"Savage Democracy" and the "Principle of Anarchy"', 107. This is one of the earliest examples of Lefort's use of the term.
66. See Wim Weymans, 'Defending Democracy's Symbolic Dimension: A Lefortian Critique of Arendt's Marxist Assumptions', *Constellations* vol. 19, no. 1 (March 2012): 75.
67. For a broader discussion of this point, see Raf Geenens, 'Democracy, Human Rights and History: Reading Lefort', *European Journal of Political Theory* vol. 7, no. 3 (July 2008).
68. See, for example, Lefort, 'Politics and Human Rights', 260, 264. Also see Flynn, *The Philosophy of Claude Lefort*, 227–8.
69. See Daniel McLoughlin, 'Post-Marxism and the Politics of Human Rights: Lefort, Badiou, Agamben, Rancière.' *Law Critique* vol. 27, no. 3 (2016): 308–9.
70. On citizens as the authors of rights, see Stefan Rummens, 'Deliberation Interrupted: Confronting Jürgen Habermas with Claude Lefort', *Philosophy and Social Criticism* vol. 34, no. 4 (2008): 393–4.
71. For a detailed discussion of Rancière's position on human rights, see Andrew Schaap, 'Enacting the Right to Have Rights: Jacques Rancière's Critique of Hannah Arendt', *European Journal of Political Theory* vol. 10, no. 1 (January 2011).
72. Flynn, *The Philosophy of Claude Lefort*, 273.
73. Lefort, 'Politics and Human Rights', 257.
74. Abensour will largely attribute Lefort's well-known concept of *permanent contestation* to E. P. Thompson, perhaps drawing in particular from his widely influential essay E. P. Thompson, 'The Moral Economy of the English Crowd in the Eighteenth Century', *Past & Present* vol. 50, no. 1 (February 1971). See Abensour, '"Savage Democracy" and the "Principle of Anarchy"', 107.

75. See, for example, Lefort, 'Politics and Human Rights', 258.
76. Peter Hallward will consider this *staging of equality* in two closely related essays. See Peter Hallward, 'Staging Equality', *New Left Review* vol. 37 (January–February 2006) and Peter Hallward, 'Staging Equality: Rancière's Theatrocracy and the Limits of Anarchic Equality', in *Jacques Rancière: History, Politics, Aesthetics*, ed. Gabriel Rockhill and Philip Watts (Durham, NC, and London: Duke University Press, 2009).
77. Lefort and Rosanvallon. 'The Test of the Political', 13.

Chapter 4

Democratisation of the Sensible: Democracy against the Police

> *So what the seventeenth- and eighteenth-century authors understand by 'the police' is very different from what we put under the term. [. . .] What they understand by 'police' is not an institution or mechanism functioning within the State, but a governmental technology peculiar to the State—domains, techniques, targets where the State intervenes.*
>
> Michel Foucault, *'Omnes et Singulatim':*
> *Toward a Critique of Political Reason*

On the Many Forms of Being-Against

Having elaborated a working concept of democracy with Lefort, we may now investigate with greater precision how the antinomies of politics plays out in various ways. For this, we will revisit the work of Rancière and Abensour in these final two chapters. Although his insights into democracy's extraordinary challenge to the archê are considerable, Rancière's project has far more to offer to the theory of the antinomies of politics. While I have argued that democracy is universally against the archê as the underlying principle of rule, this in no way exhausts what it will be found to be against in society. This is because democracy's being-against may theoretically assume as many forms as the objects it confronts and disputes in society, at different times, under different conditions. It is for this reason that what democracy is against in the modern world is often quite different from what it was originally against in antiquity, the form of its being-against always determined by the particular context in which democracy makes its appearance as an emancipatory act of politics. It is striking that, in recent decades, a number of authors appear to have independently uncovered something of what I have identified as the antinomies of politics, integrating this rather remarkable dimension of democracy into their respective theoretical frameworks. For example, it is possible to discern the groundwork for a more philosophical-anthropological analysis of a democracy against heteronomy (Cornelius Castoriadis)[1] or drawing from the roots of historical materialism, a democracy against capitalism (Ellen Wood)[2] or rediscovering the origins of its 'fugitive' proclivity in ancient Greece, even a democracy against the constraints of its own constitutionalisation (Sheldon Wolin).[3] Accordingly, in order to investigate the antinomies of politics in greater detail, for the remainder of this study, I will present two exemplary theoretical models in which democracy's being-against appears particularly pronounced and carefully evaluate how its logic plays out in each case. Keeping with the central figures considered in this study, I will advance Rancière's model of a democracy against the police and Abensour's model of a democracy against the State. While not altogether compatible, these models will serve to inform and enhance the basis of our critique, further elaborate our terms and concepts and broaden our analysis considerably. Although their projects remain quite distinct in many respects, by charting out the objects and relations of its being-against, what both Rancière and Abensour are able to perceive in democracy is precisely what I have attempted to isolate in my own analysis here: a unique political challenge in which the foundations of a given social order or particular institutional arrangement are called into question by that generic body or political subject traditionally known as the demos. If I have argued that democracy remains irreducible to a type of government or collection of institutions, however assembled and arranged, it is because it is according to this political challenge of the demos that democracy must ultimately be understood. Both Rancière and Abensour can be read to shed light on this thesis.

Let us begin with Rancière. First introduced in his volume *Disagreement*, Rancière will articulate his concept of democracy in direct opposition to what he outlines more generally as the 'order of the police'. Referencing Foucault's lectures on governmentality, Rancière understands the police according to its most comprehensive definition, much closer to its original meaning in seventeenth- and eighteenth-century Europe. Conceived as a vast set of rationalities, institutions and processes encompassing everything from the distribution of roles, functions and spaces to the exercise of authority itself, the police will be interpreted as the operative administration and management of a social order. According to Rancière, every society without exception contains this imposition of order characteristic of the police. The police concerns the organisation of the social, the technologies of productivity, security and normalisation, the smooth working order of society. It associates particular bodies and identities with particular roles, tasks and places and allocates those bodies and identities to their 'proper place' accordingly. For Rancière, this process has a symbolic dimension. The police not only involves the material distribution of the social as such, but organises the very field of perception through which this distribution is experienced and understood socially. This represents an important addition to Foucault's general concept. Therefore, after situating this more historical account of the police in the context of Foucault's larger discussion of governmentality, Rancière's rather nuanced use of the term will be significantly developed in terms of a *regime of representation*, a *government of the sensible*, a symbolic constitution that governs over both the organisation and representation of the community. Workers, women, people of colour: the police is the power to render certain bodies and certain voices *imperceptible*. This explains why Rancière chronicles the police as intrinsically hostile to the agents of democracy. At the same time, it also explains why he understands democracy's logic of dissensus as an analogous counter to the logic of the police. It is this tension or point of intersection between democracy and the police that is located at the very heart of his political theory.

What exactly does Rancière's model of a democracy against the police contribute to our analysis of the antinomies of politics? Most importantly, in this context, what Rancière's model makes abundantly clear is that democracy's being-against invariably takes the form of a defiant act of subjectivation in which the demos or political subject initiates a polemical scene challenging the categories, distributions and classifications of the police order, frustrating its basic organisation and symbolic representation of society. In all its forms, democracy requires a subject and it is only through the appearance of a subject – its acts of *dissensus*, in Rancière's terms – that democracy's opposition to what it is against will be actualised and effectuated. Democracy is not an institution or regime primarily. It is the demos *acting*. It is the emergence of a political body, whatever its name, from wherever its comes, that modifies and transforms not only the relations of the social, but how those very relations are *perceived*. Consequently, what Rancière can be said to provide the study of the antinomies of politics is a detailed theoretical interpretation of the subject through which democracy's being-against will be typically expressed. By inventing new ways of seeing and new ways of thinking about the community, its parts, places and roles, democracy's act of subjectivation creates new possibilities for both the organisation and representation of the social. As I will demonstrate, far from a fleeting agitation or disturbance of the police order, Rancière will wish to situate such acts according to a broader history or tradition of emancipation. For Rancière, this is essential to the meaning of democracy itself.

Politics and the Police: A Radical Dichotomy

In *Disagreement*, Rancière will formulate a rather peculiar notion of democracy not in isolation, but located at the juncture or intersection of two opposing logics: the logic of *equality* and the logic of the *police*. What Rancière understands as politics will be explained in terms of this encounter, nexus or 'meeting of the heterogeneous'.[4] From this, a number of implications can immediately be drawn. First, nothing can be regarded political in and of itself. Politics occurs only when there is a meeting of these two distinct logics. Anything may have the potential to become political, but only on the occasion of this encounter or confrontation of democracy with the police.[5] Secondly, by consequence, we can no longer speak of a 'pure politics'. It is the nature of politics to remain mixed, impure.[6] Politics is a composition, an alloy; not a simple substance.

More importantly, Rancière understands the manner in which these two logics collide in a very particular way. For there is no neutral context or territory in which democracy's logic of equality encounters that of the police. And Rancière remains wary of any concept that may function to conceal or cover over this inherent antagonism and opposition, implying the smooth connection between the two ('power' or 'power relations' is offered as an example of such a concept).[7] Instead, the police will be advanced in terms of a certain state of generality in which politics – as the meeting of logics, the orchestration of antagonism – appears as something of an exception to the *givenness* of this social order.[8] Although its arrangement and design will vary dramatically, it is this given order of the police that appears to classify the general state of society. *Politics is that which acts on the police.*[9] It is this notion of politics as an active agent, as something which *acts* or *acts upon*, that should not escape our attention. For it is indicative of a larger strategy in the text to first establish the police, however defined, as a kind of generic or primary category so that a more precise interpretation of politics may be at once disentangled from it and reoriented in terms of something specific that happens to it: a disruption, suspension, modification.[10] Accordingly, insofar as politics represents the setting up of an encounter or confrontation between democracy and the police, whatever it is that ultimately falls under the general category of 'the police' may therefore be established as the principal object in which democracy can be said to be against. In Rancière's model, the police is posited as the condition for democracy, as both its point of departure and its object of dispute. Democracy appears as a polemical agent that interjects moments of dissensus into the police order, calling into question the intuition of its given arrangements and classifications and opening up a space for new ways of seeing and new ways of thinking about the community, its composition and configuration. This is why as long as Rancière outlines his concept of politics with specific reference to democracy's inextricable relation to the police, his first task remains to isolate these two terms accordingly:

> Politics is generally seen as the set of procedures whereby the aggregation and consent of collectivities is achieved, the organization of powers, the distribution of places and roles, and the systems for legitimizing this distribution. I propose to give this system of distribution and legitimization another name. I propose to call it *the police*.[11]

Therefore, in rather broad strokes, Rancière introduces the police as a vast set of institutions and procedures that govern over both the organisation and representation of a community: the exercise of authority, the distribution of roles, spaces and functioning parts as well as the manner in which these systems of authority and modes of distribution are legitimised and maintained. And yet, Rancière acknowledges this rather anachronistic use of the term 'police' is not without problems. For what the concept intends to encapsulate obviously remains quite distant from what we typically associate with the term today. In Rancière's lexicon, the police will no longer signify law enforcement, a disciplinary instrument of the State, the forces of law and order, men in little blue suits (*la basse police*). Alternatively, the term is employed in its broadest connotations, resembling something of the manner in which it would have been understood in the context of the absolutist State in the seventeenth and eighteenth century.[12] It is precisely this more historical sense of the police that informs Rancière's terminology and thus must likewise frame our own analysis of the concept accordingly. Rancière certainly points us in this direction in his initial proposal of the term. Nevertheless, given its significance in his larger political project, a number of commentators have observed that the concept of the police remains rather under-theorised across Rancière's writings.[13] This criticism is entirely justified. Even in *Disagreement*, the work that situates democracy's opposition to the police at its very centre, the concept will still only receive but a few pages of the most abbreviated description. This lack of analysis could very well be seen as one of the text's greatest deficits.[14]

Foucault, the Police and *Governmentality*

In this respect, in order to appreciate the object that Rancière appears to organise his concept of democracy against, it becomes necessary, for the moment, to suspend our discussion of his own work and consider another source. In his brief exposition of this more comprehensive interpretation of the police, Rancière will on more than one occasion appeal to Foucault, whose later work considers this early modern incarnation of the police – its mechanisms, jurisdiction and destinations – in the context of his own research on *governmentality*. Although he would never incorporate this research into a proper volume, Foucault does address the topic in considerable detail in a series of lectures delivered at the Collège de France at the end of the 1970s.[15] Therefore, in attempt to establish a more substantive background for Rancière's somewhat obscure reference to the police in *Disagreement*, let us turn to Foucault.

Foucault interprets the police, in the general sense that Rancière will advance the term, as a particular historical manifestation of a larger rationality he will ultimately frame and delineate in terms of 'governmentality'. In attempt to displace the centrality of sovereignty in political thought, Foucault increasingly employs the term 'government' to cover a sweeping range of techniques, strategies, objects and domains which not only traverse the bounds of State and subject, but a number of disciplines and institutional practices ranging from economics to medicine to pedagogy to religion. Therefore, beyond its more limited reference to state administration, Foucault demonstrates that well into the eighteenth century, what may fall under the general category of government is actually quite vast, including topics as diverse as the ethics of the self, the management of the household, the moral guidance of the soul and the overseeing of public health, social welfare and economic development.[16] For this reason, Foucault will dissociate government from the comparatively narrow confines of the State, the State remaining but a single component in a complex network of actors, institutions and mechanisms involved in the governing of individuals, groups or populations.[17] Even the appearance of the 'absolutist' State in the sixteenth century will be appreciated simply in terms of a particular historical modification of the practices of government itself. Foucault regards the advent of the modern nation state merely as a type or 'episode' of this larger governmental rationality which must be granted a certain theoretical priority accordingly: the State remains an instrument or agent of government, not the reverse.[18] In this respect, Foucault may shed light on why, unlike Abensour, Rancière's model of democracy will not isolate the State as the principal object of its being-against, but rather something which remains far more expansive and all-encompassing:

> I do not, however, identify the police with what is termed the 'state apparatus.' The notion of the state apparatus is in fact bound up with the presupposition of an opposition between State and society in which the state is portrayed as a machine, a 'cold monster' imposing its rigid order on the life of society.[19]

Indeed, given the scope of government, traditionally understood, Foucault regards the very notion of 'civil' society, as a separate or autonomous sphere of society, as little more than a fairy tale.[20] It is not so much a new form of State that engenders civil society as a result, product or negation of itself, but a new form of *governmentalised* society that organises new relations of the State.[21]

Therefore, rather than restrict its location and jurisdiction to the conventional limits of the State, this broader notion of government provides Foucault with a consistent theoretical schema able to trace and decipher, under a single term, a number of practices, strategies and mechanisms applicable to a range of projects extending from the governing of self to the governing of others.[22] By organising a working framework to consider the underlying problems of government – how to govern, how to be governed, by whom, how strictly, by what methods and to what ends – what Foucault investigates under the general formula of 'governmentality' should therefore not be understood as a competing paradigm bound to a single historical epoch, but as a larger rationality coextensive with various modalities of governance potentially stretching across vast historical boundaries. It thus becomes possible, with a certain degree of consistency, to compare and evaluate, for example, a project of government specific to the Greeks (*self-legislation/self-regulation*), to the Christians (*the directing of the soul*) and to early modernity (*the management of a population*). Government, in this respect, has less to do with the imposing of laws over a sovereign territory than it does with the active organisation and arrangement of particular objects in order to effectuate particular ends deemed appropriate to those objects governed.[23] Whether it be the self, the family, workers in a factory, inmates in a prison, patients in a hospital, inhabitants of a territory or members of a population, government's primary concern is one of *comportment*: the 'conduct' of human beings.[24] Its principal task is one of guidance, the ordering and shaping of the field of possible activity.[25] Such a rationality is very much epitomised by the Hobbesian conception of man outlined in the opening pages of his treatise *On the Citizen*. Since the Greeks, Hobbes declares, the history of political thought has simply presumed man naturally fit for society, but he is not: 'Therefore, man is made fit for society not by nature, but by training (*disciplina*).'[26] It is the business of government to guide and shape, organise and arrange, manage and regulate. Government concerns not only the organised practices of governing in the strictest sense, but the active rendering of objects *governable* in the first place. It is precisely this active or positive quality of government that Rancière will associate with the police.

In a key lecture on governmentality,[27] tracing significant historical developments from the sixteenth to the eighteenth century, Foucault explains that with the collapse of feudalism, the rise of the Reformation and Counter-Reformation and the emergence of a new competitive sovereign state system in early modern Europe, the discourse on government would explode with new force.[28] This extensive body of literature would considerably augment the knowledges, techniques and objectives of government, addressing not only more traditional topics of morality, family and the affairs of the State, but also, for the first time, large-scale problems such as national economy, public health and social conditions. As a result, the very notion of government would become synonymous with these more *generalised* forms of administration and management. This is very much the context in which the police, as a new form of governmental technology, will appear. Indeed, Foucault will situate this entire literature alongside a profound *governmentalisation* of society, amalgamating a comparatively fragmented feudal system into a centralised, bureaucratic state administration (the absolutist State), governing over a newly integrated set of economic practices and policies (mercantilism), analysed, calculated and evaluated according to a new set of rational tools, methods and strategies (particularly statistics, literally 'the science of the State'). It is for this reason that, when Hegel theorises the police in the *Philosophy of Right*, it will be conceived as a 'higher guiding authority'.

To facilitate the immense undertaking of such large-scale national campaigns from economy to security to public health, this increasingly expansive notion of government would likewise require a new object: whereas it would customarily target the family, individual or subject, by the eighteenth century, government would now identify *population* as its principal aim.[29] The discovery of population would play an unprecedented role in the transformation from a more conventional sovereign authority over a territory to a more elaborate governmentalised administration of a society.[30] At once more specific and more comprehensive, population allows for a far more precise object of knowledge and systematic means to manage that object as a numerical and calculable system of *aggregate effects*, effectively implicating, for the first time, the everyday conduct of a mass body under the guidance of a sovereign authority. Consequently, by the end of the eighteenth century, it is population that would come to occupy the police at the height of its powers.[31] For Foucault, such a development is indicative of the inception of *biopower*, the management of a population very much akin to the management of life itself.[32]

To illustrate this historic expansion of government, Foucault turns to a long trend of anti-Machiavellian literature that would become prominent during the period. Although revered by his contemporaries, following his death, Machiavelli's political writings, particularly *The Prince*, would quickly fall out of favour and it would not be until the early nineteenth century that his reputation as a profound political thinker would largely be re-established. As Foucault demonstrates, across this literature critical of Machiavelli, a far more varied and wide-ranging theory of government would be developed, the rule of the prince remaining but a single form. Whereas Machiavelli's 'advice to the prince' would now be interpreted to concern the rather narrow problem of how a transcendent prince may protect and retain his sovereign authority over a principality, his many critics would be far more interested in cultivating an 'art of government' that considers the dynamics of managing a multiplicity of complex relations immanent to society itself.[33] It is in this context of an anti-Machiavellian literature that concerns itself not with the jurisdiction of the prince, but with these broader objects and technologies of government, that Foucault will isolate a new discourse on 'the police'. In its original incarnation, the police has little to do with the enforcement of laws. Rather, it is indicative of an entirely new model of government which identifies the management of society as its primary objective. Beginning in the seventeenth century, the police is simply the name of the principal mode or technique in which this management of society is carried out. The police may therefore be juxtaposed with law in the following way: whereas the law concerns universals, the police concerns particulars. Much like the judiciary, army and treasury, the police is conceived as a distinct administrative body of the State, but, unlike the judiciary, army or treasury, one whose functions remain indefinite and jurisdiction remains unlimited. As Foucault often likes to repeat: the true object of the police is *man* himself.[34]

Therefore, integrating countless sources and archival materials, Foucault's interpretation of the police may be summarised accordingly:

> So what the seventeenth- and eighteenth-century authors understand by 'the police' is very different from what we put under the term. [. . .] What they understand by 'police' is not an institution or mechanism functioning within the State, but a governmental technology peculiar to the State—domains, techniques, targets where the State intervenes.[35]

The police operates as an agent of *intervention*. It is for this reason that the police should not be confused with the State itself. It is rather the means in which the State acts directly on society in a non-juridical fashion. It represents the combined instruments, techniques, practices and strategies in which the State identifies, targets and intervenes in a wide spectrum of activities, conditions and relations of human life from infrastructure to commerce to public health to population management. The police may therefore be understood as the *actualisation* of this new model of government particular to the early modern period. It embodies the indispensable technologies and knowledges essential to a new governmentalised society. It is what renders the project of the management of society not only feasible, but effective. Whereas the prince or sovereign would traditionally be occupied with his subjects' status, virtue and obedience, what is of interest to the police is simply what men *do*: their activity, occupation, production and reproduction.[36] With a historically unprecedented degree of breadth and precision, the police functions to organise and integrate a wide diversity of human activity into the jurisdiction, authority and influence of the State:

> What, then, are the concrete tasks of police? As its instrument, it will have to provide itself with whatever is necessary and sufficient for effectively integrating men's activity into the State, into its forces, and into the development of these forces, and it will have to ensure that the State, in turn, can stimulate, determine, and orientate this activity in such a way that it is in fact useful to the State.[37]

The goal of the police is not social repression. It is to order and shape the social in such a manner that its activity is deemed useful to the State and increases its forces. Rather than a punishing mechanism devised to contend with the delinquency of a deviant minority, the primary concern of the police is to systematically enhance the general health, order and productivity of society as an integrated whole. It is what creates and ensures a well-ordered, productive and smoothly functioning society. It is precisely against this background that Rancière's reference to the police must be understood.

The Government of *the Sensible* and the Symbolic Constitution of Society: Rancière's Concept of the Police

While Rancière will not strictly correspond his own, rather nuanced concept of the police with Foucault's more contextual historical analysis, it is this general sense of an active governing agent that systematically organises, configures and arranges the social field (its parts, spaces, roles and functions) that gives Rancière cause to appeal to the term. Although abstracted from its proper historical milieu, Rancière clearly identifies something in our own society today – and indeed, perhaps something inherent to all societies in general – which merits the revival and sweeping application of the term as it was broadly understood in seventeenth and eighteenth-century Europe. What remains consistent across Foucault's and

Rancière's treatment of the police is the prominence granted to its underlying practice of social ordering, the aspiration to implement and realise the proper order of society.[38] Rancière takes the police as a symbol for the harmonious, productive society that functions without interruption and dispute. It is indicative of the well-managed, well-regulated community that organises its parts and roles according to a larger administrative framework effectively foreclosed to the complications of politics. It is for this reason that he finds the police intrinsically hostile to democracy. So, whereas Foucault contrasts the police and sovereignty, Rancière will contrast the police and politics. For Rancière, the police is synonymous with the authority to distribute order over a community, an authority that often remains indistinguishable from the very order it installs. It is in this respect that he sees the police, and the general motivating principle behind it, as in no way particular to an early modern strategy of government. Its basic formula may be found everywhere. It can be found in ancient oligarchies and medieval republics, in totalitarianism and neoliberalism alike. Indeed, it appears Rancière has difficulty envisioning a form of social existence that endures with any perpetuity beyond the dictates of a given police order. Even much of the history of political philosophy will be understood as a series of rationalisations, justifications and elaborate defences of various police orders, both concrete and ideal.[39] Most notably, Rancière reads the *Republic* as the archetype of a political philosophy whose first objective is to substitute the order of politics with that of the police. Plato calls the proper order of society 'justice'. It has many other names. Regardless, for Rancière, this substitution amounts to the effective elimination of politics from philosophical inquiry.[40] As we have seen, this remains the basis of his criticism of political philosophy.

Therefore, however indebted to the work of Foucault, rather than a governmental technology particular to the State, Rancière appears to utilise the concept to encapsulate the totality of rationalities, mentalities, operations and procedures that function to systematically organise, regulate and preserve a given order of society (covering everything from law to coercion to education to science). The police signifies the ability to impose order on a social body: it is the power to identify groups, designate parts, assign roles, allocate functions and partition spaces. Its basic presumption is that the appropriate behaviour, activity and thinking will follow from one's particular allotted part, role and function.[41] It assumes one's natural abilities and capacities both determines and is determined by one's proper place in the larger social order. This is precisely its appeal to the archê which remains at the root of every police distribution. Consequently, while he insists his employment of the term remains 'neutral' and 'nonpejorative', Rancière will identify the police in every hierarchical structure and every social arrangement that functions to assign, restrict and exclude. Whereas Foucault's analysis of the police tends to concentrate on technique and strategy, what appears to interest Rancière is primarily its *effects* on a social body.[42] It is very much from this perspective that a concept of democracy, as the appearance of a political subject that interrupts and frustrates the logic of the police, will be developed.

Rancière will associate the police with the count of the community. In both *Disagreement* and the closely related 'Ten Theses on Politics', which largely serves to distil and enumerate its most essential findings, the police will be distinguished as a particular way of identifying and dividing up the parts and shares of what is common. As opposed to a straightforward numerical count, the police engineers various intricate measuring strategies to evaluate the title, worth and share of each member of the community.[43] It calculates, appraises and assigns according to a given criterion, standard or judgement. Once again, this its appeal to the archê. In a single movement, the police establishes both what is common in the community (that which constitutes the community as a whole) and the manner in which the common of the community is divided (the dividing up of parts and shares).[44] Concerned both with what can be divided and how that division is to be carried out, the police may therefore be understood to constitute a partition (*le partage*) of the social, determining one's part, role and extent to which one participates or partakes (*avoir-part*) in the institutions of society (economic, governmental, familial, etc.). Accordingly, as a partition of the social, as the allocation of parts and shares, the police represents the solution to the longstanding problem of social organisation and distribution: of who is included, to what extent, under what conditions and to what ends.

One the more predominant features to characterise the police count is the manner in which it represents the community as a coherent body that lacks void and supplement.[45] The police offers a regulatory framework that claims to encompass the whole of the community so that all its parts are known, named and counted.[46] On at least one occasion, Rancière will describe this process in terms of *saturation*: 'The essence of the police is the principle of saturation; it is a mode of the partition of the sensible (*le partage du sensible*) that recognizes neither lack nor supplement.'⁴⁷ This principle of saturation signifies the *fullness* or *completeness* of the social, the count that excludes the very possibility of supplementation. The police order is emblematic of a distribution without remainder, without excess and without omission. It claims there is nothing unaccounted for, nothing left over or external to its mode of accounting.⁴⁸ In this regard, not only does the police function to limit, marginalise and exclude, but it embodies the power to render those excluded effectively *invisible*.

Therefore, beyond the count of the empirical parts of the community – the bodies, functions, roles and shares – Rancière is intent on establishing the police as a *regime of representation*, an agent that functions to organise and formulate the underlying constitution of society in a symbolic manner. This is a key component of Rancière's concept:

> The police is, essentially, the law, generally implicit, that defines a party's share or lack of it. But to define this, you first must define the configuration of the perceptible in which one or the other is inscribed. The police is thus first an order of bodies that defines the allocation of ways of doing, ways of being, and ways of saying, and sees that those bodies are assigned by name to a particular place and task; it is an order of the visible and the sayable that sees that a particular activity is visible and another is not, that this speech is understood as discourse and another as noise. [. . .] Policing is not so much the 'disciplining' of bodies as a rule governing their appearing, a configuration of *occupations* and the properties of the spaces where these occupations are distributed.⁴⁹

The police cannot simply be reduced to a materialism of distributed parts and shares; it is just as essential that it determine the *ineligibility* of those parts and shares distributed: how they are represented, how they are perceived and how they are experienced socially.⁵⁰ Insofar as the police stipulates the very terms of *partaking*, of inclusion and exclusion, participation and marginalisation, it must first specify the mode of perception in which those terms are inscribed. Not only does the police organise the material divisions of a shared common (*un commun partagé*), but it also likewise functions to organise the representational space in which those divisions are articulated and deciphered. The police constitutes both a particular representation of how the parts of the community are ordered and a particular ordering of how the parts of the community are represented. Its mandate is to establish the very parameters between the visible and the invisible, the sayable and the unsayable, the audible and the inaudible.[51] It is the power to name, to frame, to determine: what can be seen and what cannot, what can be heard (*logos*) and what remains indistinguishable from the incoherent fog of noise (*phônê*). Its primary concern is one of the *symbolisation* of society, the manner in which the sensible is mediated according to a given framework or design:

> The police is not a social function but a symbolic constitution of the social. The essence of the police lies neither in repression nor even in control over the living. Its essence lies in a certain way of dividing up the sensible.[52]

Essential to the police order, it could therefore be said, is nothing less than the *governance of the sensible*. For Rancière, the police intervention, regulation and management of the social extends all the way to sensory experience itself. What it governs, what it guides and shapes, is the way in which we see and hear, what we see and hear and likewise, what cannot be seen or heard at all. Although Foucault's general framework of government and governmentality still very much applies, it is here where Rancière will most decisively diverge from his research and cultivate a conception of the police particular to his own theoretical project:

> In 'Omnes et Singulatim,' Foucault conceives of the police as an institutional apparatus that participates in power's control over life and bodies; while, for me, the police designates not an institution of power but a distribution of the sensible (*le partage du sensible*) within which it becomes possible to define strategies and techniques of power.[53]

It is Rancière's contention that any relation or mechanism of power already presupposes a particular distribution of the sensible according to which that relation or mechanism of power is symbolically arranged. Moreover, this position remains consistent with one of his most elementary theses: that at the heart of every community, at the heart of every institution of the social, lies an *aesthetics*, a particular configuration and coordination of the field of the sensible, the modes of perception and forms of representation that dictate the relations and boundaries between *ways of seeing, ways of doing, ways of saying* and *ways of being*.[54] Accordingly, perhaps what ultimately constitutes the common of a community is not so much a shared identity, territory or ideology, but a dominant distribution of the sensible, a prevailing sense or modality of sense.[55] This is why Rancière can speak quite literally of a 'politics of aesthetics'. What is at stake in politics is not only the institutions and relations of society, but the very manner in which those institutions and relations are perceived and rendered intelligible. A politics of aesthetics sets forth to both challenge the limits of the perceptible and to offer new possibilities of perception, new ways of seeing and new ways of being seen. In this respect, the limits of such a politics of aesthetics can be understood to extend well beyond what Antonio Gramsci describes in his *Prison Notebooks* as the 'war of position'. For Rancière, politics is nothing less than the war of perception itself.

Aesthetics, the *distribution of the sensible*, the *police*: while the precise relationship between these key terms which populate Rancière's later work may at times be found to remain frustratingly undefined, what this conception of the police must ultimately compel us to consider is not only that every society is constituted in a symbolic manner, but that the symbolic is itself something with the capacity to be *governed*. Perhaps this is what will most sharply distinguish the symbolic as it appears in the work of Rancière and Lefort. Whereas Lefort binds a particular symbolic order to the monarchic, democratic and totalitarian regimes, Rancière appears to ascribe a general symbolic to the police itself (regardless of content and arrangement). Whereas Lefort arguably must situate politics within the context of a given symbolic field, Rancière understands politics as always external and contrary to the symbolic order of the police. Likewise, whereas Rancière associates this symbolic order with the principle of *saturation*, this is a term that Lefort would likely reserve only for totalitarianism (and even then, there is no suggestion from Lefort that the symbolic is ever itself an object of government). 'The police' is Rancière's universal term for precisely that: the totality of systems and processes that govern the symbolic constitution of society, that manage and regulate the modalities of perception operative in a social field. It is for this reason that politics cannot simply be equated with the affairs of the public. For what is public and what is private, their divisions and boundaries, are already symbolised in a particular way from the start. (This is something that the Greeks appear to have never fully grasped.) Rather, integral to the meaning of politics, Rancière argues, is the conflict over their very symbolisation.[56] Politics is the initiation of a controversy, a polemics in which the representation of the public, the private, the organisation of the community itself, is put into question and rendered an irreducible political problem.

This is the work of democracy. And, in this regard, if democracy can indeed be understood in opposition to the general order of the police as Rancière reimagines the term, perhaps what democracy must ultimately be said to be against in this context is the systematic government of the symbolic. For beyond its various modalities and strategies of social ordering, the police presides over an underlying ontology of closure, a closure that functions to restrict what is visible, what is thinkable and what is possible.[57] Although working through an entirely different paradigm, Castoriadis will routinely isolate such ontological closure as the very basis of *heteronomy*. For Rancière and Castoriadis alike, democracy represents the rupture of closure, inventing new ways of interpreting and imagining the social, its composition and configuration. According to Rancière, this rupture is indicative of the appearance of the political subject.

'Logical Revolt': Towards a Theory of the Political Subject

In the opening lines of Aristotle's *Constitution of Athens*, the demos is defined rather succinctly as those who have 'virtually no share in any aspect of government'.[58] On at least one occasion, Rancière proposes that *Disagreement* may be read in its entirety as one long commentary on these opening lines of Aristotle's text: 'In a sense, one can say that politics begins when those who have no share begin to have one.'[59] At the heart of this political struggle for a 'share' of government is a dispute over *language* itself: not only who has the right to speak, but also who has the capacity for speech and whose speech is recognised as such. This strange intersection between language and politics is one that may be traced across political theory from Aristotle to Hannah Arendt to Jürgen Habermas. When Aristotle declares man a political animal, it is not simply because he is social, but because he is in possession of *logos*. Whereas other animals merely grunt and growl, man is unique in that he is endowed with the capacity to speak, to debate, to discuss the affairs of the polis: what is just and what is unjust, how the community should be organised, what the laws that govern that community should be.[60] And yet, Aristotle is quick to qualify the implied universality of this characterisation, immediately distinguishing between those who genuinely possess *logos* and those, we can only assume, who merely possess the memetic semblance of it (slaves and, by extension, women, workers, colonised peoples, etc.). How can such a distinction be justified? The coherence of Aristotle's remarks depends entirely on the meaning of *logos*. As Rancière explains, as soon as Aristotle isolates the basis for legitimate political participation in a *logos* possessed only by a select few, it no longer corresponds to a generic human capacity for language or rational discourse, but to a symbolic division of the social.[61] The question at hand is not one of biology, physiology or cognition, but one of representation, a distribution of the sensible that organises the basic relations and proximities between speech, subjects and *logos*, a distribution indicative of the order of the police. Therefore, if *Disagreement* may be interpreted as something of an extended meditation on Aristotle's most basic political problem – who is in possession of *logos*, who is entitled to a share? – an interpretation that Rancière himself will very much endorse, it is not because language offers a foundation for politics, but because language remains the implicit object of a very particular dispute. It is precisely the inauguration of this dispute that Rancière will associate with politics. Beyond questions of justice and injustice, laws and institutions, if politics renders *logos* itself an object of controversy, it is because *logos* is never simply a matter of speech, but a particular *account* that is made of speech.[62] This is why, borrowing a term from the poet Arthur Rimbaud, when Rancière associates democracy with acts of revolt, it is revolt of a very particular kind: a 'logical revolt' that is as much a conflict over those who speak and the intelligibility of that speech as anything else.[63] Therefore, contrary to Aristotle, if language can offer no ground for politics, it is because politics represents a dispute over the interpretation of what constitutes language itself, the very distinction between *logos* and *phônê*. Whereas Aristotle appeals to language as a necessary condition for belonging to a political community, Rancière sees language as the basis of a disagreement regarding who belongs to such a community and who does not. Whereas Aristotle's political subject is the one whose words demonstrate an innate possession of *logos*, Rancière's political subject is the one whose words and, indeed, *excess* of words throw the entire symbolic division of *logos* into question. It is this political subject that concerns us here, the subject who represents an excess of words, a *literary* animal as opposed to an inherently political one,[64] whose speech embodies the capacity to disrupt and modify the sensible, rendering the symbolic order of the police inherently problematic.

From his very first work, perhaps the central question that motivates Rancière's larger political project since his infamous break with Althusser is precisely that which his former teacher systematically failed to consider: the role of the subject in the history of social emancipation.[65] For this reason, some elect to read many of Rancière's major works, contra Althusser, according to the heritage of a humanist Marxist tradition in which the subject remains an integral component of social change.[66] And yet, Rancière himself remains unequivocal that the political subject is not a sociological entity.[67] Much like Foucault, the identity, domain and appearance of the subject is never presupposed.[68] The political subject does not anticipate itself, does not exist before it acts, before it manifests a political actor. The proletariat, for example, does not exist as a political entity before it imposes itself on the workings, divisions and presuppositions of industrial capitalism, before it makes itself a problem *precisely where there was none before*. Nor is the manifestation of the political subject, consistent with Abensour's appeal to the principle of anarchy, contingent upon any particular set of socio-historical determinations. Both the origin and destination of the political subject can never be known in advance. Spontaneous, unpredictable, incalculable, Rancière largely considers the sporadic appearance of the political subject as something of an 'accident' across a long history of social domination.[69] Therefore, if class struggle does not represent the underlying motor of politics, it is because politics is the name of that which sets up this conflict between classes as parts of society in the first place.[70] Politics, in this view, is not the clash of interests, opinions or perspectives, but describes the process in which two opposing logics that count the parts of the community – that of *equality* and that of the *police* – are made to encounter one another in the form of a disagreement. The vehicle through which these two logics collide and intersect is the political subject. The political subject is something that happens, that comes into being and then falls away, provisional, local, episodic, transforming both the identity of the subject itself as well as its relations, limits and parameters as prescribed by the symbolic order of the police. For this reason, Rancière often prefers to speak of political 'subjectivation' (*la subjectivation politique*), a term more inclined to draw our attention to the process in which one or many become a political subject.[71] It is according to this process of subjectivation that democracy's being-against the police must be understood.

As we have seen, in *Hatred of Democracy*, Rancière offers a more general account of democracy as 'political' or 'anarchic' government, government based on the absence of title or qualification.

But in *Disagreement*, written a decade earlier, we encounter a somewhat different perspective. Here, democracy is formulated almost exclusively in terms of its relation to the police or, more specifically, in terms of the principal mechanism in which a given order of the police is effectively obstructed or suspended:

> Democracy is more precisely the name of a singular disruption of this order of distribution of bodies as a community that we proposed to conceptualize in the broadest concept of the police. It is the name of what comes and interrupts the smooth working of this order through a singular mechanism of subjectivation.[72]

In this context, democracy is conceived, in rather narrow terms, as politics' mode of subjectivation, the process in which an excluded or marginalised people, those previously unseen and unrecognised, abandon their allotted part or position, challenging the categories and classifications of the police, frustrating its symbolic representation of society. Democracy occurs when the sensory self-evidence of what is perceptible, intuitive, given in society is contested and called into question, when the basis of the natural correspondence between bodies, places, roles and functions is thrown back on its own inherent contingency. It reconfigures or redefines the dominant mode of perception operative in a social field. It draws the voices of those of no account, who have no right to speak, into a space of perceptibility. *Democracy represents the democratisation of perception, of the sensible itself.* This is not an inevitable process, whatever the conditions. An emancipatory politics is neither necessary nor automatic; it requires a subject and it is only through the agency of this subject – its acts of dissensus – that politics comes into being in the form of democracy. Perhaps this represents one of *Disagreement*'s most important theses. Democracy is the act of a subject. What makes an act political is not its object or location, but its form: the setting up of a dispute through a defiant demonstration of equality.[73] It is the initiation of a controversy, a polemical scene that contradicts the underlying assumptions of the police and renders new voices, new relations and new destinations possible. To become a political subject is to make oneself appear, to make oneself of some account, to impose oneself on those very spaces and times where one does not belong. Democracy begins with a new people occupying a new sphere of appearance. It is precisely the manifestation of this sphere and this people that undermines the dictates of a given distribution of the sensible.

But who is this political subject that appears in opposition to the police? In his 'Ten Theses on Politics', Rancière understands the political subject neither as the collected members of the community nor as a specific demographic unified by a shared interest or experience (for example, the working class). Rather, it will be qualified simply as the supplementary part in relation to every count of the parts of the population.[74] If the police embodies the principle of *saturation*, a distribution of the sensible that structurally precludes lack and supplement, excess and remainder, the political subject represents the surplus subject in this saturated field of experience.[75] It is the manifestation of the uncounted, the invisible remainder become flesh, the 'part without part' whose very appearance makes contentious the status of the sensible. Democracy occurs, in this view, when this surplus subject, this supplementary part, is added to the symbolic constitution of the social rendering what I have called the 'government of the sensible' intrinsically problematic. Whereas the police concerns the configuration of perception, democracy concerns its *reconfiguration*: it adds something that was not there before.[76] It produces a multiple that contradicts the very logic of the police count. This is precisely how Rancière understands acts of dissensus. Dissensus reveals a gap in the sensible, a miscount or incongruity; it demonstrates that the total is not total, the whole is not whole. It introduces a wrong (*le tort*), a torsion or twisting of logics that would otherwise never meet: the logic of equality and the logic of the police.[77] Consequently, as a surplus subject, an agent of dissensus, a manifestation of a wrong, the political subject will have no natural or constant identity. As soon as workers, women, people of colour deviate from their allotted place or position and emerge as a political subject, everything that was thought to be intuitive about their identities is effectively denatured, forced out of its obviousness.[78] Emancipation means precisely that: *escape from minority*.[79] Evading the fixity of all identifiable markers and classifications from class to race to gender, the political subject must therefore be conceptualised formally. The political subject is a floating subject, a fluctuating performer that no longer coincides with the original coordinates of its assigned place, role and function.[80] Instead, it paradoxically inhabits two worlds at once: the world of equality and the world of the police, one where it is visible and one where it is not, one where it belongs to the community and one where it remains a stranger. Politics involves the intersection of these worlds or, more to the point, the demonstration of a common world, one with a shared language and a shared *aisthesis*.[81]

Such a world may only come into being through conflict, through a certain violence to the symbolic, but it is precisely the creation of a common world, the sharing of a common stage, that allows arguments to be heard, polemical scenes to unfold and disputes to be carried out in a political fashion.

As I have argued throughout, politics is never simply conflict in itself. It is rather what modifies or reconfigures the relations of conflict; it is the conflict that makes conflict political. Workers, women, people of colour: politics requires a subject, and it is only through the emergence of a subject that politics is initiated and set in motion. For Rancière, the name of this process is *democracy*. But whereas politics will have but a single democratic form, democracy itself will experience an array of different actors, under various names, come to pass as its political agent. In part, it is for this reason that the identity of the political subject is destined to remain indeterminable. This is especially true in the modern era. Indeed, it is largely with respect to the increasing variety of political subjects that Rancière will draw the principal distinction between ancient and modern democracy. While ancient democracy witnessed the demos, the poor – those, as Aristotle explains, who have no share in government – open an arena of dispute largely played out in and for the public sphere, modern democracy, Rancière contends, experiences a proliferation of subjects whose acts of dissensus render litigious a vast range of objects at the most divergent regions of society.[82] Modern democracy can therefore be distinguished in terms of the multiplication of forms of subjectivation, which in turn multiplies the sites and matters of disagreement. By contrast, Lefort will draw his own theoretical distinction between ancient and modern democracy with respect to the manner in which power is represented symbolically. While ancient democracy perceived power as belonging to no one, identified in the middle, between citizens and principally localised in a well-defined public sphere, modern democracy, Lefort contends, experiences power as an *empty space*, occupied by a people that remains indeterminate and situated in a field with no such boundaries or limits.[83] Despite these variances, what both accounts appear to emphasise is the extent to which modern democracy effectively dislocates and multiplies the principal subject, object and location of politics: *who* the subject of democracy may be, the *objects* that democracy concerns and the *spaces* where democracy occurs. What is public and what is private, what constitutes a citizen, what determines who participates, to whom equality applies: in its modern incarnation, the solutions to these problems appear to shift and fluctuate at a far greater rate. What modern democracy is against, what it contests and disputes, becomes increasingly decentred and diversified, drawing politics into a vast spectrum of spheres of life that no doubt would have been quite foreign to the ancient Greek experience: the relations of production, racial inequities, the family, the role of women in society. But whereas Lefort's analysis considers this phenomenon against the backdrop of a symbolic horizon that renders the representation of 'the people' radically indeterminate at an ontological level, Rancière's analysis always returns to those unanticipated moments of subjectivation, the emergence of a subject whose emancipatory activity, however regional or occasional, opens up the representation of 'the people' and perpetually modifies its meaning. If this process appears more fragmented or discontinuous in Rancière, it is because, unlike Lefort, he will associate no general symbolic order with democracy itself (as an *asymbolic* political form). In Rancière's view, the political subject always manifests against the symbolic order systematically organised and managed by the police.

On Political Names

So while democracy has always meant the *power of the people*, perhaps the first lesson of modern democracy is that the identity of 'the people' is a question destined to remain unresolved in any absolute sense. Perhaps we should understand this irresolution as essential to the meaning of democracy itself. This will only further explain why Rancière will expound the political subject in formal terms. While 'the people' indeed represents the universal subject of democracy, it is a people who will invariably adopt many different names. Ancient democracy may have transformed the class known only as 'the demos' into the name of a political subject, a polemical term of controversy and dispute, but, according to Rancière, the demos simply represents the originary and most generic name for such a subject. Scattered across his writings, we encounter numerous examples of other such names drawn from history which have served a similar political function, even if those names are not typically associated with democracy in either its ancient or modern incarnation. Nevertheless, it is through an analysis of these names that the mechanism of subjectivation as a demonstration or verification of equality will be developed in greater detail.

'Pleb': Rancière will frequently recount an episode in Roman history reported by Livy often known as the secession of the plebeians. In 494 BCE, the plebs abandoned their place in the city and gathered *en masse* on the Aventine Hill demanding a treaty that would guarantee their formal recognition in the republic. The patricians promptly replied that all negotiations were out of the question given that such an accord required something impossible for a class of men whose cries and screams were indicative only of the sufferings of exhausted or mistreated animals. The patricians simply perceived no shared language in which the plebs could be engaged on common grounds. Accordingly, rather than respond with violence, the plebs discovered their power to confront and dispute this claim with speech alone. By resorting to dialogue, by demonstrating a certain equality, the plebs were able to distort the manner in which they, as a class, were perceived and understood. Consequently, compelled to recognise the plebs as autonomous speaking beings rather than simply the 'working parts' of the organic body of Rome, the patricians ultimately conceded and accepted their demands for the establishment of the plebeian tribunes. But more than the extension of citizenship, which by no means eradicated all existing inequalities, for Rancière, the real achievement of the plebeian secession was simply the recognition of the plebs themselves. Indeed, what Livy could be said to have documented is the very moment 'pleb' emerged the name of a political subject.[84]

'Woman': Rancière will also consider the example of the French playwright and outspoken advocate of the rights of women Olympe de Gouges. Although de Gouges remained a staunch proponent of the revolution, her writings and relentless criticisms of the methods of the Jacobins would ultimately lead to her arrest and execution at the height of the reign of terror. Following her sentencing at her trial, de Gouges famously protested that, if women are entitled to go to the guillotine, they should be equally entitled to go to the assembly. Her point is unequivocal: if women, excluded from the business of government, properly belong to the private, domestic sphere of life, unqualified or unfit for participating in public affairs, how is it that they may simultaneously represent a political threat to the revolution? Rancière will elaborate this blatant contradiction that de Gouges so elegantly evokes in terms of a disagreement, one in which the category of woman, affixed to an assigned role, function and place, is compromised by a profound demonstration of equality, a sharing of a common stage. By enacting her paradoxical status to the court – equal to men on the scaffold, not equal to men in the assembly – de Gouges was able to extract 'woman' from the confines of its allotted position as a gender or identity and recast it the name of a subject with new visibility and new audibility.[85]

'Proletarian': We will discover a similar case with the term 'proletarian'. In Latin, *proletarii* ('prolific people') are those who merely produce (and reproduce) without name and without status. For this reason, it provided a fitting political name for the industrial labourers of the nineteenth century. As Rancière recalls, one of its earliest and most notable uses in this sense was during the trial of the revolutionary socialist Auguste Blanqui, charged with rebellion in 1832. When asked his profession by the magistrate, Blanqui simply replied 'proletarian'. When met with objection, Blanqui responded brazenly that it is the profession of thirty million working Frenchmen deprived of political rights. So once again, we encounter something of a contradiction: for proletarian is indeed no occupation or trade in the strict sense of the term and Blanqui himself, educated both in medicine and law, was certainly no typical worker. And yet, what Blanqui's statement forced the court to acknowledge is the proletariat as a *class*. Since his archival work in the 1970s, Rancière has long rejected the proletariat as a distinct sociological group, culture or *ethos*. Rather, as Blanqui testifies, it is the name of those who do not count, those without rights or representation. It is not simply a generic term for manual labourers or workers collectively, but the name of a political subject, one that disturbs the meaning of 'worker' and 'labourer', drawing them out of their obviousness, their natural place in society. Proletariat is therefore the *politicisation* of a class, the name that distinguishes working people as a controversial problem of politics, throwing their part, role and place into question.[86]

'Jew': There are also occasions when the name of a political subject remains entirely distinct from the identity of the group that adopts it and puts it forward as a political name. This was certainly the case during May '68, when tens of thousands of French demonstrators marched through Paris chanting the slogan: 'We are all German Jews' (*nous sommes tous des Juifs allemands*). Originally something of an anti-Semitic slight levelled against Daniel Cohn-Bendit, a prominent student organiser with German-Jewish heritage, 'German Jew' was quickly reappropriated and universalised by the demonstrators themselves, clearly drawing on the still-recent memory of the atrocities experienced by those with this precarious status in Nazi Germany. It was not a matter of identification, declaring all those in the streets victims or potential victims of the State. Nor was it a matter of exploiting the crimes of the Holocaust by equating the conditions in France with those of the concentration camps. Far from a rhetorical strategy, according to Rancière, what it signalled was a process of subjectivation, one that allowed for a defiant political entity to espouse the cause of the Other: the worker, the Algerian, the poor. It was a way to discover a collective 'we' that was not there before. On the streets and behind the barricades, 'German Jew' simply became the name to assemble this 'we' and to advance this cause. Rather than a descriptive term, what it designated was an 'impossible identification', functioning to declassify 'Jew' a religious group or persecuted people and refashion it a name for an emergent political subject composed of a diverse body of students, workers and other political actors. In this sense, much like 'pleb', 'woman' and 'proletarian', it was the name not of a people, class or demographic, but the name of a wrong, a gap, a miscount that identifies a surplus or residue in the count of the police.[87]

Accordingly, political subjectivation should not be mistaken as a formula for identity politics. For the struggle of the political subject is not primarily one of identity, but of *recognition*, the recognition of something other than identity.[88] Identities are never political in and of themselves; that they are bound up with power relations is not enough. Rather, as we have seen, identities only become political when they stray from their allotted status or position, when they contest their meaning, when they become something else altogether.[89] If politics implies a certain affirmation of identity, at the same time, it also implies its categorical disavowal: a refusal or denial of the function, role or place that one has been assigned. Marx certainly understood the proletariat, for example, as the name of the class that seeks the dissolution of itself as a class.[90] The names of politics are the names of a wrong, a misnomer, a miscount. For this reason, there are no proper names for the political subject; they must be invented, borrowed, modified. If anything, it is a process of 'de-classification' or 'dis-identification'. When names become political, that is to say, when particular distributed identities disrupt their givenness and emerge the names of the uncounted, the excluded, the minority, contradicting the count of the police, they shift to a space of subjectivation losing all reference to a sociological specificity and subsequently open to anyone.[91] Therefore, if politics is not centred around an identitarian logic of the self, it is because it always passes through the location of the

Other (*heteron*) or the self as Other: the logic of subjectivation is always *heterological*.[92] The political subject is simply the form that binds the name of the Other to an axiomatic claim of equality (politics' only universal). This is true even for the subject of human rights, in which 'human' does not correspond to the species as a whole or to a form of bare life, but appears a litigious name of the disenfranchised, the subaltern, those without part, which may be invoked by anyone to assert a fundamental equality.[93] Once again, this testifies to the underlying indeterminacy of human rights on which Lefort writes extensively.

The 'History' or 'Tradition' of Emancipation

Beyond his indispensable analysis of the archê, what Rancière contributes to the theory of the antinomies of politics is a descriptive analysis of the principal agent through which democracy's being-against tends to be expressed: the political subject. Democracy cannot be thought in terms of institutions alone. It requires a subject, and it is only through the agency of a subject that democracy's opposition to what it is against will be initiated and set in motion. Even if Rancière's general account of the police is ultimately found to remain ambiguous or incomplete, this is what is essential to the concept of democracy we are pursuing here. Rancière's model of a democracy against the police theorises a democracy that opposes a general order of society in which the coordination and classification of the social is determined in advance. It disputes that women have a proper place, the working class an inherent function. In this view, what democracy refuses is the very aspiration of implementing the proper order of society, a productive, harmonious society that functions without disruption or dispute. This is precisely the notion of society that politics renders inconceivable. For Rancière, politics exists insofar as singular forms of subjectivation expose a gap in the symbolic order of the community. What may be extracted from Rancière's model, therefore, is the general postulate that the agents of democracy's being-against are in no way abstract or indeterminable, but always embodied in the political acts of a subject. Democracy is the story of how those who lack political agency come to have it. Before the name of a regime, before a set of institutions, democracy is the act of a subject. Traditionally, this subject is known as 'the demos'. As Rancière demonstrates, it has adopted many other names.

Given its centrality in *Disagreement*, some scholars find Rancière's discussion of the police lacking. For this reason, I have attempted to develop the concept substantially. Drawing heavily from Foucault, whose research serves to broaden our general formulation of government considerably, the police can be understood as a project of intervention, of social ordering, of implementing the proper order of society. For Rancière, this operation has an important symbolic dimension. What the police governs (in Foucault's sense of the term), what it manages and regulates is the symbolic of the community itself: what can be seen and what cannot, who can be heard and whose voice remains silent. Accordingly, I have sought to frame Rancière's general concept of the police as a regime of representation, a government of the sensible, an administration and management of what is visible, what is thinkable and what is possible. It not only concerns the material partition of the social, the dividing up of parts and shares, but the very modalities of perception in which those divisions and allocations are rendered intelligible. Extrapolated from a ubiquitous governmental technology particular to early modern Europe and advanced as a general formula applicable to various societies past and present, what Rancière understands as the police will inevitably assume countless different forms. Nevertheless, while he certainly acknowledges that some orders of the police remain immeasurably preferable to others, Rancière will offer no systematic historical or typological evaluation of these significant formal variations, but instead concentrates his analysis exclusively on the politics in which a particular order of the police comes to be disrupted, suspended and modified.[94] While the manifestation of such counter-powers do not go unnoticed in his own work, this is something that Foucault himself would never adequately develop. The politics of equality, Rancière submits, simply has no 'theoretical pertinence' in Foucault's project.[95]

This is arguably how Rancière distinguishes his own treatment of the police from that of Foucault. Rather than a descriptive, historical or sociological analysis, Rancière's most important work on democracy adopts a consistent political perspective *against* the police. As a challenge to a particular police order, a particular distribution of the sensible, what Rancière conceives as democracy is that which calls into question the basis of a given social order and tests the limits of what is perceptible in society. For Rancière, the conditions for democracy are nothing beyond the general order of the police itself. The police is at once its point of departure and its object of dispute. As we have seen, democracy undermines the police by introducing new subjects, new names and new voices that were not there before. It inaugurates a disagreement over what it means to speak (*logos*), what it means to be seen and what it means to have a part. By dislodging subjects from their 'proper place', by opposing the dominant representations of society, people and their capacities, democracy signifies nothing less than a radical transformation of the social: the reinvention of a relation, the rearrangement of a territory, the reconfiguration of a sensible field. Democracy not only seeks to modify our social institutions, but the very manner in which we perceive one another, our basic interactions and the spaces we inhabit in common. It is in this respect that Rancière's democracy against the police can be appreciated as a politics of aesthetics, a democratisation of perception and the organisation of perception itself.

And while some readers of *Disagreement* may find Rancière's account of democracy rather limited in scope, ultimately content with a subversive politics that appears only to momentarily disturb the smooth working order of a given police distribution, what this familiar criticism often fails to consider is the larger perspective that informs the general framework of Rancière's political project. From peasants to artisans to industrial labourers to the poor, the predominant subjects and themes that populate Rancière's political works since the 1970s will testify to a broader critique of social domination that from beginning to end is dedicated to a detailed analysis of how the limits of what is political are perpetually challenged by those who are most excluded. And as a dedicated archivist as well as a political theorist, one thing that Rancière's research will demonstrate over and over again is that the meaning of emancipation is anything but a series of fleeting rebellious acts leading nowhere. In response to those critics of *Disagreement*, Rancière thus refutes:

> I don't have a vision of history as punctuated equilibrium, where things erupt at intervals and then lapse back into platitude. [. . .] I didn't mean to suggest that equality exists only on the barricades, and that once the barricades come down it's over, and we go back to listlessness. I am not a thinker of the event, of the upsurge, but rather of emancipation as something with its own tradition, with a history that isn't just made up of great striking deeds, but also of the ongoing effort to create forms of the common different from the ones on offer from the State [. . .].[96]

However intermittent or episodic, what is clear is that Rancière envisions emancipation as a protracted, enduring process, one worthy of the terms 'history' and 'tradition'. Consequently, in this broader context, his understanding of emancipation cannot be reduced to a science of 'the event', to isolated moments or individual acts, however monumental. Just as we will discover with Abensour, emancipation is bound to a continuous struggle against modes of domination and strategies of inequality, some specific to modernity, others virtually unchanged since time immemorial. It is precisely in this context of a broader history or tradition of emancipation that Rancière's model of a democracy against the police must be situated. It is precisely in this context that we may consider Rancière's concept of democracy, much like Lefort's, according to a broader theory of democratisation.

Notes

1. See, for example, the essays contained in the English compilations Cornelius Castoriadis, *Philosophy, Politics, Autonomy* (New York: Oxford University Press, 1991) and Cornelius Castoriadis, *The Castoriadis Reader* (Oxford: Blackwell Publishers, 1997).
2. See Ellen Meiksins Wood, *Democracy against Capitalism: Renewing Historical Materialism* (Cambridge: Cambridge University Press, 1995).
3. See Sheldon S. Wolin, 'Norm and Form: The Constitutionalizing of Democracy', in *Athenian Political Thought and the Reconstruction of American Democracy*, ed. J. Peter Euben, John R. Wallach and Josiah Ober (Ithaca: Cornell University Press, 1994) and Sheldon S. Wolin, 'Fugitive Democracy', in *Democracy and Difference: Contesting the Boundaries of the Political*, ed. Seyla Benhabib (Princeton: Princeton University Press, 1996).
4. Jacques Rancière, *Disagreement: Politics and Philosophy* (Minneapolis: University of Minnesota Press, 1999), 32.
5. Ibid., 32–3.
6. See Samuel A. Chambers, 'Jacques Rancière and the Problem of Pure Politics', *European Journal of Political Theory* vol. 10, no. 3 (July 2011).
7. Rancière, *Disagreement*, 32.
8. It is for this reason that Badiou identifies Rancière's 'police' as a comparable political expression of his own more ontological 'state of the situation', a general, overarching state of being that governs over the particularities of a given situation. See Alain Badiou, 'Rancière and Apolitics', *Metapolitics* (London: Verso, 2005), 116.
9. Rancière, *Disagreement*, 33. Also see Jodi Dean, 'Politics without Politics', *Parallax* vol. 15, no. 3 (2009): 27–8.
10. See Paulina Tambakaki, 'When Does Politics Happen?', *Parallax* vol. 15, no. 3 (2009): 104.

11. Rancière, *Disagreement*, 28.
12. Ibid.
13. See, for example, Samuel A. Chambers, 'The Politics of the Police: From Neoliberalism to Anarchism, and Back to Democracy', in *Reading Rancière*, ed. Paul Bowman and Richard Stamp (London: Continuum International Publishing Group, 2011), 19 and Oliver Davis, *Jacques Rancière* (Cambridge: Polity, 2010), 96.
14. Todd May will defend Rancière against this criticism, arguing that, rather than organise his discussion of the police in a typical descriptive or analytical fashion, Rancière's writings adopt the perspective of those who are most impaired by its arrangements, systems and strategies. If May is correct, it would therefore imply that what Rancière elaborates in *Disagreement* is not so much a critique of the police itself, but its *effects* on those it dominates, excludes or neglects. See Todd May, *The Political Thought of Jacques Rancière: Creating Equality* (University Park: Pennsylvania State University Press, 2008), 118.
15. After Foucault's death, the topic of *governmentality* would largely be taken up and developed by Anglo-American scholarship in the social sciences.
16. Thomas Lemke, 'Foucault, Governmentality, and Critique', *Rethinking Marxism* vol. 14, no. 3 (2002): 50.
17. Jonathan Xavier Inda, 'Analytics of the Modern: An Introduction', in *Anthropologies of Modernity: Foucault, Governmentality, and Life Politics*, ed. Jonathan Xavier Inda (Malden: Blackwell Publishing, 2005), 1–2.
18. Michel Foucault, *Security, Territory, Population: Lectures at the Collège de France, 1977–1978* (New York: Picador/Palgrave Macmillan, 2007), 248. Also see Colin Gordon, 'Governmental Rationality: An Introduction', in *The Foucault Effect: Studies in Governmentality*, ed. Graham Burchell, Colin Gordon and Peter Miller (Chicago: University of Chicago Press, 1991), 4.
19. Rancière, *Disagreement*, 29.
20. Gordon, 'Governmental Rationality', 7.
21. Foucault, *Security, Territory, Population*, 248.
22. In this regard, Foucault makes no distinction between 'legitimate' and 'illegitimate' government, 'consensual' and 'coercive' government.
23. Inda, 'Analytics of the Modern', 4.
24. Ibid., 1.
25. Lemke, 'Foucault, Governmentality, and Critique', 52.
26. Thomas Hobbes, *On the Citizen* (Cambridge: Cambridge University Press, 1998), 21–2, 24–5. *Disciplina* may also be translated as 'education' or 'discipline'.
27. Delivered 1 February 1978 at the Collège de France as part of a course on 'Security, Territory, Population'. The topic of the police will largely be discussed on 29 March and 5 April in this lecture series.

28. Foucault, *Security, Territory, Population*, 88–9.
29. Ibid., 105.
30. See Bruce Curtis, 'Foucault on Governmentality and Population: The Impossible Discovery', *The Canadian Journal of Sociology* vol. 27, no. 4 (Autumn 2002).
31. Michel Foucault, 'The Political Technology of Individuals', *Power: Essential Works of Foucault, 1954–1984 Volume 3* (New York: The New Press, 2000), 416.
32. Foucault will often use 'biopower' and 'biopolitics' interchangeably. Although sympathetic to the general concept, Rancière takes issue with this conflation of 'power' and 'politics'. See Jacques Rancière, 'Biopolitics or Politics?', *Dissensus: On Politics and Aesthetics* (London: Continuum, 2010). For further analysis of Rancière's argument, see John McSweeney, 'Giving Politics an Edge: Rancière and the Anarchic Principle of Democracy', *Sofia Philosophical Review* vol. 3, no. 1 (2009): 124–9.
33. Foucault, *Security, Territory, Population*, 93.
34. Ibid., 322.
35. Michel Foucault, '"Omnes et Singulatim": Toward a Critique of Political Reason', *Power*, 317.
36. Foucault, *Security, Territory, Population*, 322.
37. Ibid., 322–3.
38. May, *The Political Thought of Jacques Rancière*, 42.
39. See, for example, Rancière, *Disagreement*, 63.
40. For additional insights on Rancière's position, see May, *The Political Thought of Jacques Rancière*, 42–3, and Chambers, 'The Politics of the Police', 28–9.
41. Davis, *Jacques Rancière*, 78.
42. On this point, once again see May, *The Political Thought of Jacques Rancière*, 118.
43. Gilles Labelle, 'Two Refoundation Projects of Democracy in Contemporary French Philosophy: Cornelius Castoriadis and Jacques Rancière', *Philosophy and Social Criticism* vol. 27, no. 4 (2001): 88.
44. See Maarten Simons and Jan Masschelein, 'Governmental, Political and Pedagogic Subjectivation: Foucault with Rancière', *Educational Philosophy and Theory* vol. 42, no. 5/6 (2010): 592.
45. Jacques Rancière, 'Ten Theses on Politics', *Dissensus*, 36.
46. Davis, *Jacques Rancière*, 78–9.
47. Jacques Rancière and Davide Panagia, 'Dissenting Words: A Conversation with Jacques Rancière', *Diacritics* vol. 30, no. 2 (Summer 2000): 124.
48. Chambers, 'Jacques Rancière and the Problem of Pure Politics', 306–7.
49. Rancière, *Disagreement*, 29.
50. Samuel A. Chambers, 'Police and Oligarchy', in *Jacques Rancière: Key Concepts*, ed. Jean-Philippe Deranty (Durham, NC: Acumen Publishing, 2010), 63.

51. Linsey McGoey, 'Police Reinforcement: The Anti-Politics of Organizational Life', *Reading Rancière*, 150.
52. Rancière, 'Ten Theses on Politics', 36.
53. Rancière, 'Biopolitics or Politics?', 95.
54. Rancière employs the term 'aesthetics' in a manner generally consistent with the Kantian notion of '*a priori* forms of sensibility'. See Jacques Rancière, 'From Politics to Aesthetics?' *Paragraph* vol. 28 (March 2005): 13. Also see Jacques Rancière, *The Politics of Aesthetics: The Distribution of the Sensible* (London: Continuum, 2004), 13.
55. See Katharine Wolfe, 'From Aesthetics to Politics: Rancière, Kant and Deleuze', *Contemporary Aesthetics* vol. 4 (2006).
56. See Jacques Rancière, 'Introducing Disagreement', *Angelaki: Journal of the Theoretical Humanities* vol. 9, no. 3 (December 2004): 6.
57. Bram Ieven, 'Heteroreductives – Rancière's Disagreement with Ontology', *Parallax* vol. 15, no. 3 (2009): 50.
58. Aristotle, *The Politics and The Constitution of Athens* (Cambridge: Cambridge University Press, 1996), 211.
59. Jacques Rancière, 'Democracy Means Equality', *Radical Philosophy* vol. 82 (March 1997): 31.
60. Aristotle, *The Politics and The Constitution of Athens*, 13.
61. Rancière, 'Introducing Disagreement', 5.
62. Rancière, *Disagreement*, 22–3.
63. Arthur Rimbaud, 'Démocratie', *Complete Works, Selected Letters: A Bilingual Edition* (Chicago: University of Chicago Press, 2005), 350. *Les Révoltes logiques* was also the name of an ambitious journal of history and politics founded by Rancière and others in 1975 to which he contributed a number of articles on various topics. It published regularly until 1985.
64. See Mark Robson, '"A literary animal": Rancière, Derrida, and the Literature of Democracy', *Parallax* vol. 15, no. 3 (2009).
65. See Jacques Rancière, *Althusser's Lesson* (London: Continuum, 2011). Also see Nick Hewlett, *Badiou, Balibar, Rancière: Rethinking Emancipation* (London: Continuum International Publishing Group, 2007), 84, 86.
66. For example, Jean-Philippe Deranty, 'Jacques Rancière's Contribution to the Ethics of Recognition', *Political Theory* vol. 31, no. 1 (February 2003): 138–9.
67. Jacques Rancière, 'Work, Identity, Subject', in *Jacques Rancière and the Contemporary Scene: The Philosophy of Radical Equality*, ed. Jean-Philippe Deranty and Alison Ross (London: Continuum International Publishers, 2012), 213–14.
68. Todd May, 'Jacques Rancière and the Ethics of Equality', *SubStance* vol. 36, no. 2, iss. 113 (2007): 30–1.
69. Rancière, 'Ten Theses on Politics', 35.
70. Rancière, *Disagreement*, 18.

71. The term *la subjectivation* will also be translated as 'subjectification' and 'subjectivization'. For purposes of consistency, I will be using political 'subjectivation' throughout, modifying translations when necessary. This concept should also not be confused with Foucault's use of the term 'subjectivation', which perhaps describes the subject that comes into being through its *subjection* to institutional or disciplinary practices or power relations.
72. Rancière, *Disagreement*, 99.
73. Ibid., 32.
74. Rancière, 'Ten Theses on Politics', 33.
75. Rancière and Panagia, 'Dissenting Words', 124.
76. Simons and Masschelein, 'Governmental, Political and Pedagogic Subjectivation', 594.
77. See Rancière, *Disagreement*, chapter 2.
78. Ibid., 36.
79. Jacques Rancière, 'The Uses of Democracy', *On the Shores of Politics* (London: Verso, 2007), 48.
80. Rancière, *Disagreement*, 99–100.
81. Rancière, 'Ten Theses on Politics', 37–40.
82. Rancière, *Disagreement*, 58–9.
83. Lefort offers only a few scattered remarks on his interpretation of ancient democracy. See, for example, Claude Lefort, 'The Permanence of the Theologico-Political?', *Democracy and Political Theory* (Minneapolis: University of Minnesota Press, 1988), 225–6. Also see Bernard Flynn, *The Philosophy of Claude Lefort: Interpreting the Political* (Evanston: Northwestern University Press, 2005), 158.
84. Rancière largely reads the Plebeian secession through the work of Pierre-Simon Ballanche. See Rancière, *Disagreement*, 23–6. Also see Martin Breaugh, *The Plebeian Experience: A Discontinuous History of Political Freedom* (New York: Columbia University Press, 2013), 93–4.
85. Jacques Rancière, 'Who is the Subject of the Rights of Man?' *Dissensus*, 68–9. Also see Simons and Masschelein, 'Governmental, Political and Pedagogic Subjectivation', 594–6.
86. Jacques Rancière, 'Politics, Identification, and Subjectivization', *October* vol. 61 (Summer 1992): 60–1, and Rancière, *Disagreement*, 37–8. Also see Labelle, 'Two Refoundation Projects of Democracy in Contemporary French Philosophy', 91–2.
87. Rancière, *Disagreement*, 59. Also see Kristin Ross, *May '68 and Its Afterlives* (Chicago: University of Chicago Press, 2002), 57–8.
88. See Deranty, 'Jacques Rancière's Contribution to the Ethics of Recognition'. On the topic of recognition, also consider the intriguing exchange between Axel Honneth and Jacques Rancière, *Recognition or Disagreement: A Critical Encounter on the Politics of Freedom, Equality, and Identity* (New York: Columbia University Press, 2016).

89. This process is not dissimilar from what Deleuze and Guattari call 'becoming-minoritarian' (*devenir-minoritaire*). See Gilles Deleuze and Félix Guattari, *A Thousand Plateaus: Capitalism and Schizophrenia* (Minneapolis: University of Minnesota Press, 1987).
90. Karl Marx, 'Critique of Hegel's Philosophy of Right: Introduction', *Early Writings* (London: Penguin Books, 1992), 256.
91. See Jacques Rancière, Max Blechman, Anita Chari and Rafeeq Hasan, 'Democracy, Dissensus and the Aesthetics of Class Struggle: An Exchange with Jacques Rancière', *Historical Materialism* vol. 13, no. 4 (2005): 290.
92. Rancière, 'Politics, Identification, and Subjectivization', 59–60.
93. Andrew Schaap, 'Enacting the Right to Have Rights: Jacques Rancière's Critique of Hannah Arendt', *European Journal of Political Theory* vol. 10, no. 1 (January 2011): 23.
94. As Samuel A. Chambers would likely remind us, democracy can never claim to eliminate the police *in general*. This would not be consistent with Rancière's social theory. If democracy can be said to be *against* the police, it is because it emerges against a particular incarnation of the police, a particular partition of the social and representation of society. See Chambers, 'Police and Oligarchy', 62.
95. Simons and Masschelein, 'Governmental, Political and Pedagogic Subjectivation', 603.
96. Jacques Rancière and Eric Hazan, 'Democracies against Democracy', in Giorgio Agamben et al., *Democracy in What State?* (New York: Columbia University Press, 2011), 79–80.

Chapter 5

The Politics of Emancipation: Democracy against the State

> *In modern times the French have understood this to mean that the political State disappears in a true democracy.*
> Karl Marx, *Critique of Hegel's 'Philosophy of Right'*

Social Domination and Political Emancipation: An Introduction to Abensour's General Approach to Democracy

At the same time that Rancière's work establishes democracy against the police, Abensour would develop a theory of democracy that considers its antagonistic relation to the State. Working primarily through Marx's early critique of Hegel and therefore revisiting the somewhat heterodoxical question of Marx's own contribution to democratic theory, Abensour's appropriately titled volume *Democracy against the State* represents one of the more sustained theoretical assessments of democracy's conflict with the State. Against the backdrop of Lefort's Machiavellian conception of *the political*, Abensour offers a detailed, rather idiosyncratic extrapolation of what Marx propounds, in direct contradistinction to Hegel, as 'true democracy' in which the State, as an abstract or alien form, is said to disappear. In this respect, if Abensour opposes democracy and the State, it is because, reading Marx, he identifies the State as the political alienation of the collective self-determination of the demos. Democracy, Abensour contends, represents the solution to this political alienation. In a truly innovative reading, Abensour presents democracy as the permanent 'reduction' of the State. It is what blocks or obstructs the State as an autonomous, totalising entity. At the same time, it is what generates social forms and modes of interaction other than those mediated by the State, inventing new and inclusive ways of engaging collectively in a distinctively public space. Hence, through a rather original interpretation of the young Marx, whose argument relies so heavily on Rousseau, Abensour is not only able to successfully disentangle a concept of democracy from that of the State but, at the same time, to bind it categorically to an ongoing project of emancipation. Accordingly, after placing Abensour's larger project in context and situating his political theory with respect to some of his most important sources from the Frankfurt School to Machiavelli to utopian thought, it is this conflict between democracy and the State that will be centred in our investigation of his work.

As we saw at the conclusion of the previous chapter, Rancière sees himself not as a thinker of the event or upsurge, but of a long 'history' or 'tradition' of emancipation. And yet, of the two, perhaps it is Abensour who will establish the connection between democracy, emancipation and being-against in a more definitive manner. We have already considered Abensour's compelling interpretation of savage democracy, but until now we have largely encountered Abensour as just that: an interpreter, an advocate, a reader of Lefort and Arendt. We now have the opportunity to consider Abensour's thought on democracy in its own right. While Abensour's general approach to the question of democracy may be understood to be initiated through an expressly Lefortian paradigm, at the same time, his theoretical construction of democracy reveals a decisive shift in emphasis from a form of political regime to a mode of political action.[1] Abensour takes Lefort's familiar characterisation of democracy as an open, interminable political experience, for example, as a testament to its perpetual reinvention of the possibility of political action against various forms of domination in society. This is emblematic, no doubt, of Abensour's longstanding appeal to that *savage* dimension of Lefort's thought, something which unquestionably pushes his thinking of democracy in radical new directions. In this respect, we can witness Abensour put Lefort's savage democracy to use in his own work in a highly creative and productive way. Reading Abensour, democracy appears not as a legitimate means to govern another, but as an agency of transformation and democratisation in society. It is for this reason that his theses are often taken to parallel those of Rancière. For Abensour, democracy is, in essence, something other than regime: it is a particular activity of the demos that opens up a distinct political field in which conflict is able to unfold, new social bonds are able to be forged and the desire for freedom is able to be expressed. As a form of collective action that seeks to institute inclusive, participatory and non-hierarchical models of social interaction, Abensour's understanding of democracy binds a notion of social emancipation to that enduring political struggle to establish a state of non-domination. To this vision of democracy, Abensour will at times give the name 'insurgent' democracy, a deliberately polemical term that not only intends to distinguish his own concept of democracy from other interpretations, including that of Lefort, but at the same time to isolate and identify the 'natural' target of one of its most vital conflicts: the State itself.[2] This is something that Abensour ultimately finds to be lacking in Lefort's project. Rather, approximating the work of Pierre Clastres, if Abensour frames politics as inherently contrary to the State, it is because he understands the State-form, regardless of its particular historical incarnation, as that which universally isolates the organs of power from the whole community. Democracy is theorised as the political activity that opposes this autonomy of the State, that obstructs this abstraction and monopolisation of what is 'political'. As such, democracy is conceived as nothing less than the struggle for the self-determination of the demos. It transforms, as it were, the 'power over men' into a 'power with and among men' or à la Spinoza, into the 'power to act'.[3] If Abensour appeals to the term 'insurgent' to incite such a democracy, in part it is because he regards the very idea of democracy to challenge what is most elemental to the State itself.

Abensour's model of democracy is therefore explicitly developed as a democracy *against*, a democracy whose origins and, indeed, very form are determined according to its immanent resistance to the principles of the State. It is for this reason that Abensour's work remains so essential to the antinomies of politics. For Abensour, a democracy against the State testifies to the 'always possible emergence of human struggle'. And yet, this is precisely the notion of democracy that would lead Marcel Gauchet, in a collection of interviews, to dismiss and discredit Abensour's writings as mere 'revoltism', an 'aesthetics of intransigence' leading only to the 'corruption of democracy'.[4] In response to these charges by his former colleague and onetime collaborator, Abensour would, in turn, pen an open letter that would only reaffirm his commitment to a notion of modern democracy that is not only born of a revolutionary moment, but whose very constitution remains indicative of an ongoing revolutionary impulse against the logic of the State:

> democracy is not a crystallised form [. . .] that establishes an organisation of powers and rules of the game; it is rather a continuous movement, a political action that in its very manifestation works to undo the state-form [. . .]. Democracy is the determinate institution of a conflictual space, a space against, an agonistic stage upon which two antagonistic logics confront one another: the autonomisation of the state as form, and the life of the people as action, political action.[5]

It is precisely this 'institution of a conflictual space, a space against' that interests us here. It is precisely this democracy *against* the State that I will forefront in my analysis of his work. Democracy is that which opens a space in which conflict with the State may occur. Ultimately interpreted as the struggle for self-institution and self-determination in a defiantly public sphere, according to Abensour, what is at stake for such a democracy is nothing less than the autonomy of the political itself. This is something that perhaps he first observes in Marx's critique of Hegel. It is for this reason that he identifies Marx's early work, borrowing a phrase from J. G. A. Pocock, as a 'Machiavellian moment'.[6] Hence, carefully weaving together aspects of his critical political philosophy, utopian thought and larger position against the State, this chapter will consider Abensour's pivotal reading of what Marx infers as 'true democracy'. Contrary to the longstanding philosophical tradition he denounces as 'State thought', I will demonstrate that Abensour's work helps us forge the vital connection between emancipation and being-against. This is very much at the centre of his democratic theory. Accordingly, it is Abensour's democracy against the State that will serve as our second theoretical model to investigate the antinomies of politics.

From the Frankfurt School to Lefort and Machiavelli: Abensour's Critical Political Philosophy

Compared to that of Rancière and Lefort, Abensour's work is undoubtedly the lesser known of the three in the English-speaking world. It is therefore still important to provide his project some additional context. We begin our analysis with a survey of Abensour's general approach to philosophy as a systematic tool for political critique, a theme that was already introduced in a previous chapter.[7] Insofar as Abensour situates a democracy against the State according to the broader struggle against social domination, his writings will tend to frame the concept of democracy in terms of a continuous and ever-evolving emancipatory politics. Indeed, perhaps Abensour understands emancipation as just that: not so much as the *state* of being emancipated from domination but, like Rancière, as the ongoing *process* or struggle against it. Consequently, emancipation can never be dissociated in Abensour's work from an enduring project of democratisation, a project chiefly propelled by the persistent political activity of the demos itself. And yet, alongside and inextricably interwoven with this political activity, perhaps just as essential to Abensour's understanding of emancipation is the permanent critique of domination itself, the meticulous theoretical evaluation of both those archaic modes of domination so universal throughout history as well as new strategies of domination that continually seem to appear with new institutions and new technologies.[8] It is here where Abensour locates the political and emancipatory potential of philosophy. Despite having long acknowledged the deficits of what Arendt encapsulates as the 'tradition of political philosophy' and, hence, of the so-called 'return to political philosophy' in the 1970s and 1980s (which he takes to merely announce the fashionable resurgence of its established practices and attitudes in his own day), Abensour will nevertheless affirm the importance of a rigorous philosophical critique of what he understands to be essential to the matters of politics itself, namely, the relation between domination and emancipation in society. For Abensour, the value of philosophy is its capacity to grapple with a series of fundamental political questions: *What is the nature of freedom? How do we distinguish between power, domination and authority? How do we disentangle politics and the State? What does it mean to think politics in the context of a society against the State?*[9] Drawing heavily from Lefort's lengthy interpretive study of Machiavelli, Abensour maintains that, if political philosophy cannot be reduced to a rational defence of a given social order, it is because it remains indispensable to the critical exercise of thinking emancipation in the '*here and now*' (*hic et nunc*).[10] It is here where Abensour will most dramatically distinguish his own approach from that of Rancière. While he applauds Rancière's contribution to the critique of domination in the form of the police, Abensour questions why Rancière must so fervently distance such a critique from the work of political philosophy itself, effectively discounting and discrediting its critical and emancipatory potential.[11] Positioning himself closer to Arendt and Lefort, Abensour rather opts to pit political philosophy against its very tradition so to exploit its powers of critique and interminable interrogation for political ends. Therefore, contrary to both the practice of political philosophy in the tradition of Plato and Aristotle and the academic revival of a discipline that seemingly privileges the canonical history of political thought over the issues of the present day, Abensour calls for a renewed philosophical critique of social domination organised specifically to contribute to the emancipatory struggles of today.[12] Akin to Marx's celebrated eleventh thesis on Feuerbach, Abensour is compelled by a notion of philosophy that not only interprets the world, but actively seeks to change it. This is not a philosophy that simply reflects upon the abstract topics of politics; this is a philosophy that must itself become *political*. While philosophy can never replace the political activity of the demos, it provides a critical framework through which a spectrum of contemporary social and political problems may be navigated and evaluated in the context of a larger emancipatory project towards a state of non-domination. To this end, as we have seen, Abensour will develop his critical political philosophy.

It is possible to isolate and identify three facets of Abensour's model of political thought: a critical political philosophy is one that: 1) maintains a steadfast orientation towards social emancipation; 2) offers a detailed critical analysis of the relations, institutions and technologies of domination, and 3) never obscures the vital distinction between domination and politics itself.[13] As demonstrated in a series of closely related essays, Abensour formulates the basis of his critical political philosophy through a unique intersection of the most constructive elements of critical theory and political philosophy while avoiding what he understands as the many pitfalls that afflict both theoretical types. On the one hand, while Abensour discerns critical theory (the Frankfurt School) to offer a rich, comprehensive socio-critical evaluation of modern systems of authority that can in no way be reduced to an orthodox Marxist commentary of economic exploitation, at the same time, critical theory remains curiously silent on the nature of political liberty itself, as if it can only envisage emancipation in the paradoxical terms of a freedom *from* politics itself. On the other hand, while Abensour regards more traditional examples of political philosophy to be far more inclined to explore experimental scenarios of alternative political structures and arrangements (even if only an ideal or imagined construction), at the same time, political philosophy often remains incapable of conceiving of political liberty beyond a wholly integrated model of sovereignty that not only fails to acknowledge the reality of social domination, but any semblance of the inevitable conflict and division that may threaten to disturb its serene tranquillity. Accordingly, the passage through the crossroads between critical theory and political philosophy must carefully navigate two paradigms simultaneously: a 'catastrophic' vision of domination indicative of a total domination lacking any conceivable opening for political transformation or means of escape and an 'irenic' vision of politics indicative of an idyllic politics that neglects or conceals not only the theme of domination but also the very conflict that remains so essential to the meaning of politics itself.[14] Therefore, through a series of delicate manoeuvres, Abensour will cultivate his critical political philosophy as a mode of thought that locates the very condition of emancipation in the political conflict against domination in society. Although he praises the political works of Arendt and Lefort as prime examples of philosophies that successfully avoid the hazards of both paradigmatic tendencies, Abensour discovers something of a rare forerunner of the critical political thinker with none other than Machiavelli himself. It is with Machiavelli, Abensour contends, that we encounter the first traces of a political theory that identifies the 'cradle of political liberty' in the very struggle of the people against the supremacy of the ruling classes.[15] Contrary to the still-prevailing views of Machiavelli as the prototypical 'realist' (Benedetto Croce) or quite simply 'teacher of evil' (Leo Strauss), Abensour regards Machiavelli as something of a political educator with the unique ability to help us rethink the complex dynamics of politics itself.[16] A great admirer of the tremendous achievement of Lefort's *Le Travail de l'œuvre*, beyond the opposing architectonics of the republic and the principality, Abensour reads Machiavelli to uncover something of the basic ontological status of politics itself: rather than identify the roots of political liberty in the unity and harmony of the well-ordered city, drawing from the experience of Rome, Machiavelli demonstrates that it is in fact social division, conflict, discord – particularly the clash of opposing classes or social groups – that constitutes the essence of an intrinsically contingent and unstable political field.[17] This is the basis of Abensour's allusion to the 'originary division of the social' that we encountered in our discussion of Lefort. Much like Aristotle, Machiavelli tends to approach the general question of the social through the seemingly universal division between rich and poor, the few and the many, the rulers and the ruled. And yet, beyond the clash of these two competing socio-economic groups, both *The Discourses* and *The Prince* will relate this division to a more underlying conflict between two distinct psychological types (*umori*): the grandees' desire to command and dominate and the people's desire not to be dominated.[18] Note that the implicit orientations of these opposing humours or propensities are in no way equivalent. While one class is defined by its inclined disposition towards social dominance and ascendency, the other simply expresses a negation. Perhaps a uniquely Machiavellian conception of democracy could be said to begin here: with the problem of how to formally institute the desire *not to be dominated*.[19] In any case, it is precisely this irreducible conflict of the people against the continual threat of oppression – a conflict which extends well beyond Marx's materialist conception of a historically resolvable class struggle – that Machiavelli identifies as the source and origin of the liberty and 'good laws' of the Roman Republic. It is for this reason that the Florentine secretary ultimately identifies the people, rather than the wealthy few, as the rightful guardians of liberty.[20] Consequently, it is against the backdrop of Machiavelli, or at least a Lefortian interpretation of Machiavelli, that Abensour will frame his critical political philosophy specifically designed to theorise the emancipatory dimension of social conflict integral to democratic politics. As we encountered in his essay on savage democracy, for Abensour, democracy implies just that: not only the recognition, but also the *elaboration* of the originary division of the social, the affirmation, expression and, indeed, even amplification of social conflict as the 'originary source of an ever renewed invention of liberty'.[21]

Utopia and Democracy

From Machiavelli to Arendt and Lefort to the Frankfurt School to other examples of political philosophy, Abensour assembles his critical political philosophy from a broad range of sources. And yet, beyond this rich amalgamation of theoretical tools at his disposal, perhaps Abensour would qualify that essential to his political thought is a mode of critique that remains distinctively 'utopian' in character. Rather than a commitment to an ideal society in some distant future, even a cursory survey of Abensour's utopian thought will reveal an important strategy to *think against* what is in the *here and now*. This is paramount to his general approach to politics. Without question,

Abensour is first and foremost a thinker of utopia: its function, forms and possibilities for critique. Although the concept of utopia would acquire an increasingly contentious status in twentieth-century social and political theory, it nevertheless remains a central question across much of Abensour's work from the very beginning.[22] If we cut across his many writings on this theme, Abensour argues that utopian literatures (political, literary or otherwise) cannot ultimately be appropriated as blueprints or programmes for the ideal society; they present no specific goals to be achieved, places to be discovered or fantasies to be realised. Rather than the promise of paradise, rather than a vision of a sheltered, static, harmonious existence, what interests Abensour about utopia, more structurally, is precisely what it can do to political thought: how it can shift our perspective, redirect our orientation, inform our desire. In particular, much of Abensour's earliest work on utopia is organised around the thesis that utopia has the capacity to both inspire and educate an emancipatory desire.[23] By opening up the possibility of a world other than *what is*, by constructing a new relation between the *possible* and the *actual*, utopia can disrupt the closure of the present and provoke a restless, revolutionary appetite for change. The critical function of utopia, therefore, is not to 'produce positive images, but to open breaches'.[24] Utopias remind us that the order of society is not fixed, settled, absolute. Accordingly, they can function to emancipate the imagination, motivate political action and foster a 'stubborn impulse toward liberty and justice'.[25] Far from a sublimated expression of wish-fulfilment, the concept of utopia can be taken as a symbol of hope in politics, as the desire for a better world than the one we have today. In this respect, as the perspective that adopts a critical relation to the present in the hopes of a better future to come, what Abensour calls 'the utopian' will share a striking resemblance to what Nietzsche calls 'the untimely'.

Of particular interest to Abensour is a distinct tendency in modern utopian thought that he often designates the 'new utopian spirit' (associated primarily with William Morris, Pierre Leroux, Ernst Bloch, Walter Benjamin, Martin Buber and Emmanuel Levinas).[26] Following the catastrophic failure of the 1848 revolutions, Abensour detects a decisive shift in utopian literature that would extend well into the twentieth-century experience of totalitarianism itself. Sceptical, introspective, self-critical, this new mode of utopian thought would not only recognise but incorporate the very criticisms and suspicions that came to surround utopian ideas into its very concept, shattering its mythology and refining its uses.[27] Beyond the limits of both utopian socialism and neo-utopianism, according to Abensour, the new utopian spirit signifies a 'critical reactivation' of utopian thinking that grounds its very approach to utopia in a meticulous critique of utopia itself, the form of this critique, in many respects, inspired by the works of Marx.[28] Perhaps most important for a critical political philosophy, characteristic of this new utopian spirit is the persistent critique of how the desire for emancipation so often turns into its opposite, how the utopian dream, as it were, so often collapses into an authoritarian nightmare. For Abensour, this phenomenon remains one of the more troubling political problems of modern times. It is for this reason that he returns again and again to the question of utopia. As Abensour demonstrates, it is the first task of this new utopian spirit to break the circle of this 'dialectic of emancipation', to place utopia against itself, to at once extract its political and emancipatory potential, to draw out its revolutionary desire, while at the same time instructing this desire in the risks of the utopian promise, thereby fashioning utopia into a critical tool and preventing its concept from settling into a model for society to simply implement, realise or reproduce. What remains is the idea of utopia in pure form (as a 'no-place' [*ou-topos*]; perhaps this is already inscribed in Thomas More's original concept from the start).[29] By voiding itself of content – specific goals, designs, destinations – utopia thus returns a strategy of critique, offering a critical evaluation of both the conditions of our own society as well as the desire for those conditions to be otherwise. This is precisely what interests Abensour about utopias. Utopias offer no models, no solutions, but represent a *critical displacement of what is* in thought, inviting us to imagine the possibility of a radical alterity of the *here and now*.[30] As Deleuze submits in his own vernacular, the very concept of utopia binds the critique of the present milieu to an absolute deterritorialisation of thought. Consequently, for Deleuze: 'it is with utopia that philosophy becomes political and takes the criticism of its own time to its highest point.'[31]

In this regard, as the criticism of its own time, as the impetus towards the possible, the different, the otherwise, we may very well discern a certain *against* in the very structure of utopia itself. If we follow Abensour's analysis, perhaps the utopian experience could ultimately be described as one of estrangement; it generates a certain distance, assumes a critical perspective, calls into question the status of the existing state of affairs.[32] Accordingly, utopia could be seen to initiate a mode of political thinking oriented against what is often presumed to be simply *given* in society. Essential to the utopian imagination is the capacity to think otherwise, to resist the present, to adopt a critical relation to *what is*. *Utopia is the political expression of thinking against*. Although seldom a topic of utopian studies and rarely explored, this remains an indispensable dimension of its concept. As soon as utopia is dissociated from a representation of a distant mythical paradise completely divorced from our present experience and made to collide with the reality of our social conditions as an instrument of critique, utopia takes the distinctive form of an against. Perhaps it is here where Abensour discovers its true political potential. Perhaps it is here where we will discover its connection with democracy. One of the more prominent questions across Abensour's work is the precise relationship between utopia and democracy, a problem that is incessantly being worked out over the course of his authorship.[33] While Abensour clearly identifies both utopia and democracy as examples of emancipatory projects, one at the level of thought, the other at the level of a social collective, perhaps their most striking point of intersection must ultimately be located here: with the against itself. Just as utopia represents a distinct mode of thought oriented *against* the conditions of the present and desires their transgression, democracy represents a distinct political activity oriented *against* the relations of domination and strives for their transformation. Hence, perhaps democracy could be said to be utopian insofar as it demonstrates the capacity to think against the conditions of the present and utopia could be said to be democratic insofar as it demonstrates a desire for a more participatory, more egalitarian society. Although Abensour does not seek to synthesise or assimilate these terms, but to hold their intersection perpetually in tension, one informing the other,[34] this interpretation at least provides a possible response to that enduring question he incessantly revisits throughout his authorship: *How to at once democratise utopia and utopianise democracy?*[35]

Therefore, just as we were able to locate a *savage* dimension of Abensour's concept of democracy, opening up that concept and pushing its interpretation towards its most radical point, we will likewise detect an important *utopian* dimension of that concept as well. Although utopia can provide no coherent picture of the form of society that democracy inevitably seeks to create, interestingly, it does appear to embody the anatomy of the against that we found to be so imperative to its politics. *Emancipatory, savage, utopian*, this is the constellation that forms the basis of the concept of democracy that Abensour's critical political philosophy will advance. This is the democracy that he ultimately posits against the State.

Against the State: Clastres contra Hobbes

Accordingly, in addition to savage democracy and utopian thought, our survey of the background of Abensour's mature work on democracy must likewise consider the groundwork for his position against the State itself. A decade before his meditation on Marx's 'true democracy', this is a theme that will first be encountered in a highly original critique of the political philosophy of Thomas Hobbes. In his later volume *Utopia: From Thomas More to Walter Benjamin*, Abensour writes: 'It is only in a refutation of Hobbes, in the enunciation of an Anti-Hobbes that utopia can come into existence.'[36] Insofar as utopia offers no blueprint, no design for us to follow, but instead, drawing from More's original concept, inspires us to continuously ponder new ways of improving the conditions of our social existence beyond the inscribed limits of *what is*, Abensour understands More's fabled island society to contain something revelatory about the nature of social institutions themselves: contrary to Hobbes, rather than a means to hinder and restrict the innately destructive, egotistical, 'wolf-like' nature of man, institutions are themselves suggestive of our rather fraternal social being and testify to the importance of organising human life *in common*. The very concept of utopia insists we reflect upon the kind of world in which we want to live and more to the point, how we wish to relate to one another as human beings. It is in this sense that More can be read to offer something of an uplifting rebuttal to Hobbes's far more infamous account of human nature and society. And yet, beyond his reading of Thomas More, there is another, perhaps more important respect in which Abensour can be understood to organise his political thought against Hobbes, namely, as a resistance to his notorious argument for the necessity and inevitability of the State itself. On this question, Abensour will draw not from utopian thought, but from the political anthropology of Pierre Clastres.

The State, its origin and function, as well its position and status in the history of political thought, is a problem that Abensour will initially explore in an important essay now translated as 'The Counter-Hobbes of Pierre Clastres'.[37] Here, Abensour will appeal to Clastres as a means to resist a familiar custom of political philosophy to represent the nature of society as an experience of instability, volatility and perpetual strife necessitating the supremacy of the State as an autonomous, overarching authority, a custom that Abensour finds particularly emblematic of Hobbes's *Leviathan*. As

Abensour explains, this counter-Hobbesian tendency that extends across Clastres's work (perhaps most explicit in *Archaeology of Violence*) can be taken to refute and even reverse many of the English philosopher's most underlying assumptions about society, the State and societies without States. From Hobbes to Friedrich Engels to many of his own contemporaries in the field of political anthropology, as we have already encountered, Clastres highlights modern political thought's profound inability to approach those societies past and present that lack a State from any perspective other than that of State societies themselves.[38] Perhaps this is most apparent with Hobbes himself. As is well known, Hobbes's contractualism moves to establish the legitimacy of the State by virtue of its juxtaposition with its supposed opposite: the state of nature. Spectacularly characterised as the condition of perpetual war of 'every man against every man', the state of nature (which Hobbes would occasionally associate with the Indigenous peoples of the Americas) is defined precisely by its *absence* of social institutions, law and justice, peace and security, a condition in which human life, plagued by constant danger and fear, is destined to remain 'solitary, poor, nasty, brutish and short'.[39] Therefore, beyond the general distinction between instituted society and this hopelessly mythical state of nature, Hobbes can be read to establish an even more dramatic opposition: that of the permanent state of war and the absolute sovereignty of the State.[40] Unifying the body politic in the singular will of the sovereign, Hobbes expounds the State as the formal transcendence of the primal conditions of war; it is what suppresses and abolishes the natural causes of conflict and warfare so indicative of human nature. This is precisely the narrative of the State that Abensour seeks to overturn with the aid of Clastres. As Abensour demonstrates, Clastres's extensive research on primitive societies in South America may be encapsulated by three theses, all of which Abensour frames as contrary to Hobbes in nature: 1) primitive societies, that is, societies without States, are societies nonetheless; 2) the political institution of such societies is established not through the unifying principles of the State, but through war; 3) war is not the inevitable condition of *every man against every man* symptomatic of the brutish state of nature, but itself an instituted political campaign specific to stateless societies ultimately aimed against the emergence of the State itself.[41] Hence, according to Abensour, Clastres's 'Copernican revolution' of the Hobbesian paradigm may be expressed accordingly: if Hobbes posits the State against war, Clastres posits war against the State.[42] Through his extensive fieldwork, Clastres comes to understand war in this context neither as the condition of savage people in their natural state of existence (Hobbes) nor as the breakdown of exchange relations among tribes (Claude Levi-Strauss), but as the primary strategy of primitive societies to at once generate social bonds, collectively retain the social formation of their homogeneous, indivisible communities (without hierarchy, coercion or formal division between ruler and ruled) and, most important, to combat the perpetual threat of the appearance of a unitary, autonomous authority external to the community itself.[43] In short, primitive societies are societies at war with the State. This is the basis of their politics.

But Abensour goes further. In attempt to expound the logic of democracy's being-against, I have already made an argument for the analogous structure of the against as it appears both in primitive societies and democracy alike.[44] But in his own work, Abensour appeals to Clastres for a different reason. With implications extending well beyond the immediate framework of the Hobbes–Clastres debate, by turning to Clastres to challenge the underlying suppositions of Hobbes, Abensour discovers a way to effectively disturb what he identifies more broadly as the paradigm of 'State thought' (*pensée de l'État*) so pervasive across much of political thought.[45] Abensour is not alone in his assessment. Working through those very counter-Hobbesian themes in Clastres themselves, Gilles Deleuze and Félix Guattari, in *A Thousand Plateaus*, will reflect upon philosophy's strange fixation with the State over the course of its long history. Not only does political philosophy tend to centre its analysis around the relations of the State (king and subject, sovereign and people, governor and governed), it also appears to organise its very models of thought around the terms of the State itself: *its* principles, *its* mechanisms, *its* goals. Thus, in both thought and analysis, political philosophy is often inclined to adopt the perspective of the State. It props itself up with the State, draws from its authority, even fashions itself after the State's own image (Plato's philosopher-rulers). In exchange, philosophy offers a defence of the State, supplying a basis for its rationality, its universality, its raison d'être. The State is presented as the most rational and harmonious organisation of a community, the greatest freedom, a moral force. Therefore, in many respects anticipating Abensour's position, Deleuze and Guattari understand the history of political philosophy predominately as the history of State thought, this bizarre symbiosis between philosophy and the State perhaps reaching its height with Hegel (in which the

State is expressed as a historical manifestation of *absolute spirit*).[46] Hence Abensour's recourse to Clastres. Beyond the anthropological argument, Abensour advances the work of Clastres in attempt to liberate political thought from the centrality of the State, to call into question the legacy of State thought from Plato to Hobbes to Hegel, a philosophy devised in service of the State and committed to a representation of the State as not only inherently legitimate, but the necessary, inevitable and most desirable form of human coexistence. In so doing, Abensour encourages us to rethink the philosophical status of the State itself, to dislodge politics from the State and, following Clastres, to put forward a model of politics in opposition to the State. As Abensour submits, regardless of its historical incarnation, as the formal separation of the organs of power from the whole community, the State remains eternally an instrument of domination, a mode of coercion and exclusion in society. It is here, interestingly, where Abensour will encounter resistance from Lefort.

In his own assessment, Lefort finds Clastres's general concept of the State rather one-dimensional and limited in scope. Although he accepts many of Clastres's basic postulates of primitive societies, Lefort rejects that the State may be theorised as transcendent or 'detached' from an otherwise integrated and undivided social body. What Clastres ultimately fails to provide, he contends, is a sufficient account of both what determines legitimate and illegitimate authority within a society's institutions as well as its symbolic dimension which extends well beyond them. For this reason, Lefort finds no reason to accept Clastres's presentation of the State as it supposedly manifests in tribal communities as its universal form. While Clastres never claims that all State societies suffer from one and the same oppression, the eternal risk of the mutual exclusivity of primitive and State societies, according to Lefort, is that it inadvertently functions to render all forms of the State equivalent. The State, Lefort claims, possesses no such uniformity. The State, as it appears in the totalitarian society and the democratic society, for example, is not the same State. Consequently, contrary to Abensour, Lefort will reject that the State may be epitomised by coercion and repression absolutely. For Lefort, this only obscures its many nuances.[47] As a result, perhaps this explains why Abensour's mature work on democracy will tend to distance itself from Lefort somewhat, concluding that Lefort's concept of democracy ultimately remains too bound up with law and the State, its continuing struggle for new rights and more inclusion merely serving to legitimate and expand the State's very authority.[48] And yet, perhaps Abensour's criticism itself risks obscuring Lefort's own many nuances. In one of his last published essays 'Nation et souveraineté', Lefort may be interpreted as offering a final meditation on how we may ultimately unravel an analysis of politics from that of the State.[49] Indeed, although it is true that much of Lefort's more descriptive political analysis of the democratic society does indeed retain a place for the State, at the same time, does it not also provide us a way to think democracy outside and beyond the State itself?[50] Could even the most uncompromising demands of a *savage* democracy really be reconciled with a State system as Abensour's later writings on insurgent democracy ultimately suggest? Almost appearing to anticipate such objections, Lefort writes: 'It is often said that the power of the State is increasing as a result of these new demands, but the extent to which it is being challenged tends to be forgotten.'[51] As he continues elsewhere:

> Such demands are rooted in the awareness of right. However substantial they may be, and whatever changes they might introduce into [. . .] every sphere of administration, they do not seek to be resolved by the action of state power. They stem from a domain that the state cannot occupy.[52]

Is Abensour guilty here of forgetting those moments in Lefort that serve to challenge the sovereignty of the State, that locate what is most important about democracy in a domain well beyond its grasp? Regardless, what remains clear enough is that it is not Lefort who is the source of Abensour's general concept of the State, but Clastres. If Abensour finds Lefort's treatment of the State dangerously ambiguous, Clastres's political anthropology provides a more unequivocal picture of what is most constitutive of the State-form itself. Both in philosophy and in politics, Clastres helps Abensour to think against the State. This will prove essential to his concept of democracy.

Marx's 'Machiavellian Moment': Hegel, Sovereignty and Political Alienation

Having established Abensour's general position on the State, we may now turn to his reading of Marx. If State thought indeed discovers its fullest expression with Hegel, as Deleuze and Guattari suggest, then perhaps it is fitting that Abensour develops his mature theory of democracy not with Lefort primarily, but with a young Marx defiantly opposed to Hegel's speculative theory of the State. In 1843, after the suppression of the *Rheinische Zeitung*, the liberal journal for whom he had been writing since the completion of his doctoral thesis, Marx took the opportunity to revisit and re-evaluate Hegel's political thought. The result was a lengthy manuscript in which he prepared a paragraph-by-paragraph critique of the final section of the *Philosophy of Right* devoted to the question of the State. Although abandoned unpublished, only appearing in 1927, this critique would showcase both the depths of Marx's humanism as well as his increasing distance from the Hegelian roots which he would so often be associated. At the heart of the manuscript, Marx challenges the cogency of Hegel's abstract State and, reversing his very logic, arrives at the position that with 'true democracy' (*wahre Demokratie*) the State itself disappears. This forms the basis of Abensour's exegetical volume *Democracy against the State*, a detailed study that may function at once as a monograph on the political thought of the young Marx before his so-called 'economic turn' and as a broader philosophical contribution to the theory of democracy itself, one that does not fail to locate the *against* at its very centre. Therefore, just as his earliest work on utopia would situate Marx's larger political project in a productive, ongoing dialogue with the utopian tradition, Abensour's mature work on democracy would return to Marx once again, this time bringing to light this often forgotten or overlooked democratic moment in Marx's thought.

While Abensour does not seek to contradict or overturn established Marxist scholarship, the general framework through which he approaches the young Marx will be found to be entirely unique. Drawing from Pocock's landmark study which itself could be taken to circumvent a certain 'State thought', tracing an alternative, republican paradigm from Florentine humanism to the American Revolution by way of Machiavelli and James Harrington, Abensour identifies a distinct 'Machiavellian moment' with Marx himself, situating his early writings according to a vibrant republican tradition of civic humanism and secular political inquiry.[53] It is this Machiavellian moment that directs Abensour's study from beginning to end. What is the connection between Marx and Machiavelli? Contrary to Althusser, it is not Gramsci who provides the link between the two.[54] Rather, Abensour detects something of Machiavelli's critical political inquiry in Marx's very writings themselves. Although Marx does not explicitly draw from Machiavelli's works (throughout this early period, Marx will reference Spinoza more than Machiavelli), Abensour nevertheless maintains that Marx's political and philosophical positions reveal a general perspective consistent with the spirit of a modern republicanism very much epitomised by Machiavelli himself. What are the markers of such a republicanism worthy of the name 'Machiavelli'? Once again, it is not a question of realism. As Abensour outlines in the opening pages of the text, modern republican thought initiates a civic humanism that recentres the human being as a self-determining historical subject and political actor. It rehabilitates the ancient virtue of *vita activa*, advocating the active participation of citizens in the public affairs of the city. Refusing to deduce politics from theology or morality, liberating the *res publica* from the bonds of the theological-political, it grasps the political realm as *something in itself*, as something worldly, historical, contingent, rendering the organisation of society and the institutions of government both susceptible to crisis and available to modification. Against Augustine, it therefore reorients the problems of politics away from the heavenly city of God, fastening them firmly in the present, grounded in the historical conditions of the social, however rife with conflict and division. Perhaps most importantly, as best demonstrated by Machiavelli himself, modern republican thought revives a philosophical tradition of radical questioning that reconsiders the very enterprise of political thought itself: *What are the conditions for a philosophical thinking of the political? How are we to think political affairs? What is the status of the political itself? What is the place of the political in the constitution of the social realm? What is the specific character of political modernity?*[55] In this respect, the Machiavellian moment could very well be understood to function as something of a test for Marx's thought.[56] Not only does Abensour's approach give prominence to a Marx that can in no way be said to be ideologically bound to a metaphysics of history or underlying economic foundation of society, but it also uncovers a Marx who has the capacity to offer great insight into the object of politics itself: the self-determination of the demos, the institution of political equality and what Marx understands more generally as 'human emancipation'.[57] In his critique of Hegel, this is precisely what Marx associates with true democracy.[58] Hence, by reading the young Marx according to a rich tradition of modern republican thought, Abensour is able to bind a sustained meditation on the nature of the political to a rather unconventional conception of democracy as *human emancipation*, a democracy that

Abensour understands not only as a battle against the State, but a battle for the autonomy of the political itself. For this reason, Abensour's *Democracy against the State* cannot be taken as a mere commentary on Marx, its underlying theses clearly a testament to its author's broader pursuit of a more emancipatory conception of democracy. Accordingly, the validity of Abensour's conclusions about democracy should not be evaluated solely on the merits of his hermeneutical strategies in the text. While his interviews repeatedly pay tribute to Marx's 1843 *Critique* as a watershed moment in his own investigation of democracy,[59] what Abensour discovers in Marx is something he undoubtedly holds to have far greater significance for the understanding of democracy itself. Certainly, a theory of a democracy against the State does not begin and end with Marx. Marx simply provides a single political philosophical passage through which it may be encountered. It is this encounter that Abensour's volume ventures to explore.

By any account, the evolution of Marx's thought in the 1840s is nothing short of astonishing. In order to isolate this Machiavellian moment in Marx – a moment that would prove to be very momentary indeed – Abensour traces the development of his early political thought from the 1842 articles in the *Rheinische Zeitung* to the pivotal 1843 writings (particularly the momentous critique of Hegel that uncovers the autonomy of the political) to the more widely scrutinised *Economic and Philosophic Manuscripts* of the following year (in which the analysis of the political would first be eclipsed by economics, a theme which would largely dominate Marx's thought until the events of the Paris Commune nearly thirty years later). Briefly, if we follow Abensour's reading, still very much inspired by the example of the French Revolution, the *Rheinische Zeitung* articles repeatedly assail the Prussian monarchy as an antiquated relic of the *ancien régime*, ultimately making a case for the so-called 'rational State' (liberated from its absolutist and theological underpinnings) as the basis for modern, secular political life. Here, interestingly, it is the State, purged of its theological dimension, that is identified as the emancipatory location of politics. By Abensour's own account, such a position undoubtedly testifies to what Lefort could very well diagnose as a larger fissure in the premodern theological-political symbolic, facilitating not only a new political language, but a new representation of politics itself. But, by 1843, Abensour detects a decisive shift in the object of this political critique. Whereas the 1842 articles are intent on dismantling the theological apparatus of the Prussian Christian State, the principal task that comes to occupy Marx a year later is more universal: namely, to 'unmask' the alienating consequences of the State itself.[60] It is only through a critical rereading of Hegel that Marx would encounter the problem. Although alienation obviously remains a predominant theme across Ludwig Feuerbach's widely influential *Essence of Christianity*, it is Hegel's utter mystification of the State that would prompt Marx to grant the concept its first thoroughly political treatment. In this regard, while Marx's theory of alienation is customarily associated with the proletarian experience of alienated labour under the conditions of capitalist production as formulated in the *Economic and Philosophic Manuscripts*, Abensour locates a distinctively *political* alienation, identically structured, at the centre of his critique of Hegel drafted a year earlier.[61] It is by way of this problem of political alienation in Hegel's *Philosophy of Right* that Marx would come to a more systematic criticism of the modern State itself. It is here that politics is finally disentangled from the State and appears for the first time, as in Clastres, in opposition to it.

A work of enormous depth and complexity, perhaps Hegel's *Philosophy of Right* must ultimately be located *between* historicism and idealism. For it is organised neither as a description or defence of the present-day Prussian State nor as an elaborate promotion of Hegel's own preferred society. Rather, what it seeks to establish are the logical conditions of rational freedom (what Hegel eventually associates with 'ethical life'). Its basic supposition is that, beyond abstract right and subjective morality (Hegel finds even Kant's moral universalism too subjective), freedom necessitates a broader rational ordering of social institutions that organise and coordinate particular interests according to universal ends. Following lengthy discussions of the family and civil society, this is ultimately discovered in the supremacy of the State. Neither liberal nor absolutist in tenor, Hegel's conception of the modern State, said only to manifest at a given historical juncture (where the conditions of slavery and feudalism have been overcome [*aufheben*]), will immediately resemble something of a nuanced constitutional monarchy. And yet, beyond the more narrow confines of the 'political State proper', Hegel understands the historical actualisation of the State as *Idea* to represent something far more profound: in its most realised form, personified by the singularity of the crown, the State represents nothing less than the organic unity of society, the rational integration of the family and civil society within itself as a higher form and universal end. It is therefore not difficult to decipher that the

State is designed to serve a very particular purpose within Hegel's larger theoretical project. Universal, rational, necessary, what the logic of the State formally resolves is precisely the underlying historical problem the *Philosophy of Right* ultimately seeks to overcome: what Hegel perceives as the emergence of a major schism in modern Prussian society. Hegel's philosophy is one of reconciliation. His political philosophy is no exception.[62] At least in Marx's estimation, what Hegel's concept of the State functions to reconcile is the formal division between what he understands as *political* society on the one hand (government, the administrative bureaucracy) and *civil* society on the other (namely, that sphere of society between family and government, private and universal: the sphere of the market economy, organised into corporations and overseen by the police).[63] For Hegel, the State is the ultimate expression of unity and identity in modern society. Hegel conceives the State as a universal form, self-sufficient, an end in itself, that both logically anticipates and teleologically completes its finite moments as external necessity, higher authority and absolute end, harmonising particular and universal, part and whole, in an immanent expression of its actualised Idea. We have thus arrived at the basis of Marx's criticism.

Although Marx readily acknowledges the materiality of the problem, clearly appreciating the significance of an increasingly divided society, his manuscript is quick and unreserved in its rejection of its formal resolution in the *Philosophy of Right*. According to Marx, Hegel's concept of the State is able to repair such a divide only *in appearance*, at the level of abstraction. Indeed, much of Marx's criticism of Hegel will be devoted to what he perceives as the mystification of the State as Idea. Rather than *right*, he charges, Hegel makes logic, abstract reality, his principal subject and theorises the State according to the logical categories of this abstract reality consequently.[64] The State thus appears not as a political institution of society but, as in Hobbes, as an autonomous entity eternally set out against it. Defined in its most abstract terms, the State's relation to the social becomes one of externality, of formal opposition, the family and civil society rendered but finite moments of the finality of the State as Idea. Realised only in their transcendence, the family and civil society exist not for themselves, but for the universality of the State, their empirical existence governed not by themselves but by an abstract logic that remains entirely *alien* to them.[65] Hegel's speculative philosophy therefore remains for Marx an irreparable categorical inversion: it mistakes the abstract for the concrete, the predicate for the subject. It privileges an abstract reality over the material conditions of political life. It sacrifices the self-institution of the social for the sake of the harmony of a higher form. For it is not the State that conditions the family and civil society, Marx repeatedly interjects, but the family and civil society that condition the State. What Hegel's theory of the State systematically fails to recognise, Marx likely drawing here from Rousseau, is that it is the people – *'the whole demos'* – that represents the material source and active agent of their very constitution. Quite the opposite, in Hegel's view, in the absence of the unifying form of the State, the people are destined to remain but a 'formless mass'.[66]

This attitude would serve to raise an important question for Marx that would inevitably shift his critique to the more general problem of the State itself: *Is sovereignty ultimately enshrined in the monarch or in the people?*[67] In what is undoubtedly for Abensour some of the most revealing passages of the *Critique*, Marx will approach this question through a formal juxtaposition of monarchy and democracy. While a number of Lefort's essays deploy a similar strategy, by retracing Marx's steps, Abensour takes this theoretical exercise to a very different end. Insofar as Hegel establishes sovereignty a property of the State, expressed symbolically by the uniformity of the *monos*, he regards any notion of popular sovereignty to rely upon a confused, 'wild idea of the people'. For this reason, Hegel situates democracy at the limit of what is sovereign, its constitution therefore something of a contradiction of itself. But Marx sees the categories very much reversed: 'Hegel proceeds from the State and conceives of man as the subjectivized State; democracy proceeds from man and conceives of the State as objectified man.'[68] In a radical reversal, if it is not the *monos*, as an abstract part, but the demos, as a whole, that represents the source and origin of the constitution of the social, then it is democracy and not monarchy, that properly expresses the sovereign element both in form and substance: 'In democracy the *formal* principle is identical with the *substantive* principle. For this reason it is the first true unity of the particular and the universal.'[69] Following Marx's logic, Abensour can therefore distinguish monarchy as the constitution in which a singular part, abstracted from the whole, determines the character of the whole from a fixed point, so that the demos is subsumed under but one form of its existence: the constitution itself. Democracy, rather, is the constitution in which the constitution itself remains merely a facet of the self-determination of the demos, appearing only as a moment of the people and thus not as the State as an abstract form. Simply put, democracy is the constitution in which the whole is dominated by no single part. According to Marx, this remains its distinguishing characteristic: 'In democracy no moment acquires a meaning other than what is proper to it. Each is really only a moment of the *demos* as a whole.'[70] Therefore, if Marx understands democracy as the exception to every other constitution, it is because the democratic constitution is that which does not abstract itself from the form of its self-institution, but remains a dimension of the demos as its originary subject. For this reason, just as Spinoza calls democracy the most 'natural' constitution,[71] Marx regards it the most 'generic'. It is precisely this generality that Marx claims will ultimately resolve the question of the constitution itself:

> Democracy is the solution to the *riddle* of every constitution. In it we find the constitution founded on its true ground: *real human beings* [. . .]. The constitution is thus posited as the people's *own* creation. The constitution is in appearance what it is in reality: the free creation of man.[72]

Thus conceived, Abensour can declare democracy the true political expression of the self-determination of the demos, monarchy its formal abstraction. It is in this sense that Marx understands democracy as the *truth* of monarchy and monarchy democracy *falsified*. Whereas democracy explains itself, only through democracy can monarchy be explained. Whereas democracy makes the constitution for man, monarchy makes man for the constitution.[73] Against Hegel's own typological hierarchy, Marx will therefore diagnose monarchy a democracy in degenerated form, a democracy in contradiction with itself. Monarchy is the democratic constitution severed from its instituting subject. It remains nothing less than the formal *alienation* of the self-determination of the demos. This is precisely how Marx comes to understand the modern State itself:

> If in a democracy the political State exists separately from its content and is distinguished from it, it nevertheless exists itself only as a *particular* content, as a particular *form of existence* of the people. By contrast, e.g. in the monarchy, this particular moment, the political constitution, assumes the significance of the *universal*, determining and dominating all particulars. In democracy the State as particular is *only* particular, and as universal it is the real universal; i.e. it is not something determinate set off against other contents. In modern times the French have understood this to mean that the *political State disappears* in a true democracy.[74]

The State is the constitution of the social made abstract. It not only assumes autonomy over the demos as such but also dominates its particular moments as a universal form. This is ultimately what renders the State incompatible with democracy. This is not merely a logical determination. Cutting through the rigidity of his formal analysis, Abensour demonstrates that, beyond the opposition between monarchy and democracy, what Marx's critique boldly uncovers is the underlying antagonism between democracy and the State itself. *Democracy is not a State-form; democracy is against the State.* It is in this respect that Marx, no doubt indebted to Rousseau once again, can proclaim *true* democracy the State's formal disappearance.[75] Democracy means the State ceases to be the dominant moment. When the State remains merely a moment, it is no longer the State. Consequently, emblematic of an emancipatory politics antithetical to the State, the very notion of true democracy obliges Marx to entirely reconsider the place of politics itself. As its association with the State, as an abstract form, begins to break down, Marx must re-establish the political realm precisely according to that from which the State is ultimately abstracted: *the whole demos*. For Abensour, this is Marx's Machiavellian moment.

'True' Democracy and the *Reduction* of the State

Abensour reads Marx's critique of Hegel to restore the State to the demos. But in this respect, perhaps the structure of Marx's argument is not entirely unique. Perhaps Marx merely repeats what is simply axiomatic to Rousseau: that sovereignty remains in its only legitimate form an expression of the people rather than the State. Indeed, Marx does appear to share a certain affinity with that spontaneous 'democratic moment' of contract theory in which the whole collectively institutes itself a political society. And yet, as I have suggested, while there is little doubt of Rousseau's importance for Marx during this period,[76] only further supporting the claim of a republican heritage, Abensour himself will not frame Marx's conclusions according to the question of sovereignty primarily. Rather, from Marx's critique of the State, Abensour will draw three important theses: 1) politics pertains not to the workings of the State, but to the emancipation of the demos; 2) democracy is the form in which this emancipation takes place; 3) in democracy, the State, as the domination of the demos, becomes a privileged site of political conflict. This gives us much to consider. Let us begin with the demos itself. As Abensour recounts, uncovering the alienating properties of the State, Marx is compelled to ground the political according to the demos as its true subject and original source. And yet, we must proceed with care. For this does not announce the discovery of a new archê. On this, Abensour is unequivocal. As we encountered with Rancière, the archê functions to divide a social body according to an abstract principle of rule. And indeed, essential to the division between governor and governed, ruler and ruled, Abensour does not fail to detect the workings of the archê at the foundation of every State. But binding a concept of the political to the demos *as a whole* rather has the effect of a negation: what it refuses, what it denies, is the monopolisation of the political moment in the guise of an abstract State. The generality of the demos thus affirms the very opposite of the specificity of the archê: *that politics has no proper subject*. The true subject of politics is precisely the subject that is not a proper subject at all. It is for this reason that the demos can never serve as a suitable archê. This is something we observed with Rancière. Rather than a particular class or disenfranchised body, Marx's appeal to 'the whole demos' will recall the demos of Rancière's anarchic title, the empty form that signifies that generic equality of *'anyone at all.'* For Rancière, this anarchic equality is politics' only foundation. For the very same reasons, the same can be said of the demos as a whole. They remain identical expressions. Consequently, Rancière would likely regard Marx's concept of the demos not a vague abstraction, but indicative of that essential anarchy beneath every hierarchical structure, that underlying equality implicit in every system of inequality. At least for Abensour, there can be no true democracy without reactivating this underlying anarchic impulse that rises up against the archê of the State.[77] As he writes elsewhere, drawing not from Marx, but from Levinas, it is anarchy, the very multiplicity of the social itself, that ultimately frustrates the unity and totality of the State: 'It disturbs the State in a radical way, that is to say by shaking the State in its roots and its foundation.'[78]

Adopting the language of Étienne de La Boétie, the formula of Abensour's democracy against the State can therefore be expressed in the following way: the 'all ones' (*tous uns*) against the 'all One' (*tous Un*).[79] This expression allows us to further clarify Abensour's terms. The only difference, he suggests, between Rancière's democracy against the police and the democracy against the State he here attributes to Marx is their respective objects in question: whereas the police refers to government or governmentality, a vast instrumental machinery of social partition and allocation, the State refers to a more unified, totalising structure.[80] Monolithic, centralised, universal, the State is a system of integration and mediation, a unifying, organising entity that posits itself as a fixed point over and beyond the plurality of the demos. Perhaps this is why Hegel finds the State to be best expressed by a monarchy and why Karl Popper finds the totalitarian State of the twentieth century to represent its logical conclusion.[81] For Abensour, the State is not only a privileged point among many, but also the point that determines all other points through itself; it is not only the One that isolates itself from the multiple, it is the One that dominates the multiple from above. So whereas Foucault regards the State as but a type or episode of government which traverses the bounds of State and society, Abensour understands the State as a form severed from society and eternally set out against it. As in Clastres, the State is therefore the entity that lends itself nicely to the concentration of power, to the isolation of the organs of power from the whole community. By contrast, Abensour associates the demos, contrary to the State, with plurality, free creation and ongoing self-institution. In direct contradistinction to the rigidity and fixity of the State, in the spirit of William Godwin, he characterises the life of the demos as dynamic, plastic, innovative and transformational.[82] And while at times he finds Marx's presentation of the demos to forget the insurmountable conflict and division so apparent to Machiavelli (where the *whole* is never the *united*), Abensour perceives all these qualities in Marx's general concept of the demos as well.[83] Marx speaks of the '*fluidity*' of the instituting activity, precisely that which becomes the object of hypostasis under the dictates of the State-form.[84] Echoing Godwin, Abensour will therefore establish a stark irreconcilable opposition between two irreducible terms: the State = *the One, the total, the fixed*, the demos = *the multiple, the fluid, the mutational*. This is given an almost ontological expression. Democracy posits a creative, self-differentiating multiplicity against a static, integrated uniformity. It is the politics of becoming against being. *A Bergsonian democracy*. This is the basis and substance of its conflict with the State:

> This conflict arises from the contrast between the qualities of life – dynamism, the continuous flux of experience, impulsion, overflowing spontaneity – and the characteristics of form as a crystallization that acts as a power of conservation in view of maintaining the cohesion of the whole.[85]

As a moment of the demos reified, the State represents the crystallisation or petrification of the creative self-instituting activity of the demos. Democracy is that which resists the predominance of this reified moment. What it seeks to restore is the *form* of the State to the *life* of the demos. Its basic mechanism is what Abensour calls 'reduction'.

Abensour will put forward a theory of reduction – arguably one of his most important concepts – as the centrepiece of true democracy and the key to understanding its being-against the State: 'By bringing to light reduction and its consequences, Marx was able to show as clearly as possible that the struggle against the State, as a form, is inscribed in the heart of democratic logic.'[86] If Marx's thesis of democracy ultimately relies upon a notion of its constitutional exceptionality, Abensour finds this exceptionality primarily expressed in the implementation of reduction. This operation is unique to democracy alone. Here, the relation between constitution and demos, part and whole, remains distinct from every other constitutional form. Simply put, in democracy, the constitution – or the objectification of the demos in the form of a constitution – is rendered the object of a reduction.[87] This does not imply the effacement of the constitution itself (this is where Abensour differs from Sheldon Wolin).[88] Nor is it simply a matter of the devolution of a centralised authority to more local or regional administration. Rather, in democracy, reduction is the very mechanism through which this objectification of the demos occurs. Although never explicitly defined, political objectification may be appreciated as the manner in which the demos institutes, represents and encounters itself in an objective form. As with Lefort, a society can never experience itself directly (for Lefort, this is the entrance of the symbolic). Constitution is the *becoming-objective* of the demos, the giving itself a form, the making itself an object of social organisation and legislation. Reduction is the process that ensures this constitution, this moment of objectification, remains an ongoing process. Therefore, if democracy does not achieve the status of an abstract State, it is because its constitution is perpetually subjected to reduction. This is its primary strategy against the autonomy of the State. Democracy is not simply the name of the constitution reduced; it is the very exercise of reduction. Modern democracy, it could be said, appears in the eighteenth century as the reduction of monarchy (this is its revolutionary origin). It is what counters the State by reducing the constitution to what it is: a single moment of the demos and nothing more. This is how Abensour interprets

Marx when he declares democracy to make the constitution for man as opposed to man for the constitution. Democracy means the constitution remains at all times subordinate to the demos and never an agent of its domination. It is specifically in this sense that the State can be said to disappear. In this context, the disappearance of the State does not attest to the obsolescence and eventual 'withering away' of the State apparatus under the conditions of a realised communism. In true democracy, what disappears is the very presence of an abstract organising principle, a universal that monopolises the particular, a total that dominates its parts. As an instrument of the self-determination of the demos, this is precisely what reduction seeks to preclude and forestall. How should this unique mechanism of democracy be understood? Reduction entails blocking the State's means of transfiguration. It obstructs or impedes the very channels through which political objectification achieves a certain independence onto itself. It prevents that which constitutes the demos from becoming an integrated, organising principle. It is here where Abensour's democracy against the State approximates something of Clastres's society against the State. It testifies to a politics that demands a certain institutional awareness, a constant determination of limits, a mindfulness of the always possible threat of the emergence or re-emergence of the State. For the State will always struggle to neutralise democracy, to resist reduction, to block blocking. For this reason, democracy's relation to the State must always remain critical, vigilant. To be a democrat is to take on the task of constantly surveying the State, navigating its contours, determining its limits. As Rousseau grasped with great clarity: 'Man's natural dispositions for or against servitude therefore have to be judged not by the degradation of enslaved Peoples but by the prodigious feats of all free Peoples to guard against oppression.'[89]

Against Hegel, who renders the State a subject and Hobbes, who grants his Leviathan the status of a 'mortal god', part of what reduction implies for Abensour is the recognition that however alien or abstract in appearance, the State itself remains quintessentially a human object. This is why for Marx, democracy unravels the riddle of the constitution itself. The constitution reduced is the constitution resolved. This alone can have a liberating effect. At the origin of every constitution, monarchy and democracy alike, Marx discerns a trace of the free creation of man. The State is a social construct, nothing more. The distinction lies in monarchy's capacity to close off, distort and distance this moment of free creation from its original instituting subject, at once elevating its constitution to that of a State and diminishing the demos to a mere moment of its existence.[90] Consequently, as an abstract form, the State can appear as if it presides over society from a place beyond the demos itself, occupying something of the 'religious sphere' beyond the earthly realm of political intervention.[91] In this respect, much like the commodity of capitalist production, we may detect a certain fetishism inherent to the State-form itself. *Alienation, reification, fetishism*: before his critique of capital, all these terms are already very much inscribed in Marx's early critique of the State. Democracy is that which dispels this mystification. In so doing, the basis of political alienation is conjured away. Reduction reveals the State for what it is: anthropological, institutional, artificial. It thereby inhibits the inclination to dissociate the State from the original human activity that instituted it. In the language of Castoriadis, it reconciles the 'instituting' and 'instituted' moments of society. It immerses the constitution in the very process that produced it. Reduction initiates something of an eternal return, the process of perpetually returning to the original moment of institution. Reduction may therefore be understood as the operation that exposes the State to politics, that renders the State a political problem precisely by re-establishing its essential relation to the political realm, the realm of the demos as a whole. The politicisation of the State is its restitution, its restoration or return to the very condition implicit in its origin: the self-institution of the demos. The general formula for reduction may therefore be expressed as follows: *reduction = recognition = resolution = restitution*. Accordingly, Abensour finds reduction itself to consist of multiple facets or dimensions: first, reduction is the moment of 'going back', the moment of returning or restoring the constitution to the condition of its original instituting activity; second, by redirecting the constitution back to its origin, it allows for what is realised in the constitution to be extended infinitely across other dimensions of social life.[92] Put another way, reduction contains both a negative and productive element: the very blocking that prevents the abstraction of the political moment is at the same time what inspires the propagation of politics itself, the introduction of the political to other objects, parts, places and spheres of society.[93] Hence, for Abensour, the mechanism of reduction is itself the very condition of extension (*irrigation*): 'It is as if the movement of the return to an originary subject triggers a release, a retroaction of the subject's activity into every field that requires its energy.'[94] This extension may be interpreted in the following manner. The reduction of the

State, the very resolution of the problem of political alienation, is at once the irrigation of politics itself, granting it new life and new energies. It sets politics in motion, reanimates it, exposing it to institutions and social relations beyond the limits of those traditionally ascribed to the State itself. For Abensour, a theory of a democracy against the State is therefore a theory of democratisation, a democracy in perpetual motion and expansion. As that 'impetuous river' incessantly overflowing its riverbanks, Abensour sees democracy's resistance to the State constantly mutating into new forms with new disputes and new polemics at increasingly diverse corners of society. Accordingly, if we follow Abensour, reduction can be said to be composed of three isolatable moments or stages: *reduction, blocking* and *extension*:

> It is this latter stage which allows for the irrigation of all the other spheres of the life of a people, according to a democratic mode of being, in such a way that we can say that all holds to democracy.[95]

Democracy is the politicisation of the objects its appears against. It exposes, as it were, what it is against to a political field, calling into question its underlying foundations and challenging its basic suppositions. Reduction, therefore, should not be confused as a process of relinquishing the political to the domain of civil society. This is precisely what distinguishes Abensour's reading of Marx from that of Pierre Rosanvallon. Offering his own interpretation of the 1843 *Critique*, Rosanvallon identifies the *political* with the State, the *social* with civil society. This results in a reading of true democracy as the 'reabsorption' of the political into the social and the realisation of a society 'immediate to itself', attesting to a rather naive liberal vision of the 'self-sufficiency' of a distinctively apolitical civil society.[96] On the contrary, Abensour understands true democracy as a battle for the autonomy of the political itself. Democracy reminds us that politics is not subject to the State. It has a logic all of its own. At the same time, it demonstrates that civil society is never itself essentially *apolitical*. Politics is the very stage upon which the question of the autonomy or heteronomy of the demos is played out.[97] It has no proper domain. If anything, Abensour submits, today civil society must be *repoliticised*, set up as a place of conflict, a site of confrontation between the people and the grandees.[98] And while the State apparatus remains a structure that arguably can never itself be democratised, this does not deter democracy from politicising the State, that is, from challenging the State and rendering it a political problem. This is implicit in its reduction. For this reason, Abensour finds a democracy against the State to reveal with great clarity what is at stake in the political realm itself: an experience of universality, the negation of domination, the establishment of an isonomic public space.[99] Although an activity invariably wrought with incessant struggle, Abensour regards politics as just that: a lived expression of the open, perhaps unresolvable question of how people can live together in such a way as to realise 'liberty and free will'. This is not a question that can be monopolised by the State.

Insurgent Democracy

Despite Abensour's considerable reliance on his 1843 critique of Hegel, Abensour's theory of a democracy against the State should not be conflated with the work of the young Marx too hastily. Rather, Abensour will put an entirely new concept on offer. For Marx, 'true democracy' and the 'disappearance of the State' are expressions which amount to the same. Accordingly, the *truth* of democracy functions to deny the very proposition of a democratic State. Indeed, the so-called 'democratic State' appears to attest to the integration, mediation and moderation of democracy, a democracy reconciled with the State-form (Abensour understands Tocqueville's project very much in this sense). In opposition to such a project, which in light of Marx's critique can only be found to be inherently contradictory, Abensour will propose an alternative: 'insurgent' democracy.[100] For Abensour, this is the proper name of a democracy against the State:

> In truth, democracy is not a political regime. Beyond being the conflictive political institution of the social, it is an action, a form of political activity that is distinctive in its eruption of the demos onto the public stage, its opposition to the grandees, its struggle to end domination. It is not a matter of a momentary act, but of a continuous activity over time, always ready to push back in the face of the obstacles it encounters. It is a complex process, constantly reinventing itself in order to better persevere and defeat the counter-movements that threaten its destruction and return to a state of domination. This is insurgent democracy.[101]

Retaining his proximity to Machiavelli, if Abensour seeks a model of politics that locates the very condition of emancipation in that originary division of the social, in that irreducible conflict of the plebs against the agents of domination, he discovers such a model with insurgent democracy. But does Abensour really require a new concept? What exactly is it that distinguishes insurgent democracy from savage democracy, that which Abensour, more than anyone, not only defends, but elaborates considerably? And given savage democracy's stubborn lack of formula or foundation, what are the grounds for such a distinction? Perhaps the issue is one of precision, of specificity. Perhaps the radical openness that savage democracy brings to the concept ultimately lacks the kind of definition and demarcation Abensour now is looking for. Although he takes so much from Lefort's vision of democracy, what Abensour's later work calls 'insurgent' democracy can be understood as the democracy that specifically adopts the State as its 'natural' or 'favoured' target.[102] Lefort's savage democracy, he now claims, explicitly identifies no such target. These remarks signal a remarkable shift in Abensour's appraisal of savage democracy. Although he accepts savage democracy as a suitable expression for the dissolution of the markers of certainty, for the repeated test of indeterminacy, the logic of savage democracy, he ultimately determines, is not *necessarily* anti-statist.[103] It is insurgent democracy that embodies this very necessity.[104] Perhaps insurgent democracy could therefore be thought as a savage democracy inscribed with a new object, a new target. Perhaps it takes everything that is savage about democracy, as it were, to what Abensour understands as its logical conclusion, its absolute end: *a democracy against the State*. We occasionally encounter this interpretation in the scholarship.[105] At the same time, however indebted to the young Marx, perhaps insurgent democracy announces a concept of democracy that is no longer theoretically dependent on the critical framework of his 1843 *Critique*. In many respects, Marx's argument for democracy simply reverses the formal logic of Hegel's abstract theory of the State. Insurgent democracy is bound by no such logic. Instead, Abensour draws its basic framework from a still relatively obscure tradition of revolutionary activity that sporadically manifests throughout modern history.[106] As a concept, insurgent democracy traces that unique political genealogy from the Paris Commune to the German Revolution of 1918 to the Spanish Civil War to the council movement of the Hungarian Revolution to the May '68 revolts.[107] We could no doubt add a number of other examples to this list as well. For Abensour, what defines each of these events is a spontaneous irruption of the demos against the agents of the State. What we find at the root of insurgent democracy, therefore, is a rejection of the State as the natural or inevitable basis of social organisation. It invites us to consider the very possibility of a political community founded upon something other than the State: the self-determination of the demos, a state of non-domination, an ongoing experiment in political freedom.

Insurgent democracy is a democracy in perpetual conflict with the State, a democracy that not only accommodates conflict, but embraces and multiplies it. This is its defining feature. And yet, this conflict is not limited to the traditional confines of the State itself.[108] Insurgent democracy does not situate itself immanent to the State, but locates its primary site of conflict in an altogether different space: outside, beyond and against the State. It is the democracy that occurs in the streets and public squares, that which is often regarded peripheral or irrelevant by the State itself. It is what opens up a space for political action. It is what initiates an agonistic scene which organises and coordinates the essential opposition between the people and the State:

> In a Rousseauist vocabulary, insurgent democracy can be defined as an arising of the body of the people against the body of the State; in other words, the expression of the political rapport as it proceeds from the true subject, the 'whole demos'.[109]

Insurgent democracy represents the irreconcilable clash of two distinct bodies: the demos and the State. And yet, always maintaining a relation of externality, insurgent democracy does not ultimately seek to seize the State or occupy its institutions, but to resist it, carving out new political spaces, devising alternative social structures and generating new forms of social bonds. Insurgent democracy is not a new theory of revolution. It is the endless quest to discover horizontal, non-hierarchical, non-contractual modes of what Arendt calls *'being-together'*. It is therefore a question of creating the very conditions of new and inclusive ways of engaging collectively in the public realm.[110]

Occupying an entirely different space than the State, insurgent democracy likewise situates itself in a temporality all of its own. Clearly drawing from that pivotal moment of the French Revolution, that brief interval between regimes, it corresponds to the time *in between* two State forms; it struggles against the State on two fronts at once: the State of the *ancien régime* and the new State to come.[111] To some extent, even beyond those rare revolutionary moments, every political struggle must contend with the State of the old regime, its history, its burdens, its relics. At the same time, we are often confronted with the State's perpetual restructuring and reform, its modernisation and rationalisation (in Max Weber's sense of the term). Insurgent democracy installs itself precisely in the caesura between these two incarnations of the State, in that very opening, paradoxically, that refuses installation and permanent forms.[112] It occupies, as it were, that revolutionary moment, a time between the radical opening up of a system and its rapid reconsolidation. This is a temporality that lacks all reference to identity and self-presence. It is an experience defined only by incessant conflict on all sides, a permanent contestation. It is the first task of insurgent democracy to preserve this caesura, to maintain this rupture or opening for political action. It is precisely through this window that social transformation and democratisation may occur.

Although insurgent democracy may appear to have a rather precarious status, eternally anchored in the present, between regimes, destined to lack a certain stability or constancy, Abensour finds no reason to presume its inherent incompatibility or outright antagonism with institutions.[113] What exactly is democracy's relationship to institutions? This is a question we have largely neglected throughout this study. We cannot do it justice here. But Abensour's comments will certainly help us frame and orient this question for future consideration. Abensour remarks that his critics often take issue with what is perceived to be his purely 'negative' conception of democracy (a democracy against), one that disregards positive institutions for the sake of binding democracy to the insurrectionary event. But this misconstrues Abensour's work and, indeed, the antinomies of politics itself. Nevertheless, it is a criticism that legitimately raises a number of questions regarding the institution of insurgent democracy itself, a topic that Abensour would eventually address in a subsequent preface to *Democracy against the State*. In principle, Abensour maintains, insurgent democracy is neither hostile nor resistant to institutional engagement. A democracy against the State is not inevitably a democracy against institutions. On the contrary, institutions can endow political experience with a certain sustainability. They can help insurgence to endure over time, to connect its present moment to events of the past and even to anticipate and prepare for events of the future. And yet, given its objectives and orientation, insurgent democracy's engagement with institutions will naturally remain *selective*. Even so, Abensour's criteria is relatively intuitive and straightforward: insurgent democracy distinguishes between those institutions that promote, support and advance the political action of the demos and those that discourage, prohibit or suppress it, those institutions that subscribe to a politics of liberty and non-domination and those that retreat from such a project, those institutions that block and inhibit the desire of the grandees and those that allow their ambition to circulate freely.[114] This is not the meeting or convergence of a vital, transient insurgence and a stable, institutional framework. Neither is it the old question of spontaneity and organisation. Institutions do not function to legislate or govern insurgence, giving it shape or direction. Their interaction is far more nuanced. Here, Abensour finds it helpful to distinguish between institutions and laws. Turning to an early essay by Deleuze, who himself draws principally from David Hume (a great thinker of institutions), Abensour explains that an institution is more of a matrix than a framework, a model or blueprint that engenders, creates and develops.[115] Deleuze understands an institution as a *system of anticipation*: whereas laws intend to limit or prohibit action, institutions provide a positive model for it, whereas laws rely on penalty, institutions appeal to freedom: 'Such a theory will afford us the following political criteria: tyranny is a regime in which there are many laws and few institutions; democracy is a regime in which there are many institutions and few laws.'[116] For Deleuze, an institution is an organisation of means. It is essentially positive, innovative, a *way* of acting or acting in concert. This is the concept of an institution best suited to insurgent democracy. Far from an obstruction or impediment to its cause, Abensour sees institutions as something of a launch pad for democracy, their durability and continuity allowing for new possibilities of invention and intervention. While institutions can inform and sustain insurgence, insurgence can direct and orient institutions. Institutions can be a friend to the against. They can themselves be positioned against the State. This is just as true for Abensour and democracy as it is for Clastres and primitive societies.

In Summary: Rancière's Democracy against the Police and Abensour's Democracy against the State

In his conclusion to *Democracy against the State*, Abensour returns his inquiry to the present, to the *here and now*: 'Are we at a Machiavellian moment today?'[117] Do we have the capacity, as Machiavelli did, to think political matters *politically*? For Abensour, the legacy of figures like Arendt, Merleau-Ponty and Lefort suggest that a Machiavellian moment is still very much upon us. It is not a matter of returning to Marx or even to Machiavelli, but rather of returning to *politics* itself. Before a question of government or law, politics is a question of emancipation. This is the fundamental link Abensour's work seeks to re-establish. Emancipation is the object of politics, democracy its form. Unlike Castoriadis and Lefort, Abensour does not draw a consistent conceptual distinction between *politics* and *the political* (*la politique* and *le politique*). Rather, it is qualified simply as the ongoing project to establish a state of non-domination. For Abensour, the State presents a formidable challenge to such a project. In this regard, perhaps Marx's revelation of the irreconcilable conflict between democracy and the State must be thought an indispensable facet of what a Machiavellian moment would have to recognise and consider today. On the problem of the State, Abensour often finds Lefort's formal opposition between democracy and totalitarianism at once too limited and too absolute. For the State is certainly not democratic if it is not totalitarian. At times, he rather finds it necessary to introduce a third term: *the authoritarian State*, that which is neither 'democratic' or 'totalitarian', but signals the accelerated degeneration of our own political institutions without falling into totalitarianism absolutely.[118] A rapidly changing world inevitably brings with it the potential for new authorities and new instruments of repression. For Abensour, this is the use of philosophy. Abensour envisions the critical political philosopher as something of a 'watchman' of authoritarian tendencies in society.[119] The philosopher patrols, surveys, identifies and diagnoses the spaces, relations and technologies of domination, their emergence and evolution. Accordingly, a critical political philosophy can reveal just how exposed the so-called democratic form of society often is to subversion, corruption and authoritarianism, not only from without, but *from within*. For Abensour, perhaps this only further demonstrates the necessity of a robust and vigilant insurgent democracy.

Although Abensour ultimately distinguishes the two theoretically, where insurgent democracy and true democracy inevitably collide and intersect is in their conception of a democracy explicitly oriented *against the State*.[120] Indeed, this is a theme to which Marx himself would eventually return in 1871 following the events of the Paris Commune. However, in contrast to his early critique of Hegel, now it is no longer a question of the formal 'disappearance' of the State, but of a political programme to 'break' or 'smash' modern State power itself.[121] Now it is not simply monarchy, but every form of State that is explicitly called into question. The State is the entity that not only dominates the plurality of the demos as universal form, but at the same time, isolates and consolidates the organs of power into the hands of the few. As demonstrated by the fate of the Paris Commune, this can be an egregiously violent act. The State-form is neither neutral nor instrumental. Against Lenin, it contains no revolutionary potential. For Marx himself, this is the lesson of the Paris Commune. It was the position of the anarchists from the beginning. Ultimately a struggle for self-determination, a democracy against the State strives to *reduce* the State, to generate modes of association other than those on offer by the State, creating new and inclusive ways of engaging collectively in a distinctively public space. As he defiantly informs Gauchet, Abensour is committed to such a concept of democracy, a democracy that embraces conflict rather than conceals it, that multiplies the spaces of collective invention, that circulates the desire for autonomy and inspires experiences of political freedom.[122] In this regard, perhaps we should take care not to contrast Marx's true democracy with some false or incomplete interpretation of democracy, but to understand its 'truth' to reveal and call attention to something essential about the meaning of democracy itself: that democracy is not a State-form; democracy is against the State.

We have now encountered two contemporary models of the antinomies of politics: Rancière's democracy against the police and Abensour's democracy against the State. My aim has not simply been one of comparison, nor a straightforward survey of their theses. Although we have observed many correspondences and points of intersection, in each case I have largely situated my analysis *within* the conceptual framework of each author, as a visitor or traveller, evaluating concepts, establishing relations, testing limits and boundaries. My goal has ultimately been one of extraction: to isolate and draw out a general theory of the *against* intrinsic to the antinomies of politics in order to consider its objects, logic, and broader social and political implications. The against is not a consequence of democracy. It is immanent to its very form. Whether it identifies the police or the State as its primary object, democracy is always generated in the form of an against, an against which is at all times integral to its composition, orientation and institutional expression. A theory of democracy's being-against is therefore a theory of a politics of transformation, a politics that initiates change precisely through its immanent resistance to that which it is against. Both Rancière and Abensour represent exceptional thinkers of democracy in that the against is never overlooked, concealed or marginalised in their work. While their respective theories of democracy differ in many respects, by fixing the against at the centre of its concept, they help us think democracy in new and productive ways: not as a regime, government or institution primarily, but as a profound challenge to oppressive, hierarchical and exclusionary arrangements and practices in society. Perhaps in many ways, they complement each other well. Against the backdrop of Foucault's concept of governmentality, Rancière provides a critique of the police organised around the problem of the proper order of society. Against the backdrop of Marx's concept of sovereignty, Abensour provides a critique of the State organised around the problem of political alienation. While Rancière sees democracy as the disruption of the police, Abensour understands democracy as the reduction of the State. While Rancière grounds politics according to the claim of equality, Abensour centres politics around the question of emancipation. Whereas Abensour lacks a detailed account of the political subject as the primary agent or actor of democracy, this can readily be found in Rancière. Whereas Rancière is curiously reticent on the ultimate goals and objectives of democracy, this is something Abensour is only too willing to articulate. Although both offer a substantive critique of what Arendt understands as the tradition of political philosophy, while Rancière elects to circumvent and abandon the discipline entirely, Abensour endeavours to refashion and remodel it a critical political philosophy. Ultimately, the object is not to synthesise or harmonise the two or to overlook their many tensions and discrepancies, but to gather from each new insights into the forms and practices of democracy's emancipatory, transformative politics. Democracy is the democratisation of society, its institutions and relations. But this democratisation is neither a natural nor inevitable process. It often occurs only through conflict, that is, in the form of a being-against. Both Rancière and Abensour help us to understand this.

Notes

1. James D. Ingram, *Radical Cosmopolitics: The Ethics and Politics of Democratic Universalism* (New York: Columbia University Press, 2013), 199.
2. See Miguel Abensour, 'Of Insurgent Democracy', *Democracy against the State: Marx and the Machiavellian Moment* (Cambridge: Polity, 2011).
3. Miguel Abensour and Michel Enaudeau, *La Communauté politique des 'tous uns': désir de liberté, désir d'utopie* (Paris: Belles Lettres, 2014), 94.

4. Marcel Gauchet, *La Condition historique* (Paris: Stock, 2003), 160. Also see James D. Ingram, 'The Politics of Claude Lefort's Political: Between Liberalism and Radical Democracy', *Thesis Eleven* vol. 87, no. 1 (2006): 41.
5. Miguel Abensour, 'Lettre d'un "révoltiste" à Marcel Gauchet converti à la "politique normale"', *Réfractions* no. 12 (2004): 164, as quoted in Ingram, 'The Politics of Claude Lefort's Political', 44. For a detailed comparison of the projects of Abensour and Gauchet as 'students' of Lefort, see Ingram's insightful article. For an additional perspective on Abensour's polemical response to Gauchet, see Warren Breckman, *Adventures of the Symbolic: Post-Marxism and Radical Democracy* (New York: Columbia University Press, 2013), 180–1.
6. J. G. A. Pocock, *The Machiavellian Moment: Florentine Political Thought and the Atlantic Republican Tradition* (Princeton: Princeton University Press, 2003).
7. See my introduction to Chapter 3.
8. Abensour finds much of the history of political philosophy to conceal the reality of social domination, whereas his own political philosophy places the question of domination at its very centre. See Gilles Labelle, 'La philosophie politique et le "choix du petit" dans le travail de Miguel Abensour', *Monde commun* vol. 1, no. 1 (Autumn 2007): 44.
9. Miguel Abensour, 'De quel retour s'agit-il?' *Les Cahiers de Philosophie* no. 18 (1994): 8.
10. Miguel Abensour, 'Philosophie politique critique et émancipation?', *Politique et Sociétés* vol. 22, no. 3 (2003): 120.
11. See, for example, Miguel Abensour, 'Pour une philosophie politique critique?', *Pour une philosophie politique critique* (Paris: Sens & Tonka, 2009), 286.
12. Patrice Vermeren, 'Equality and Democracy', *Diogenes* vol. 55, no. 4 (2008): 59.
13. Abensour, 'Pour une philosophie politique critique?', 267.
14. Ibid., 294. Also see Abensour and Enaudeau, *La Communauté politique des 'tous uns'*, chapter 6.
15. Abensour, 'Philosophie politique critique et émancipation?', 137, and Abensour, 'Pour une philosophie politique critique?', 311–13.
16. Martin Breaugh, 'From a Critique of Totalitarian Domination to the Utopia of Insurgent Democracy: On the "Political Philosophy" of Miguel Abensour', in *Thinking Radical Democracy: The Return to Politics in Postwar France*, ed. Martin Breaugh et al. (Toronto: University of Toronto Press, 2015), 240.
17. See Abensour's comments in Abensour, 'Sur le chemin de Machiavel', *Pour une philosophie politique critique*. Also see Claude Lefort, *Machiavelli in the Making* (Evanston: Northwestern University Press, 2012), part 3, chapter 3.

18. Niccolò Machiavelli, *The Discourses* (London: Penguin Books, 2003), 116, and *The Prince* (Chicago: Chicago University Press, 1998), 39.
19. For a related democratic interpretation of Machiavelli, see John P. McCormick, *Machiavellian Democracy* (Cambridge: Cambridge University Press, 2011).
20. Machiavelli, *The Discourses*, 116.
21. Miguel Abensour, '"Savage Democracy" and the "Principle of Anarchy"', *Democracy against the State*, 105.
22. Utopia is the topic of Abensour's doctoral thesis *Les Formes de l'utopie socialiste-communiste. Essai sur le communisme critique et l'utopie*, completed under the supervision first of Gilles Deleuze and then Charles Eisenmann in 1973.
23. See Christine Nadir's helpful essay 'Utopian Studies, Environmental Literature, and the Legacy of an Idea: Educating Desire in Miguel Abensour and Ursula K. Le Guin', *Utopian Studies* vol. 21, no. 1 (2010). Also see Ruth Levitas, *Utopia as Method: The Imaginary Reconstitution of Society* (Houndmills and New York: Palgrave Macmillan, 2013), 113–16.
24. Miguel Abensour, 'L'homme est un animal utopique', *L'Homme est un animal utopique: Utopiques II* (Paris: Sens & Tonka, 2013), 278, as quoted in Christopher Holman, 'Machiavelli's Two Utopias', *Utopian Studies* vol. 29, no. 1 (2018): 89.
25. Miguel Abensour, 'Persistent Utopia', *Constellations* vol. 15, no. 3 (2008): 407.
26. Abensour will introduce the 'new utopian spirit' in Miguel Abensour, 'The History of Utopia and the Destiny of its Critique', in *Political Uses of Utopia: New Marxist, Anarchist, and Radical Democratic Perspectives*, ed. S. D. Chrostowska and James D. Ingram (New York: Columbia University Press, 2016), 39–49.
27. Ibid., 39–40. Also see Breaugh, 'From a Critique of Totalitarian Domination to the Utopia of Insurgent Democracy', 247.
28. Abensour, 'The History of Utopia and the Destiny of its Critique', 43. Abensour will refuse to position Marx simply as a crass proponent of 'scientific socialism' which systematically jettisons its original utopian dimension. Abensour rather reads Marx as a significant contributor to the rich utopian tradition.
29. Abensour's most important discussion of Thomas More can be found in Miguel Abensour, *Utopia: From Thomas More to Walter Benjamin* (Minneapolis: Univocal, 2017).
30. Abensour, 'Persistent Utopia', 418.
31. Gilles Deleuze and Félix Guattari, *What is Philosophy?* (New York: Columbia University Press, 1994), 99.
32. Levitas, *Utopia as Method*, 119.
33. This arguably culminates in the recently translated Miguel Abensour, 'Utopia and Democracy', in *The Weariness of Democracy:*

Confronting the Failure of Liberal Democracy, ed. Jason Powell Frausto and Sarah Vitale (Cham, Switzerland: Palgrave Macmillan, 2020). On the intersection of utopia and democracy, also see Paul Mazzocchi, 'Excavating Abensour: The Dialectics of Democracy and Utopia at a Standstill', Constellations vol. 22, no. 2 (June 2015).
34. Martin Breaugh, 'Le lien social entre utopie et démocratie', in *Critique de la politique. Autour* de Miguel Abensour, ed. Anne Kupiec and Étienne Tassin (Paris: Sens & Tonka, 2006), 91.
35. See Abensour, 'Utopia and Democracy', 28, as well as Abensour and Enaudeau, *La Communauté politique des 'tous uns'*, 381. On this question of 'democratising' utopia and 'utopianising' democracy, also see Manuel Cervera-Marzal, *Miguel Abensour: critique de la domination, pensée de l'émancipation* (Paris: Sens & Tonka, 2013), 169–72.
36. Abensour, *Utopia*, 54.
37. Originally included in the commemorative volume edited by Miguel Abensour, *L'Esprit des lois sauvages: Pierre Clastres ou une nouvelle anthropologie politique* (Paris: Seuil, 1987). Also see Cervera-Marzal, *Miguel Abensour*, 48–51.
38. Miguel Abensour, 'The Counter-Hobbes of Pierre Clastres', in *Thinking Radical Democracy*, 90–1.
39. Thomas Hobbes, *Leviathan: Parts One and Two* (Upper Saddle River: Prentice-Hall, 1958), 106–7.
40. Abensour, 'The Counter-Hobbes of Pierre Clastres', 100.
41. Ibid., 101–2.
42. Ibid., 111. Also see Abensour and Enaudeau, *La Communauté politique des 'tous uns'*, 71.
43. Abensour, 'The Counter-Hobbes of Pierre Clastres', 103–5.
44. In Chapter 3 above.
45. Martin Breaugh, 'Critique de la domination, pensée de l'émancipation. Sur la philosophie politique de Miguel Abensour', *Politique et Sociétés* vol. 22, no. 3 (2003): 56.
46. See Gilles Deleuze and Félix Guattari, *A Thousand Plateaus: Capitalism and Schizophrenia* (Minneapolis: University of Minnesota Press, 1987), 374–6.
47. See Claude Lefort, 'Dialogue with Pierre Clastres', *Writing: The Political Test* (Durham, NC: Duke University Press, 2000). This essay also originally appeared in Abensour's edited volume *L'Esprit des lois sauvages*. Also see Bernard Flynn, *The Philosophy of Claude Lefort: Interpreting the Political* (Evanston: Northwestern University Press, 2005), 94–8. For additional remarks on Lefort's position on the State, see Antoon Braeckman, 'The Hermeneutics of Society: On the State in Lefort's Political Theory', *Constellations* vol. 25, no. 2 (June 2018).
48. Abensour, 'Of Insurgent Democracy', xxxii. Also see Mazzocchi, 'Excavating Abensour', 293.

49. See Claude Lefort, 'Nation et souveraineté', *Le Temps présent: Écrits 1945–2005* (Paris: Belin, 2007).
50. Marc G. Doucet, 'Thinking Democracy beyond Regimes: Untangling Political Analysis from the Nation-State', in *Claude Lefort: Thinker of the Political*, ed. Martín Plot (Houndmills, Basingstoke, Hampshire: Macmillan, 2013), 166–72.
51. Claude Lefort, 'Human Rights and the Welfare State', *Democracy and Political Theory* (Minneapolis: University of Minnesota Press, 1988), 43.
52. Claude Lefort, 'Politics and Human Rights', *The Political Forms of Modern Society: Bureaucracy, Democracy, Totalitarianism* (Cambridge, MA: MIT Press, 1986), 264.
53. See Cervera-Marzal, *Miguel Abensour*, 91–6. In addition to Pocock's *The Machiavellian Moment*, Lefort's *Machiavelli in the Making* undoubtedly remains a second important source for Abensour's uniquely 'Machiavellian' reading of Marx. See Farhang Erfani, 'Fixing Marx with Machiavelli: Claude Lefort's Democratic Turn', *Journal of the British Society for Phenomenology* vol. 39, no. 2 (May 2008): 201.
54. See Louis Althusser, *Machiavelli and Us* (London: Verso, 1999). Even when Lefort explores some of the parallels in the work of Marx and Machiavelli (their decisive break with idealist philosophy, their rejection of a distinctively apolitical Christian morality), he will rely on Gramsci's 'Notes on Machiavelli' as his initial point of departure. See Claude Lefort, 'Reflexions sociologiques sur Machiavel et Marx: la politique et le réel', *Les Formes de l'histoire* (Paris: Gallimard, Folio-Essais, 2000).
55. Abensour, *Democracy against the State*, 5.
56. Max Blechman, 'Translator's Introduction: To Think Emancipation Otherwise', *Democracy against the State*, x.
57. See Karl Marx, 'On the Jewish Question', *Early Writings* (London: Penguin Books, 1992).
58. For a more extensive survey of Marx's concept of democracy beyond the 1843 *Critique*, see Vasilis Grollios, 'Marx and Engels' Critique of Democracy: The Materialist Character of their Concept of Autonomy', *Critique* vol. 39, no. 1 (2011). On the question of democratic participation in Marx, see Patricia Springborg, 'Karl Marx on Democracy, Participation, Voting, and Equality', *Political Theory* vol. 12, no. 4 (November 1984).
59. See, for example, Abensour's remarks in Abensour and Enaudeau, *La Communauté politique des 'tous uns'*, chapter 5, and Miguel Abensour, Jean-Luc Nancy and Jacques Rancière, 'Instances démocratiques', *Vacarme* vol. 48, no. 3 (Summer 2009): 9–10.
60. Abensour, *Democracy against the State*, 32–3.
61. Abensour is not the first to observe this theme in the 1843 *Critique*. Perhaps one of the earliest references to 'political alienation' in this

sense appears in Ralph Miliband, 'Marx and the State', *The Socialist Register* vol. 2 (1965): 280. Nicholas Churchich will devote an entire chapter to the concept in Nicholas Churchich, *Marxism and Alienation* (Rutherford: Fairleigh Dickinson University Press, 1990), chapter 9.
62. See G. W. F. Hegel, *Elements of the Philosophy of Right* (London: Oxford University Press, 1962), 12, 222–3. Also see Michael O. Hardimon, 'The Project of Reconciliation: Hegel's Social Philosophy', *Philosophy & Public Affairs* vol. 21, no. 2 (Spring 1992).
63. Hegel is the first to use the term 'civil society' in this manner. Before Hegel, 'political' and 'civil' society were terms largely employed interchangeably and simply intended to oppose what is 'natural' to man. Both Tocqueville and Marx would follow Hegel in this basic terminological distinction.
64. Karl Marx, 'Critique of Hegel's "Philosophy of Right"', *Early Writings*, 72–3.
65. Ibid., 62–3.
66. See Hegel, *Elements of the Philosophy of Right*, 183, and Marx, 'Critique of Hegel's "Philosophy of Right"', 86–7.
67. Marx, 'Critique of Hegel's "Philosophy of Right"', 86.
68. Ibid., 87.
69. Ibid., 88.
70. Ibid., 87.
71. Baruch Spinoza, *Theological-Political Treatise* (Indianapolis: Hackett Publishing Company, 2001), 179.
72. Marx, 'Critique of Hegel's "Philosophy of Right"', 87.
73. Ibid.
74. Ibid., 88. For additional insights into this important passage, see Simon Critchley, 'True Democracy: Marx, Political Subjectivity and Anarchic Meta-politics', in *Radical Democracy: Politics between Abundance and Lack*, ed. Lars Tonder and Lasse Thomassen (Manchester: Manchester University Press, 2005).
75. If we assume, not without justification, that by 'the French' Marx is thinking principally of Rousseau. See Robert Fine, *Political Investigations: Hegel, Marx, Arendt* (London: Routledge, 2001), 75.
76. Perhaps Lucio Colletti remains the authority on the link between Rousseau and Marx. See Lucio Colletti, *From Rousseau to Lenin: Studies in Ideology and Society* (New York: Monthly Review Press, 1974).
77. Abensour, 'Of Insurgent Democracy', xl–xli.
78. Miguel Abensour, 'An-archy between Metapolitics and Politics', *Parallax* vol. 8, no. 3 (2002): 17.
79. Miguel Abensour, 'Is There a Proper Way to Use the Voluntary Servitude Hypothesis?', *Journal of Political Ideology* vol. 16, no. 3 (2011): 341.

80. Abensour, 'Of Insurgent Democracy', xxxiv.
81. See Karl Popper, *The Open Society and Its Enemies* (Princeton and Oxford: Princeton University Press, 2013).
82. Abensour, *Democracy against the State*, 59.
83. Martin Deleixhe presumes Lefort would likely take issue with Marx's notion of 'the whole demos', perhaps finding in it the kernel of the totalitarian logic of the 'people-as-one'. See Martin Deleixhe, 'La démocratie radicale et la critique du marxisme', *Raisons politiques* vol. 75, no. 3 (2019): 38.
84. Abensour, *Democracy against the State*, 65.
85. Ibid., 93.
86. Abensour, 'Of Insurgent Democracy', xxxiii.
87. Abensour, *Democracy against the State*, 53.
88. See Sheldon S. Wolin, 'Norm and Form: The Constitutionalizing of Democracy', in *Athenian Political Thought and the Reconstruction of American Democracy*, ed. J. Peter Euben, John R. Wallach and Josiah Ober (Ithaca: Cornell University Press, 1994).
89. Jean-Jacques Rousseau, 'Discourse on the Origin and Foundations of Inequality among Men', *The Discourses and Other Early Political Writings*, ed. Victor Gourevitch (Cambridge: Cambridge University Press, 2005), 177.
90. Abensour, *Democracy against the State*, 60.
91. Marx, 'Critique of Hegel's "Philosophy of Right"', 89.
92. Abensour, *Democracy against the State*, 56.
93. Ibid., 65.
94. Ibid., 56–7.
95. Abensour, 'Of Insurgent Democracy', xxxiii.
96. Pierre Rosanvallon, 'Marx and Civil Society', *Democracy Past and Future* (New York: Columbia University Press, 2006), 162–3.
97. Abensour, *Democracy against the State*, 71.
98. Abensour, 'Of Insurgent Democracy', xxxvii–xl. For further analysis of the repoliticisation of civil society, see Jordi Riba, 'What is Old and New in our Democracies?', in *The Weariness of Democracy: Confronting the Failure of Liberal Democracy*, 61.
99. Abensour, *Democracy against the State*, 92.
100. Abensour will originally outline insurgent democracy in the foreword to the second French edition and preface to the Italian edition of *Democracy against the State*.
101. Abensour, Nancy and Rancière, 'Instances démocratiques', 11 (translation by Brian Singer).
102. Abensour, 'Of Insurgent Democracy', xxxiii–xxxiv.
103. Ibid., xxxi–xxxii. Also see Breaugh, 'Le lien social entre utopie et démocratie', 87.
104. For further analysis of Abensour's pivot from savage democracy to insurgent democracy, see Cervera-Marzal, *Miguel Abensour*, 133–6.

105. See, for example, Mazzocchi, 'Excavating Abensour', 295.
106. Abensour and Enaudeau, *La Communauté politique des 'tous uns'*, 136.
107. To take up but one of these examples, Paul Mazzocchi considers how Abensour's notion of insurgent democracy plays out with respect to the German Revolution. See Paul Mazzocchi, 'Insurgent Democracy and the German Councils', in *The German Revolution and Political Theory*, ed. Gaard Kets and James Muldoon (Cham, Switzerland: Palgrave Macmillan, 2019).
108. Abensour, 'Of Insurgent Democracy', xl.
109. Ibid.
110. Breaugh, 'From a Critique of Totalitarian Domination to the Utopia of Insurgent Democracy', 242–3.
111. Abensour, 'Of Insurgent Democracy', xxxv. For a discussion of insurgent democracy in the context of the French Revolution, see Sophie Wahnich, 'Démocratie insurgeante et révolution française', in *Désir d'utopie: politique et émancipation avec Miguel Abensour*, ed. Manuel Cervera-Marzal and Nicolas Poirier (Paris: L'Harmattan, 2018).
112. Abensour, 'Of Insurgent Democracy', xxxv.
113. Miguel Abensour, 'Insurgent Democracy and Institution', *Democracy against the State*, xxv.
114. Ibid., xxvi. As something of an archetypal example, Abensour sites the people's right to insurrection included in the stillborn French constitution of 1793. Also see Riba, 'What is Old and New in our Democracies?', 59.
115. Abensour, 'Insurgent Democracy and Institution', xxvii.
116. Gilles Deleuze, 'Instincts and Institutions', *Desert Islands and Other Texts* (Los Angeles: Semiotext(e), 2004), 19–20.
117. Abensour, *Democracy against the State*, 89.
118. Abensour, 'Pour une philosophie politique critique?', 314–15.
119. Breaugh, 'Critique de la domination, pensée de l'émancipation', 69.
120. For a broader discussion on the relation between insurgent democracy and true democracy, see Abensour and Enaudeau, *La Communauté politique des 'tous uns'*, chapter 5.
121. Karl Marx, 'The Civil War in France', *Later Political Writings* (Cambridge: Cambridge University Press, 1996), 186. Also see Abensour, *Democracy against the State*, chapter 6 and Patrick Cingolani, 'Interprétation de l'insurrection communale. La démocratie, l'état et la politique', in *Critique de la politique. Autour de Miguel Abensour*.
122. Abensour, 'Lettre d'un "révoltiste" à Marcel Gauchet converti à la "politique normale"', 162. Also see Ingram, 'The Politics of Claude Lefort's Political', 41.

Conclusion: *'Hic et nunc'* – the Use of Philosophy and the Critique of the Present

> *When someone asks 'what's the use of philosophy?' the reply must be aggressive, since the question tries to be ironic and caustic. Philosophy does not serve the State or the Church, who have other concerns. It serves no established power. [. . .] Philosophy is at its most positive as critique, as an enterprise of demystification.*
> Gilles Deleuze, *Nietzsche and Philosophy*

In a perceptive, but now completely obscure lecture on the issues of democracy, theologian and utopian socialist Henry James Sr (father of philosopher William James and novelist Henry James) will introduce the topic of democracy according to what it 'protests'. For the elder James, what democracy counters and opposes are those all too familiar claims to rule epitomised by the regimes of monarchy and aristocracy:

> Against these two claims, Democracy is a protest. It denies the claim of any one man to govern other men, and the right of any one class to govern other classes. [. . .] Thus the Democratic idea exhibits a purely negative development. It is revolutionary, not formative. It is born of denial.[1]

Rather than a form, James sees democracy as a destroyer of forms, rather than an institution, a denial of established institutions. This denial is inscribed in its very inception and indeed, for James, what must define democracy itself. He continues:

> Democracy is not so much a new form of political life as a dissolution or disorganisation of the old forms. It is simply a resolution

of government into the hands of the people, a taking down of that which has before existed, and a re-commitment of it to its original sources [. . .].[2]

Thus, however rudimentary in its presentation and at times naively utopian in its outlook, James is able to see something in democracy that many cannot: the *against* that remains so indispensable to the idea of democracy itself. While the meaning of democracy is certainly not limited to what it is against, this aspect of democracy is often what is lacking from its history and analysis. It is precisely this lack of analysis that has compelled this study. Democracy is not simply a question of a particular society or institution; it is a question of how societies and institutions that are not democratic become so. It is a question of democratisation and social emancipation. Democracy is never constituted in a void. It appears as a particular encounter or confrontation. It takes the form of a being-against. This is what I have called the 'antinomies of politics'. The against propels democracy forward, informs its targets and objectives, galvanises its resolve towards a more participatory, more egalitarian society. Democracy introduces a polemics to the polis; it initiates a unique political controversy and dispute. It throws what it means to govern and what it means to be governed into question. It renders the foundations of a given social order intrinsically problematic. This is not a natural or inevitable process. It is the act of a subject, the demos simply being its original and most generic name. The antinomies of politics is therefore emblematic of a democracy that binds the persistent democratisation of society to that distinct challenge of the demos, the excluded, those who do not count and do not have a voice. Democracy is the story of how those who lack political agency come to have it. Rather than a grand revolutionary moment, it testifies to a long trajectory, a becoming, a history or tradition of emancipation. Democracy is the democratisation of society, its institutions and relations. This is the strange tautology through which democracy must ultimately be understood.

Through a series of exegetical studies, of Rancière, Lefort and Abensour, this is the basic concept of democracy I have sought to develop and advance. Although their projects differ considerably and are bound to no single framework, each of these authors offer a certain resistance to the customary strategies of formulating and evaluating what is called 'democracy' today. Indeed, reading these figures, each individually and all together, a whole discourse on democracy appears to be called into question. Democracy will no longer correspond to a State-form, a collection of institutions or a style of government. Rather, their writings provide us the necessary tools to effectively disentangle its concept, so that it may be thought anew and put to use in creative and productive ways. Their work challenges us to explore the limits and potentials of what the *power of the people* can mean. At the same time, it invites us to re-examine those arrangements and structures in our own society that claim to be 'democratic'. Inscribed in their respective theories of democracy, therefore, is a sustained critique of the present and the way in which the general concept of democracy is often received and accepted today. It is precisely this resistance, this critique of the present, that renders their work on democracy *political*.

From Plato to Hobbes to Hegel, it quickly became apparent that much of what comes down to us under the guise of political philosophy is not in fact political at all. Rather, in the assessment of Arendt, Castoriadis, Rancière, Abensour and others we have encountered, political philosophy has routinely functioned to conceal and obscure the political question, neutralise its polemics, resolve what it is that makes it inherently controversial. At least since Plato, that this tradition begins with a tenacious campaign against democracy is no coincidence. With but a few exceptions, political philosophers have consistently functioned to shelter rule from the problems of politics, supplant politics with reason, order, absolution, supply it a rational foundation, undermine its anarchic condition. This is emblematic of the paradigm that Abensour associates with 'State thought', the philosophy that organises its models and analyses around the terms and relations of the State, the sovereign, governor and governed, ruler and ruled. And yet, however pervasive across its history, contrary to Rancière, I have made the case that political philosophy's critical and emancipatory potential should not be discounted too quickly. Indeed, as we have seen, against the predominance of State thought, political philosophy can itself be placed against its very tradition, making *another political philosophy* possible, one that returns not to the foundations of its tradition but, as Abensour has appealed, to the *matters of politics* themselves, the problem of domination and the possibilities of emancipation. Abensour is not alone in this view. Castoriadis would likely remind us that it is no accident that politics and philosophy have a common origin, a common birthplace. They are but two expressions of the project of autonomy, a project first betrayed by Plato himself.[3] Throughout this study, we have encountered three general interpretations of philosophy useful to politics: philosophy as an enterprise of demystification (Deleuze); as interminable questioning (Lefort); as permanent critique (Abensour). If we follow Deleuze, perhaps what ultimately makes philosophy political is not so much the topics it examines or themes it considers, but the manner in which the concepts it generates can be put to use in a practical and critical way. As we have seen, it is certainly true for Abensour, who studied under Deleuze, that philosophy does indeed contain a political and emancipatory potential. According to Deleuze, philosophy is not a descriptive science. It does not strive to simply represent the world in thought. Rather, the task of philosophy is to navigate and evaluate particular problems of our own time, our own historical milieu. Lefort is therefore entirely correct to locate political inquiry in the *here and now*, but this in no way limits the work of philosophy to a simple matter of grasping the conditions of the present state of affairs. Rather, much like Nietzsche, Deleuze understands the first task of philosophy as being to counter, to challenge the present time and help us to *think against* it. This is the basis of what Nietzsche calls 'the untimely' and Abensour 'the utopian'. In each case, what is realised is a political expression of thinking against, a resistance to *what is*, a critique of the present in the hopes of a better future to come. This is the use of philosophy. It is here and in this sense that philosophy becomes political.

Thus, insofar as it represents a protracted exercise in concept construction, perhaps this study of democracy may ultimately be considered *Deleuzian*. Perhaps there is something about our own present time, our own *here and now*, that desperately calls for a new concept of democracy. By placing the against at the centre of its concept, my hope is that we may think democracy – its origins, aspirations and institutions – in new and productive ways. Along with a whole language of rights and equality, the concept of democracy can itself be fashioned as an instrument through which a comprehensive critique of the present may be initiated and carried out. For Abensour, essential to the meaning of emancipation is the permanent critique of domination. It is in this respect that he envisions political philosophy not simply as a theoretical discipline but, like Marx, as a tool with the power to *change*. This is the first objective of his own critical political philosophy.

Perhaps the problem of democracy inevitably becomes a philosophical one as soon as we arrive at that inescapable question: *How should democracy be thought?* This is the broader question that underlies this entire study. It is a question we have returned to again and again. As we discovered with Lefort, part of what democracy means is that there is no final word on its meaning. Democracy will refuse its mastery or monopolisation by a proclaimed authority or class of purported experts. This refusal is rendered explicit by what Lefort calls 'savage' democracy. Admittedly, my use of Lefort in this project may be found rather peculiar. Although he can certainly be read to theorise a democracy against the regimes of monarchy and totalitarianism, I have not drawn on Lefort to consider yet another model of the antinomies of politics. Instead, I have revisited those rather enigmatic references to savage democracy as an occasion to reflect upon the larger philosophical problem of *thinking* democracy itself, of organising its concept for political use. As Abensour testifies, savage democracy highlights the indetermination that stubbornly refuses to grant democracy finality, closure or resolution, raising the entire question of democracy over and over again. Loosening the constraints that so often circumscribe its limits, rather than define democracy with greater precision, we found savage democracy to throw the concept into question, keeping the idea of democracy unsettled and perpetually open. In Deleuze's terminology, perhaps savage democracy could be said to describe a democracy *deterritorialised*. From the French Revolution to May '68, while Lefort tends to utilise the 'savage' qualifier to illuminate those more transformative moments that punctuate democracy's modern history, its sheer indeterminacy will oblige his readers to incessantly return to the question of what is most essential to democracy itself. 'It is as if "savage" connotes the inexhaustible reserve of turmoil that soars above democracy.'[4] It cautions us not to reduce democracy to a government or institution too quickly. It prompts us to conceive democracy in terms of what it can do, what it can become and what it can transform. Accordingly, savage democracy not only functions to prevent the closure of the question of democracy, but also urges us to perpetually push our thinking of democracy ever further. By evoking everything that is revolutionary about democracy, the savage emancipates the concept from all the limitations that typically restrict and confine what democracy can be and what it can mean, allowing us to reimagine it according to its most creative and transformative dimensions and capacities. It is in this respect that savage democracy can be taken as something of a heuristic device, an exercise of thought. It is a symbol for the ambition, indeed the risk, of thinking democracy in unconventional ways. It means distancing its concept from those mitigated, domesticated representations of democracy so ubiquitous today. It means organising its concept according to its most uncompromised and resilient incarnation: its political acts of emancipation, its endless capacity for conflict and contestation, its enduring momentum towards a more participatory and egalitarian society. Such a concept is imperative to the theory of the antinomies of politics.

One of the implications of such a theory is that it appears to necessitate we revise our entire approach to politics. This was very much implicit in our initial point of departure. As Arendt recounts, where the tradition of political philosophy systematically fails is in its almost methodical obscuration of politics itself, its routine displacement of the problems of politics for the problems of government, sovereignty and the affairs of State. For Arendt, this underlying fixation with rule effectively cancels out the very basis of political inquiry from philosophy altogether, creating considerable challenges for thinking about politics in its own right. For this reason, she advocates the extraction of politics from various models of rule. This is just as essential to her own phenomenology of political activity as it is to our theory of democracy here. Politics cannot be reduced to a general framework dictated solely by the problem of how a given class of rulers, governors, sovereigns and kings are to exercise their rule over a community. Rather, following the example of Arendt, by circumventing the philosophical tradition and revisiting the historical origins of the term, we found that, in its original Greek inception, politics describes something quite different. Politics is not the foundation upon which one rules another; it is the condition in which the foundation of rule is called into question. Politics is that which renders the polis, its laws and institutions, inherently problematic. It is what renders controversial the very nature of government and who has the right to govern. It is here where we witness the etymological connection between 'polis', 'politics' and 'polemics'. As for Christian Meier, politics implies the *politicisation* of that which was not political before: it widens the community's inclusion in the deliberation of the affairs of the polis; it makes public the question of the public, common the question of the common. Politics reveals that there is no proper order of society, that the problem of the organisation of the social is one destined to remain unresolved in any absolute sense. To Castoriadis's point, there is no abstract model of society provided by nature or intended by the gods. There is no ultimate closure to the question of the good, the just, the true. What is so profound about the Greek invention of politics, therefore, is precisely what Plato cannot tolerate about it: politics exposes the polis and the representation of the polis to an irreducible field dictated only by the rule of *doxa* and *agon*. What the formal institution of *doxa* and *agon* unconditionally denies is that there somewhere exists an underlying truth of society, accessible, decipherable, realisable. The *political* society is the one that recognises, represents and, indeed, explicitly institutes the condition of its very indeterminacy, the contingency of the social, the lack of an absolute foundation. This is precisely the impetuous, unpredictable experience aboard Plato's allegorical ship of democracy. As Lefort illustrates so successfully, democracy's only foundation is the experience of indeterminacy itself, that which is not a proper foundation at all. This is why, beyond the politicisation of the polis, the making political what was not political before, politics may also describe a condition, the very condition that remains particular to democracy itself. This is the very condition that Plato decries as *anarchy*.

As we discovered, what isolates democracy from every other regime is its merciless dissolution of the archê. This is the universal of democracy's being-against. Democracy is against the archê wherever and whenever it appears. No meaningful sense of equality is possible as long as the archê remains intact, unchallenged. Equality is anarchic or it is nothing at all. The archê is that mysterious principle that haunts so much of political thought and analysis. At the basis of every hierarchy, every claim of privilege and priority, of a proper order of society, a proper allocation of parts and roles, it is there: posited, imposed, naturalised, rationalised. It functions not only to formally divide the categories of governor and governed, ruler and ruled, but to distribute the community across these categories according to some abstract standard or criterion. The archê therefore intends to resolve the problem of qualification, of entitlement, of who is entitled to rule. It claims to discover a basis, a genuine foundation for the reason why one rules another, the few rule the many. For this reason, it represents the closure of politics, the effacement of its condition. As soon as the archê is postulated theoretically, the organisation of the social is discerned a rational problem as opposed to a political one. This inaugurates a philosophical project of deciphering the grounds, the underlying principles, which claim to account for various hierarchical relations and systems of rule. But, as Plato observes with great clarity, democracy is that strange anomaly which not only lacks a proper archê itself, but operates to undermine the archê of every other order. What it disputes, what it renders intrinsically problematic, is the very basis upon which any such entitlement to rule may be ultimately established. By disrupting the foundations upon which rulers distinguish themselves from the rest of the community, democracy reveals the inherent artificiality and arbitrariness of every hierarchical relation. By exposing the essential groundlessness upon which the apparatus of rule is constructed, it reveals the sheer contingency of every social order. As John Keane will attest, democracy involves the *denaturing* of power. It demonstrates that, whether it be birth, wealth, virtue or expertise, every conventional standard to rule is just that: convention and convention alone. This is why Rancière can uncover an essential anarchy beneath every hierarchical relation, an underlying equality implicit in every system of inequality. Democracy is that which replaces the order of the archê with the order of politics. It not only deposits the problems of the polis in the hands of the community itself, but also institutes those problems in such a way that they remain political and ultimately irreducible. Democracy is not the rule of the demos. It is that which challenges the very division between ruler and ruled. This is what it means to be against the archê.

As preserved in its very name, democracy is that without archê, without measure. As such, it can make no claim, no reference to any principle or standard of rule. Beyond the field of politics itself, it has recourse to no foundation, no frame of reference which may validate its claims or justify its institutions. Democracy can provide no absolution, no guarantee. There is simply no proper archê of the demos to which the demos may appeal. Indeed, the generality or indecipherability of 'the demos' renders the very logic of the archê inoperative. This is precisely what is expressed by Rancière's 'anarchic title' and Abensour's 'demos as a whole'. Rather, from ancient times, democracy means only this: the *power of the people* (the *kratos* of the demos). But in this respect, what exactly is meant by 'power' and, more importantly, what is meant by 'people' is something that appears destined to remain indeterminate. This is not simply a consequence of democracy. This is the basis of its strategy. Accordingly, perhaps this entire study could be read as a series of interpretations of what the *power of the people* can mean, in different contexts, at different moments: the *power of the people* is the power of those without title or qualification to subvert and destroy the archê, making problematic the very foundation that divides governor and governed, ruler and ruled, revealing an underlying anarchic equality (Chapter 2); the *power of the people* is the power of the excluded, the marginalised, the *invisible* to manifest a political subject and dispute the categories, classifications and distributions of the police, frustrating its symbolic representation of society and creating new possibilities of perception (Chapter 4); the *power of the people* is the power of those subject to the State to reduce its unifying, totalising structure to but a single moment of the demos, generating alternative social arrangements, new public spaces and new forms of social bonds (Chapter 5). These interpretations are in no way contradictory. Nor are they exhaustive. On the contrary, particularly in the modern world, the expression of the *power of the people* appears to take on multiple forms, in different places, at different times. As Lefort and Rancière seem to concur, the experience of modern democracy is one of increasing political conflicts engendered by an increasingly diverse body of actors unfolding at increasingly divergent regions of society. Who the subject of democracy may be, the objects that democracy concerns and the spaces where democracy occurs all appear, in its modern incarnation, to be broadened exponentially. Perhaps this is what ultimately distinguishes modern democracy from its ancient antecedent. In this regard, perhaps the precise meaning of the *power of the people* can only be appreciated against the backdrop of its particular struggle, its particular objective, its particular mode of being-against. Beyond the politics of Athens, this remains a testament to the proliferation of the against and its forms in the modern world.

And yet, as the *power of the people*, democracy cannot be thought a natural or inevitable process of a society. It requires a subject, and it is only through the agency of a subject that its challenge to what it is against may be initiated and set in motion. This is particularly important for Rancière. In *Disagreement*, Rancière defines democracy in terms of a political mode of subjectivation, the manifestation of a subject that disputes the prevailing distribution of the social via a defiant claim of equality. Although at times this definition may appear rather narrow, it serves as an important reminder that the underlying agents of democracy, its powers or forces, must ultimately be located in the political activity of a subject. Traditionally this subject is known as the demos, but, as Rancière demonstrates, it may adopt many names. According to Rancière, the political subject is not a sociological entity; it cannot be ascertained by demographic, identity or interest. Nor is the political subject bound necessarily to a specific set of conditions, social, historical or economic. Akin to the 'principle of anarchy' to which Abensour appeals, both its origin and destination can never be known in advance. Rather, Rancière regards the appearance of the political subject as something unpredictable, incalculable, *accidental*. Whenever the marginalised, the excluded, the poor, abandon their allotted status, part or position and challenge the prevailing categories of a given social order, a distinct political subject comes into being. The political subject is that which imposes itself on those very places and times to which it does not belong. It is that which makes itself of some account. It makes problematic what was not problematic before. It throws the established correspondence between bodies, spaces, roles and functions back on its own inherent contingency, transforming at once the identity of the subject itself as well as its prescribed relations, limits and parameters in society. For Rancière, this is an act of dissensus, the enactment of a wrong. What Rancière provides this study, therefore, is a working theory of the subject. It concerns the question of agency, of instrumentality, that which Althusser inexcusably ignores. Even beyond the scope of Rancière's model, this is essential for locating the against more generally. In democracy, more than an institution, the against is embodied in the activity of a subject. It is through the subject that the against primarily finds expression. Being-against is a subject acting. It is therefore quite phenomenal. It can be seen and it can be heard. It has a name and it has a face. It is voiced, demonstrated, performed, by one or by many, in public buildings or in the streets. It intervenes, opposes, contests and protests. It calls into question and it holds to account. In this regard, if Abensour associates democracy with the qualities of spontaneity, free creation and ongoing self-institution, it is because democracy remains inextricably bound to the demos as a *living* subject.

At the same time, this emphasis on the subject and the agency of the subject does not intend to diminish the significance of institutions. As we saw with Abensour, even an 'insurgent' democracy is aided by a robust institutional engagement. An institution is a *system of anticipation*, an organisation of means; it provides a positive model for action, a *way* of acting or acting in concert. It is therefore quite senseless to oppose democracy and institutions in general. Rather, my argument is simply that democracy remains irreducible to its institutions and cannot be defined by them. However its institutions are organised and arranged, there is always something of democracy that exceeds them. Consequently, the institutional question is one that does not anticipate democracy, but logically follows from it. The question must be framed in terms of *which* institutions best serve democracy and which do not, *which* institutions best express democracy and which do not. When can an institution be considered democratic? Quite simply, a 'democratic' institution is one that facilitates, fosters and sustains democracy's radical democratising initiatives as opposed to neutralising, curtailing or inhibiting them. Democracy seeks out institutions that bolster and broaden its project of democratisation. The very concept of democratisation implies that the limits of democracy are never absolute, never determined in advance. As a politics of transformation, democratisation means just that: perpetually confronting its own arbitrary limits. The impetus of this process, its motive force, is the against. The against, it could be said, situates democracy precisely according to its margins, according to what obstructs, denies or negates it. This is why it is so crucial for a theory of democracy to closely examine the objects it confronts and disputes in society. In the final chapters, we considered two such objects in detail: the *police* and the *State*. While other models of the antinomies of politics could have been considered, there is something of these two objects that appears to merit particular attention. As theorised by Rancière, the problem of the police is emblematic of the aspiration to implement the proper order of society. The police can be taken as a symbol for the harmonious, productive society sheltered from the complications of politics, the well-managed, well-regulated community that functions without disruption or dispute. It determines what is public and what is private, who is included and who is excluded, who can be seen and heard and who remains invisible. The police is a regime of representation, a government of the sensible, an administration and management of what is visible, what is thinkable and what is possible. It not only concerns the distribution of the social, but its symbolic constitution, the very modes of perception that render such a distribution intelligible. Likewise, as theorised by Abensour, the problem of the State is emblematic of the socio-historical phenomenon of political alienation. The State is the constitution of the social abstracted from the political dimension of its very institution and thus isolated from the demos as its originary subject. As a moment of the demos reified, it represents the crystallisation of its creative, self-instituting activity, its everlasting invention and innovation. The State is a system of integration, unification and mediation that elevates itself over and beyond the plurality of the demos. As an abstract organising principle, a total that dominates its parts, it not only assumes autonomy over the demos, but monopolises its particular moments as a universal form. For this reason, as we saw with Clastres, it is a form that very much facilitates the concentration of power, the isolation of the organs of power from the whole community. Clearly, the challenges that the police and the State present to the project of democracy are considerable. And yet, for Rancière and Abensour, they are precisely what animate and reanimate a defiant and resilient democracy against. As Abensour proclaims on more than one occasion: 'democracy is the always possible emergence of human struggle.' More than any other statement, perhaps this best encapsulates the meaning of the antinomies of politics.

Perhaps the lesson of Machiavelli is that politics must always remain a question particular to the *here and now* (*hic et nunc*). It must be grounded firmly in the present, according to the conditions and situations of today. Likewise, perhaps the lesson of Nietzsche is that philosophy must always remain contrary to the present. It must counter *what is* and help us to think against it. As I have argued throughout, this is precisely how the practice of philosophy should be approached. A *political* philosophy is one that puts its concepts to use, as a critical tool, as a means to critique the present. The concept of democracy must be organised accordingly. As a concept, democracy need not simply represent the society that so boastfully calls itself a 'democracy' today. It can be forged an instrument of critique. It can help us evaluate the present state of our institutions and relations. It can help us identify modes of domination and strategies of emancipation. It can help us clarify how we desire the future of our society to be. It can help us resist the existing order and participate in its transformation. Without question, the first two decades of the twenty-first century have experienced no shortage of social turmoil and civil unrest. In addition to the Arab Spring and Occupy Wall Street which captured much attention, we have witnessed pro-democratic activism in Hong Kong, the Gulabi Gang in India, the Yellow Vest protests in France, anti-austerity movements in Greece and Spain, Black Lives Matter in the United States, Idle No More in Canada and, most recently, the profound resistance to the theocratic regime in the streets of Iran. But, at the same time, we have also witnessed a distressing rise in populism, the increasing prominence of right-wing nationalism, the troubling ascendancy of figures like Donald Trump and the widespread vilification of Muslims, immigrants and refugees. It would appear, therefore, that for the present moment and for the foreseeable future, we will have much to critique. And democracy will have much to be against.

Notes

1. Henry James, 'Democracy and Its Issues', *Lectures and Miscellanies* (New York: Redfield, 1852), 1–2.
2. Ibid., 4.
3. This is a major theme in Castoriadis. See, for example, the essays contained in Cornelius Castoriadis, *Philosophy, Politics, Autonomy* (New York: Oxford University Press, 1991).
4. Miguel Abensour, '"Savage Democracy" and the "Principle of Anarchy"', *Democracy against the State: Marx and the Machiavellian Moment* (Cambridge: Polity, 2011), 106.

Bibliography

Abélès, Marc. *Thinking beyond the State*. Translated by Phillip Rousseau and Marie-Claude Haince. Ithaca: Cornell University Press, 2017.
Abensour, Miguel. 'Against the Sovereignty of Philosophy over Politics: Arendt's Reading of Plato's Cave Allegory.' Translated by Martin Breaugh. *Social Research* vol. 74, no. 4 (Winter 2007): 955–82.
Abensour, Miguel. 'An-archy between Metapolitics and Politics.' *Parallax* vol. 8, no. 3 (2002): 5–18.
Abensour, Miguel. *Democracy against the State: Marx and the Machiavellian Moment*. Translated by Max Blechman and Martin Breaugh. Cambridge: Polity, 2011.
Abensour, Miguel. 'De quel retour s'agit-il?' *Les Cahiers de Philosophie* no. 18 (1994): 5–8.
Abensour, Miguel (ed.). *L'Esprit des lois sauvages: Pierre Clastres ou une nouvelle anthropologie politique*. Paris: Seuil, 1987.
Abensour, Miguel. *Hannah Arendt contre la philosophie politique?* Paris: Sens & Tonka, 2006.
Abensour, Miguel. 'The History of Utopia and the Destiny of Its Critique.' In *Political Uses of Utopia: New Marxist, Anarchist, and Radical Democratic Perspectives*. Edited by S. D. Chrostowska and James D. Ingram. New York: Columbia University Press, 2016.
Abensour, Miguel. *L'Homme est un animal utopique: utopiques II*. Paris: Sens & Tonka, 2013.
Abensour, Miguel. 'Is There a Proper Way to Use the Voluntary Servitude Hypothesis?' Translated by Roald Creagh. *Journal of Political Ideology* vol. 16, no. 3 (2011): 329–48.
Abensour, Miguel. 'Lettre d'un "révoltiste" à Marcel Gauchet converti à la "politique normale".' *Réfractions* no. 12 (2004): 159–64.
Abensour, Miguel. 'Philosophie politique critique et émancipation?' *Politique et Sociétés* vol. 22, no. 3 (2003): 119–42.

Abensour, Miguel. 'Persistent Utopia.' Translated by James Ingram. *Constellations* vol. 15, no. 3 (2008): 406–21.
Abensour, Miguel. *Pour une philosophie politique critique*. Paris: Sens & Tonka, 2009.
Abensour, Miguel. *Utopia: From Thomas More to Walter Benjamin*. Translated by Raymond N. MacKenzie. Minneapolis: Univocal, 2017.
Abensour, Miguel. *Utopiques II*. Paris: Sens & Tonka, 2013.
Abensour, Miguel and Michel Enaudeau. *La Communauté politique des 'tous uns': désir de liberté, désir d'utopie*. Paris: Belles Lettres, 2014.
Abensour, Miguel, Jean-Luc Nancy and Jacques Rancière. 'Instances démocratiques.' *Vacarme* vol. 48, no. 3 (Summer 2009): 8–17.
Agamben, Giorgio et al. *Democracy in What State?* Translated by William McCuaig. New York: Columbia University Press, 2011.
Althusser, Louis. *Machiavelli and Us*. Translated by Gregory Elliot. London: Verso, 1999.
Apperley, Alan. 'Hobbes on Democracy.' *Politics* vol. 19, no. 3 (September 1999): 165–71.
Arendt, Hannah. *Between Past and Future*. London: Penguin Books, 2006.
Arendt, Hannah. *The Human Condition*. Chicago: University of Chicago Press, 1998.
Arendt, Hannah. *On Revolution*. London: Penguin Books, 2006.
Arendt, Hannah. *The Promise of Politics*. Edited by Jerome Kohn. New York: Schocken Books, 2005.
Aristotle. *The Politics and The Constitution of Athens*. Edited by Stephen Everson. Cambridge: Cambridge University Press, 1996.
Badiou, Alain. *Metapolitics*. Translated by Jason Barker. London: Verso, 2005.
Benhabib, Seyla (ed.). *Democracy and Difference: Contesting the Boundaries of the Political*. Princeton: Princeton University Press, 1996.
Bilakovics, Steven. *Democracy without Politics*. Cambridge: Harvard University Press, 2012.
Bourg, Julian. *From Revolution to Ethics: May 1968 and Contemporary French Thought*. Montreal: McGill-Queen's University Press, 2007.
Bowman, Paul and Richard Stamp (eds). *Reading Rancière*. London: Continuum International Publishing Group, 2011.
Braeckman, Antoon. 'The Hermeneutics of Society: On the State in Lefort's Political Theory.' *Constellations* vol. 25, no. 2 (June 2018): 242–55.
Breaugh, Martin. 'Critique de la domination, pensée de l'émancipation. Sur la philosophie politique de Miguel Abensour.' *Politique et Sociétés* vol. 22, no. 3 (2003): 45–69.
Breaugh, Martin. *The Plebeian Experience: A Discontinuous History of Political Freedom*. Translated by Lazer Lederhendler. New York: Columbia University Press, 2013.

Breaugh, Martin, Christopher Holman et al., *Thinking Radical Democracy: The Return to Politics in Postwar France*. Toronto: University of Toronto Press, 2015.

Breckman, Warren. *Adventures of the Symbolic: Post-Marxism and Radical Democracy*. New York: Columbia University Press, 2013.

Burchell, Graham, Colin Gordon and Peter Miller (eds). *The Foucault Effect: Studies in Governmentality*. Chicago: University of Chicago Press, 1991.

Caillé, Alain. 'Claude Lefort, the Social Sciences and Political Philosophy.' *Thesis Eleven* vol. 43, no. 1 (1995): 48–65.

Castoriadis, Cornelius. *The Castoriadis Reader*. Edited by David A. Curtis. Oxford: Blackwell Publishers, 1997.

Castoriadis, Cornelius. *Ce qui fait la Grèce. 1 D'Homère à Héraclite*. Paris: Seuil, 2004.

Castoriadis, Cornelius. *Figures of the Thinkable*. Translated by Helen Arnold. Stanford: Stanford University Press, 2007.

Castoriadis, Cornelius. *Philosophy, Politics, Autonomy*. Edited by David A. Curtis. New York: Oxford University Press, 1991.

Cervera-Marzal, Manuel. *Miguel Abensour: critique de la domination, pensée de l'émancipation*. Paris: Sens & Tonka, 2013.

Cervera-Marzal, Manuel and Nicolas Poirier. *Désir d'utopie: politique et émancipation avec Miguel Abensour*. Paris: L'Harmattan, 2018.

Chambers, Samuel A. 'Jacques Rancière and the Problem of Pure Politics.' *European Journal of Political Theory* vol. 10, no. 3 (July 2011): 303–26.

Chollet, Antoine. 'L'énigme de la démocratie sauvage.' *Esprit* no. 451 (January–February 2019): 136–46.

Chomsky, Noam. *Chomsky on Anarchism*. Edited by Barry Pateman. Oakland: AK Press, 2005.

Churchich, Nicholas. *Marxism and Alienation*. Rutherford: Fairleigh Dickinson University Press, 1990.

Clastres, Pierre. *Archaeology of Violence*. Translated by Jeanine Herman. Los Angeles: Semiotext(e), 2010.

Clastres, Pierre. *Society against the State: Essays in Political Anthropology*. Translated by Robert Hurley. New York: Zone Books, 1987.

Colletti, Lucio. *From Rousseau to Lenin: Studies in Ideology and Society*. Translated by John Merrington and Judith White. New York: Monthly Review Press, 1974.

Curtis, Bruce. 'Foucault on Governmentality and Population: The Impossible Discovery.' *The Canadian Journal of Sociology* vol. 27, no. 4 (Autumn 2002): 505–33.

Dallmayr, Fred. 'Postmetaphysics and Democracy.' *Political Theory* vol. 21, no. 1 (February 1993): 101–27.

Davis, Oliver. *Jacques Rancière*. Cambridge: Polity, 2010.

Dean, Jodi. 'Politics without Politics.' *Parallax* vol. 15, no. 3 (2009): 20–36.

Deleixhe, Martin. 'La démocratie radicale et la critique du marxisme.' *Raisons politiques*, vol. 75, no. 3 (2019): 29–44.
Deleuze, Gilles. *Difference and Repetition*. Translated by Paul Patton. London: Continuum, 2001.
Deleuze, Gilles. 'Instincts and Institutions.' *Desert Islands and Other Texts*. Translated by Michael Taormina. Los Angeles: Semiotext(e), 2004.
Deleuze, Gilles. *Nietzsche and Philosophy*. Translated by Hugh Tomlinson. New York: Columbia University Press, 2006.
Deleuze, Gilles and Félix Guattari. *A Thousand Plateaus: Capitalism and Schizophrenia*. Translated by Brian Massumi. Minneapolis: University of Minnesota Press, 1987.
Deleuze, Gilles and Félix Guattari. *What is Philosophy?* Translated by Hugh Tomlinson and Graham Burchell. New York: Columbia University Press, 1994.
Deranty, Jean-Philippe (ed.). *Jacques Rancière: Key Concepts*. Durham, NC: Acumen Publishing Limited, 2010.
Deranty, Jean-Philippe. 'Jacques Rancière's Contribution to the Ethics of Recognition.' *Political Theory* vol. 31, no. 1 (February 2003): 136–56.
Deranty, Jean-Philippe. 'Rancière and Contemporary Political Ontology.' *Theory and Event* vol. 6, no. 4 (2003).
Deranty, Jean-Philippe and Alison Ross (eds). *Jacques Rancière and the Contemporary Scene: The Philosophy of Radical Equality*. London: Continuum International Publishers, 2012.
Derrida, Jacques. *Specters of Marx: The State of the Debt, The Work of Mourning, and the New International*. Translated by Peggy Kamuf. New York: Routledge, 2006.
Erfani, Farhang. 'Fixing Marx with Machiavelli: Claude Lefort's Democratic Turn.' *Journal of the British Society for Phenomenology* vol. 39, no. 2 (May 2008): 200–14.
Ferguson, Adam. *An Essay on the History of Civil Society*. Edited by Fania Oz Salzberger. New York: Cambridge University Press, 1995.
Ferrari, G. R. F. *City and Soul in Plato's Republic*. Chicago: University of Chicago Press, 2005.
Fine, Robert. *Political Investigations: Hegel, Marx, Arendt*. London: Routledge, 2001.
Finley, M. I. *Democracy Ancient and Modern*. New Brunswick: Rutgers University Press, 1985.
Flynn, Bernard. 'Democracy and Ontology.' *Research in Phenomenology* vol. 38, no. 2 (2008): 216–27.
Flynn, Bernard. *The Philosophy of Claude Lefort: Interpreting the Political*. Evanston: Northwestern University Press, 2005.
Foucault, Michel. *The History of Sexuality Volume I: An Introduction*. Translated by Robert Hurley. New York: Vintage Books, 1990.
Foucault, Michel. *Power: Essential Works of Foucault 1954–1984 Volume 3*. Edited by James D. Faubion. New York: The New Press, 2000.

Foucault, Michel. *Security, Territory, Population: Lectures at the Collège de France, 1977–1978*. Edited by Michel Senellart. New York: Picador/Palgrave Macmillan, 2007.

Frausto, Obed, Jason Powell and Sarah Vitale (eds). *The Weariness of Democracy: Confronting the Failure of Liberal Democracy*. Cham, Switzerland: Palgrave Macmillan, 2020.

Gauchet, Marcel. *La Condition historique*. Paris: Stock, 2003.

Geenens, Raf. 'Democracy, Human Rights and History: Reading Lefort.' *European Journal of Political Theory* vol. 7, no. 3 (July 2008): 269–86.

Gerçek, Salih Emre. 'From Body to Flesh: Lefort, Merleau-Ponty, and Democratic Indeterminacy.' *European Journal of Political Theory* vol. 19, no. 4 (2017): 571–92.

Godway, Eleanor M. 'Wild Being, the Prepredicative and Expression: How Merleau-Ponty Uses Phenomenology to Develop an Ontology.' *Man and World* vol. 26, no. 4 (1993): 389–401.

Goldman, Samuel. 'Beyond the Markers of Certainty: Thoughts on Claude Lefort and Leo Strauss.' *Perspectives on Political Science* vol. 40, no. 1 (2011): 27–34.

Grollios, Vasilis. 'Marx and Engels' Critique of Democracy: The Materialist Character of their Concept of Autonomy.' *Critique* vol. 39, no. 1 (2011): 9–26.

Guthrie, William Keith Chambers. *A History of Greek Philosophy, Vol. 1: The Earlier Presocratics and the Pythagoreans*. Cambridge: Cambridge University Press, 2000.

Hall, Robert W. *Political Thinkers: Plato*. London: G. Allen & Unwin, 1981.

Hallward, Peter. 'Jacques Rancière and the Subversion of Mastery.' *Paragraph* vol. 28, no. 1 (March 2005): 26–45.

Hallward, Peter. 'Staging Equality.' *New Left Review* vol. 37 (January–February 2006): 109–29 Hamilton, Alexander, James Madison and John Jay. *The Federalist*. Cambridge: Cambridge University Press, 2003.

Hardimon, Michael O. 'The Project of Reconciliation: Hegel's Social Philosophy.' *Philosophy & Public Affairs* vol. 21, no. 2 (Spring 1992): 165–95.

Hegel, G. W. F. *Elements of the Philosophy of Right*. Translated by T. M. Knox. London: Oxford University Press, 1962.

Hendley, Steven. 'Reconsidering the Limits of Democracy with Castoriadis and Lefort.' *Reinterpreting the Political: Continental Philosophy and Political Theory*. Edited by Lenore Langsdorf, Stephen H. Watson and Karen A. Smith. Albany: State University of New York Press, 1998.

Hewlett, Nick. *Badiou, Balibar, Rancière: Rethinking Emancipation*. London: Continuum International Publishing Group, 2007.

Hobbes, Thomas. *Leviathan: Parts One and Two*. Upper Saddle River: Prentice-Hall 1958.

Hobbes, Thomas. *On the Citizen*. Edited by Richard Tuck and Michael Siverthorne. Cambridge: Cambridge University Press, 1998.

Holman, Christopher. 'Machiavelli's Two Utopias.' *Utopian Studies* vol. 29, no. 1 (2018): 88–108.

Honneth, Axel and Jacques Ranciére. *Recognition or Disagreement: A Critical Encounter on the Politics of Freedom, Equality, and Identity*. Edited by Katia Genel and Jean-Philippe Deranty. New York: Columbia University Press, 2016.

Howard, Dick. *The Primacy of the Political: A History of Political Thought from the Greeks to the French and American Revolutions*. New York: Columbia University Press, 2010.

Howard, Dick. *The Specter of Democracy*. New York: Columbia University Press, 2002.

Ieven, Bram. 'Heteroreductives – Rancière's Disagreement with Ontology.' *Parallax* vol. 15, no. 3 (2009): 50–62.

Inda, Jonathan Xavier (ed.). *Anthropologies of Modernity: Foucault, Governmentality, and Life Politics*. Malden: Blackwell Publishing, 2005.

Ingram, James D. 'The Politics of Claude Lefort's Political: Between Liberalism and Radical Democracy.' *Thesis Eleven* vol. 87, no. 1 (2006): 33–50.

Ingram, James D. *Radical Cosmopolitics: The Ethics and Politics of Democratic Universalism*. New York: Columbia University Press, 2013.

James, Henry. *Lectures and Miscellanies*. New York: Redfield, 1852.

Kant, Immanuel. *Political Writings*. Edited by H. S. Reiss. Cambridge: Cambridge University Press, 1991.

Kantorowicz, Ernst. *The King's Two Bodies: A Study in Mediaeval Political Theology*. Princeton: Princeton University Press, 1957.

Keane, John. *The Life and Death of Democracy*. London: Simon & Schuster, 2009.

Kupiec, Anne and Étienne Tassin (eds). *Critique de la politique. Autour de Miguel Abensour*. Paris: Sens & Tonka, 2006.

Labelle, Gilles. 'La philosophie politique et le "choix du petit" dans le travail de Miguel Abensour.' *Monde commun* vol. 1, no. 1 (Autumn 2007): 44–63.

Labelle, Gilles. 'Two Refoundation Projects of Democracy in Contemporary French Philosophy: Cornelius Castoriadis and Jacques Rancière.' *Philosophy and Social Criticism* vol. 27, no. 4 (2001): 75–103.

Laclau, Ernesto and Chantal Mouffe. *Hegemony and Socialist Strategy: Towards a Radical Democratic Politics*. London: Verso, 2001.

Lefort, Claude. *Complications: Communism and the Dilemmas of Democracy*. Translated by Julian Bourg. New York: Columbia University Press, 2007.

Lefort, Claude. *Democracy and Political Theory*. Translated by David Macey. Minneapolis: University of Minnesota Press, 1988.

Lefort, Claude. *Éléments d'une critique de la bureaucratie*. Paris: Gallimard, 1979.
Lefort, Claude. *Machiavelli in the Making*. Translated by Michael B. Smith. Evanston: Northwestern University Press, 2012.
Lefort, Claude. *The Political Forms of Modern Society: Bureaucracy, Democracy, Totalitarianism*. Edited by John B. Thompson. Cambridge, MA: MIT Press, 1986.
Lefort, Claude. 'Reflexions sociologiques sur Machiavel et Marx: la politique et le réel.' In *Les Formes de l' histoire*. Paris: Gallimard, Folio-Essais, 2000.
Lefort, Claude. *Le Temps présent: Écrits 1945–2005*. Paris: Belin, 2007.
Lefort, Claude. *Writing: The Political Test*. Translated by David A. Curtis. Durham, NC: Duke University Press, 2000.
Lefort, Claude and *Anti-mythes*. 'An Interview with Claude Lefort.' Translated by Dorothy Gehrke and Brian Singer. *Telos* no. 30 (1976): 173–92.
Lefort, Claude and Pierre Rosanvallon. 'The Test of the Political: A Conversation with Claude Lefort.' *Constellations* vol. 19, no. 1 (March 2012): 4–15.
Lefort, Claude and Paul Thibaud. 'La communication démocratique.' *Esprit* no. 9–10 (September–October 1979): 34–44.
Legros, Martin. 'Qu'est-ce que la démocratie *sauvage*? De Claude Lefort à Miguel Abensour.' In *Critique de la politique. Autour de Miguel Abensour*. Edited by Anne Kupiec and Étienne Tassin. Paris: Sens & Tonka, 2006.
Lemke, Thomas. 'Foucault, Governmentality, and Critique.' *Rethinking Marxism* vol. 14, no. 3 (2002): 49–64.
Lévêque, Pierre and Pierre Vidal-Naquet. *Cleisthenes the Athenian: An Essay on the Representation of Space and Time in Greek Political Thought from the End of the Sixth Century to the Death of Plato*. Translated by David A. Curtis. Atlantic Highlands: Humanities Press, 1996.
Lévi-Strauss, Claude. *The Savage Mind*. Chicago: University of Chicago Press, 1966.
Levitas, Ruth. *Utopia as Method: The Imaginary Reconstitution of Society*. Houndmills and New York: Palgrave Macmillan, 2013.
Lummis, C. Douglas. *Radical Democracy*. Ithaca: Cornell University Press, 1996.
Machiavelli, Niccolò. *The Discourses*. Edited by Bernard R. Crick. London: Penguin Books, 2003.
Machiavelli, Niccolò. *The Prince*. Translated by Harvey C. Mansfield. Chicago: Chicago University Press, 1998.
Manent, Pierre. *Tocqueville and the Nature of Democracy*. Translated by John Waggoner. Lanham: Rowman & Littlefield, 1996.
Marchart, Oliver. *Post-foundational Political Thought: Political Difference in Nancy, Lefort, Badiou and Laclau*. Edinburgh: Edinburgh University Press, 2007.

Markell, Parchen. 'The Rule of the People: Arendt, Archê, and Democracy.' *The American Political Science Review* vol. 100, no. 1 (February 2006): 1–14.
Marx, Karl. *Early Writings*. Translated by Rodney Livingstone and Gregor Benton. London: Penguin Books, 1992.
Marx, Karl. *Later Political Writings*. Translated by Terrell Carver. Cambridge: Cambridge University Press, 1996.
May, Todd. 'Jacques Rancière and the Ethics of Equality.' *SubStance* vol. 36, no. 2, iss. 13 (2007): 20–36.
May, Todd. *The Political Thought of Jacques Rancière: Creating Equality*. University Park: Pennsylvania State University Press, 2008.
May, Todd. 'Rancière and Anarchism', in *Jacques Rancière and the Contemporary Scene: The Philosophy of Radical Equality*. Edited by Jean-Philippe Deranty and Alison Ross (London: Continuum International Publishers, 2012), 117–28.
Mazzocchi, Paul. 'Excavating Abensour: The Dialectics of Democracy and Utopia at a Standstill.' *Constellations* vol. 22, no. 2 (June 2015): 290–301.
Mazzocchi, Paul. 'Insurgent Democracy and the German Councils.' In *The German Revolution and Political Theory*. Edited by Gaard Kets and James Muldoon. Cham, Switzerland: Palgrave Macmillan, 2019.
McCormick, John P. *Machiavellian Democracy*. Cambridge: Cambridge University Press, 2011.
McLoughlin, Daniel. 'Post-Marxism and the Politics of Human Rights: Lefort, Badiou, Agamben, Rancière.' *Law Critique* vol. 27, no. 3 (2016): 303–21.
McSweeney, John. 'Giving Politics an Edge: Rancière and the Anarchic Principle of Democracy.' *Sofia Philosophical Review* vol. 3, no. 1 (2009): 113–36.
Meier, Christian. *The Greek Discovery of Politics*. Translated by David McLintock. Cambridge: Harvard University Press, 1990.
Merleau-Ponty, Maurice. *The Visible and the Invisible*. Translated by Alphonso Lingis. Evanston: Northwestern University Press, 1968.
Miliband, Ralph. 'Marx and the State.' *The Socialist Register* vol. 2 (1965): 278–96.
Moore, J. M. *Aristotle and Xenophon on Democracy and Oligarchy: Translations with Introductions and Commentary*. London: Chatto & Windus, 1975.
Morin, Edgar, Claude Lefort and Jean-Marc Coudray. *Mai 1968: la Brèche*. Paris: Fayard, 1968.
Mouffe, Chantal. *The Democratic Paradox*. London: Verso, 2000.
Nadir, Christine. 'Utopian Studies, Environmental Literature, and the Legacy of an Idea: Educating Desire in Miguel Abensour and Ursula K. Le Guin.' *Utopian Studies* vol. 21, no. 1 (2010): 24–56.

Nancy, Jean-Luc. *The Truth of Democracy*. Translated by Pascale-Anne Brault and Michael Naas. New York: Fordham University Press, 2010.
Nelson, Bryan. 'New Earth, New People: Deleuze, Democracy and the Politics of the Future.' In *Movements in Time: Revolution, Social Justice and Times of Change*. Edited by Cecile Lawrence and Natalie Churn. Cambridge: Cambridge Scholars Publishing, 2012.
Nietzsche, Friedrich. *Untimely Meditations*. Translated by R. J. Hollingdale. Cambridge: Cambridge University Press, 2011.
Ober, Josiah. *The Athenian Revolution: Essays on Ancient Greek Democracy and Political Theory*. Princeton: Princeton University Press, 1996.
Ober, Josiah. 'The Original Meaning of 'Democracy': Capacity to Do Things, Not Majority Rule.' *Constellations* vol. 15, no. 1 (2008): 3–9.
Pappas, Nickolas. *Plato and the Republic*. London: Routledge, 1995.
Plato. *Complete Works*. Edited by John M. Cooper and D. S. Hutchinson. Indianapolis: Hackett Publishing Company, 1997.
Plot, Martín (ed.). *Claude Lefort: Thinker of the Political*. Houndmills, Basingstoke, Hampshire: Macmillan Publishers Limited, 2013.
Pocock, J. G. A. *The Machiavellian Moment: Florentine Political Thought and the Atlantic Republican Tradition*. Princeton: Princeton University Press, 2003.
Polybius, *The Histories: Books 5–8*. Translated by W. R. Paton. Cambridge: Harvard University Press, 1972.
Popper, Karl. *The Open Society and Its Enemies*. Princeton and Oxford: Princeton University Press, 2013.
Rancière, Jacques. *Althusser's Lesson*. Translated by Emiliano Battista. London: Continuum, 2011.
Rancière, Jacques. 'Democracy Means Equality.' *Radical Philosophy* vol. 82 (March 1997): 29–36.
Rancière, Jacques. *Disagreement: Politics and Philosophy*. Translated by Julie Rose. Minneapolis: University of Minnesota Press, 1999.
Rancière, Jacques. *Dissensus: On Politics and Aesthetics*. Translated by Steven Corcoran. London: Continuum, 2010.
Rancière, Jacques. 'From Politics to Aesthetics?' *Paragraph* vol. 28 (March 2005): 13–25.
Rancière, Jacques. *Hatred of Democracy*. Translated by Steve Corcoran London: Verso, 2007.
Rancière, Jacques. *The Ignorant Schoolmaster: Five Lessons in Intellectual Emancipation*. Translated by Kristin Ross. Stanford: Stanford University Press, 1991.
Rancière, Jacques. 'Introducing Disagreement.' Translated by Steven Corcoran. *Angelaki: Journal of the Theoretical Humanities* vol. 9, no. 3 (December 2004): 3–9.

Rancière, Jacques. 'Is There a Deleuzian Aesthetics?' Translated by Radmila Djordjevic. *Qui Parle* vol. 14, no. 2 (Spring/Summer 2004): 1–14.

Rancière, Jacques. *The Method of Equality: Interviews with Laurent Jeanpierre and Dork Zabunyan*. Malden: Polity Press, 2016.

Rancière, Jacques. *On the Shores of Politics*. Translated by Liz Heron. London: Verso, 2007.

Rancière, Jacques. *The Philosopher and His Poor*. Translated by John Drury, Corinne Oster and Andrew Parker. Durham, NC: Duke University Press, 2003.

Rancière, Jacques. 'Politics, Identification, and Subjectivization.' *October* vol. 61 (Summer 1992): 58–64.

Rancière, Jacques. *The Politics of Aesthetics: The Distribution of the Sensible*. Translated by Gabriel Rockhill. London: Continuum, 2004.

Rancière, Jacques, Max Blechman, Anita Chari and Rafeeq Hasan. 'Democracy, Dissensus and the Aesthetics of Class Struggle: An Exchange with Jacques Rancière.' *Historical Materialism* vol. 13, no. 4 (2005): 285–301.

Rancière, Jacques, Todd May, Benjamin Noys and Saul Newman. 'Democracy, Anarchism and Radical Politics Today: An Interview with Jacques Rancière.' *Anarchist Studies* vol. 16, no. 2 (2008): 173–85.

Rancière, Jacques and Davide Panagia. 'Dissenting Words: A Conversation with Jacques Rancière.' *Diacritics* vol. 30, no. 2 (Summer 2000): 113–26.

Rimbaud, Arthur. *Complete Works, Selected Letters: A Bilingual Edition*. Translated by Wallace Fowlie. Chicago: University of Chicago Press, 2005.

Roberts, Jennifer Tolbert. *Athens on Trial: The Antidemocratic Tradition in Western Thought*. Princeton: Princeton University Press, 1994.

Robson, Mark. '"A literary animal": Rancière, Derrida, and the Literature of Democracy.' *Parallax* vol. 15, no. 3 (2009): 88–101.

Rockhill, Gabriel and Philip Watts (eds). *Jacques Rancière: History, Politics, Aesthetics*. Durham, NC, and London: Duke University Press Books, 2009.

Rosanvallon, Pierre. *Democracy Past and Future*. Edited by Samuel Moyn. New York: Columbia University Press, 2006.

Ross, Kristin. *May '68 and its Afterlives*. Chicago: University of Chicago Press, 2002.

Rousseau, Jean-Jacques. *The Discourses and Other Early Political Writings*. Edited and translated by Victor Gourevitch. Cambridge: Cambridge University Press, 2005.

Rousseau, Jean-Jacques. *The Social Contract*. Translated by Maurice Cranston. London: Penguin Books, 1968.

Rummens, Stefan. 'Deliberation Interrupted: Confronting Jürgen Habermas with Claude Lefort.' *Philosophy and Social Criticism* vol. 34, no. 4 (2008): 383–408.

Samaras, Thanassis. *Plato on Democracy*. New York: P. Lang, 2002.
Santas, Gerasimos. 'Plato's Criticism of the Democratic Man in the Republic.' *The Journal of Ethics* vol. 5 no. 1 (2001): 57–71.
Schaap, Andrew. 'Enacting the Right to Have Rights: Jacques Rancière's Critique of Hannah Arendt.' *European Journal of Political Theory* vol. 10, no. 1 (January 2011): 22–45.
Shapiro, Michael J. 'Radicalizing Democratic Theory: Social Space in Connolly, Deleuze and Rancière.' In *The New Pluralism: William Connolly and the Contemporary Global Condition*. Edited by David Campbell and Morton Schoolman. Durham: Duke University Press, 2008.
Schumpeter, Joseph A. *Capitalism, Socialism, and Democracy*. New York: Harper, 1950.
Schürmann, Reiner. *Heidegger on Being and Acting: From Principles to Anarchy*. Translated by Christine-Marie Gros. Bloomington: Indiana University Press, 1987.
Simons, Maarten and Jan Masschelein. 'Governmental, Political and Pedagogic Subjectivation: Foucault with Rancière.' *Educational Philosophy and Theory* vol. 42, no. 5/6 (2010): 588–605.
Spinoza, Baruch. *Political Treatise*. Translated by Samuel Shirley. Indianapolis: Hackett Publishing Company, 2001.
Spinoza, Baruch. *Theological-Political Treatise*. Translated by Samuel Shirley. Indianapolis: Hackett Publishing Company, 2001.
Springborg, Patricia. 'Karl Marx on Democracy, Participation, Voting, and Equality.' *Political Theory* vol. 12, no. 4 (November 1984): 537–56.
Steinmetz-Jenkins, Daniel. 'Claude Lefort and the Illegitimacy of Modernity.' *Journal for Cultural and Religious Theory* vol. 10, no. 1 (Winter 2009): 102–17.
Tambakaki, Paulina. 'When Does Politics Happen?' *Parallax* vol. 15, no. 3 (2009): 102–13.
Tanke, Joseph J. *Jacques Rancière: An Introduction*. London: Continuum International Publishers, 2011.
Thompson, E. P. 'The Moral Economy of the English Crowd in the Eighteenth Century.' *Past & Present* vol. 50, no. 1 (February 1971): 76–136.
Thoreau, Henry David. *The Essays of Henry D. Thoreau*. Edited by Lewis Hyde. New York: North Point Press, 2002.
Tocqueville, Alexis de. *Democracy in America*. Two volumes. Edited by Phillips Bradley. New York: Vintage Books, 1990.
Tønder, Lars and Lasse Thomassen (eds). *Radical Democracy: Politics between Abundance and Lack*. Manchester: Manchester University Press, 2005.
Vermeren, Patrice. 'Equality and Democracy.' *Diogenes* vol. 55, no. 4 (2008): 55–68.
Vamvacas, Constantine J. *The Founders of Western Thought: The Presocratics*. Dordrecht: Springer, 2009.

Weymans, Wim. 'Deepening Democracy through Contestation? Lefort and Gauchet on May 1968 and its Legacy.' *The Tocqueville Review* vol. 41, no. 1 (April 2020): 121–39.

Weymans, Wim. 'Defending Democracy's Symbolic Dimension: A Lefortian Critique of Arendt's Marxist Assumptions.' *Constellations* vol. 19, no. 1 (March 2012): 63–80.

Whitman, Walt. *Leaves of Grass*. Minneapolis: First Avenue Editions, 2015.

Wolfe, Katharine. 'From Aesthetics to Politics: Rancière, Kant and Deleuze.' *Contemporary Aesthetics* vol. 4 (2006).

Wolin, Sheldon S. 'Norm and Form: The Constitutionalizing of Democracy.' In *Athenian Political Thought and the Reconstruction of American Democracy*. Edited by J. Peter Euben, John R. Wallach and Josiah Ober. Ithaca: Cornell University Press, 1994.

Wolin, Sheldon S. *Politics and Vision: Continuity and Innovation in Western Political Thought*. Princeton: Princeton University Press, 2004.

Wood, Ellen Meiksins. *Democracy against Capitalism: Renewing Historical Materialism*. Cambridge: Cambridge University Press, 1995.

Žižek, Slavoj. *On Belief*. New York: Routledge, 2001.

Index

Abensour, M., 3–4, 6–9, 10, 12, 15, 16, 19, 20, 21, 30–33, 39, 41, 46, 50, 70, 72, 77, 78, 79–80, 81, 84, 86, 87, 88, 89, 93, 96–8, 100, 101, 102, 103, 104, 105, 106, 114, 115, 120, 132, 143, 149–68, 170–86, 195, 196, 197, 198, 201, 203, 204, 205
  on the allegory of the cave, 30–3
  on Clastres, 88, 151, 160–4, 176
  on critical political philosophy, 10, 14, 41, 79, 152–6, 158, 159, 184, 186, 197
  on emancipation, 4, 12, 19, 79, 80, 97, 98, 143, 150, 151, 152, 153, 154, 155, 158, 166–7, 172, 179–80, 184, 186, 196, 197
  on the Frankfurt School (critical theory), 150, 154, 155, 156
  on Hobbes, 88, 160–2, 163, 176
  on insurgent democracy, 12, 16, 151, 164, 179–83, 184, 203
  on Lefort, 150, 151, 153, 155, 156, 163–4, 167, 180, 183, 184; *see also* savage democracy (Lefort)
  on Machiavelli, 10, 79, 149, 150, 153, 155–6, 165–6 174, 179–80, 183–4; *see also* 'Machiavellian moment' (Pocock)
  on Marx, 149–50, 152, 154, 158, 160, 164–79, 180, 183–5, 186, 197
  on politics, 151, 153, 155, 163, 172, 178, 179–80, 184, 186, 196
  on Rancière, 153–4, 173–4
  on reduction, 149–50, 175–9, 186
  on savage democracy *see* savage democracy (Lefort)
  on the State, 12, 50, 86, 106, 115, 120, 149–50, 151–2, 153, 159, 160–86, 202, 204–5
  on State thought, 162–3, 164–5, 196
  on 'true' democracy, 149, 152, 160, 165, 166, 171–2, 173, 175, 176, 178, 179, 184, 185
  on utopia, 150, 152, 156–9, 160, 165
absolute spirit (Hegel), 163
absolutist State *see* State, the

abstract right, 168
abstract State *see* State, the
Adorno, T., 88
Aeschylus, 23
aesthetics (Rancière), 8, 128–9
   politics of, 129, 142
Agamemnon, 57
agon, 27, 39, 40, 61, 200
   agonistic stage/agonistic scene, 152, 181
aisthesis, 134; *see also* aesthetics (Rancière)
Alcaeus, 23
aletheia see truth
alienated labour, 168
alienation, 168; *see also* political alienation
allegory of the cave (Plato), 30–3, 54
allegory of the ship (Plato), 22–9, 32, 53, 66, 95, 200
Althusser, L., 7, 132, 165, 203
American Revolution, 165
anarchic condition, 22, 28, 32, 38–9, 41, 61, 65, 72, 96, 196
anarchic equality *see* equality
anarchic title *see* Rancière, J.
anarchism, 35, 49–50, 58, 185
anarchy/anarchic, 3, 21, 25, 46, 47, 48, 61, 65, 70, 71, 72–3, 95–8, 106, 173, 200, 201; *see also* anarchic condition
Anaximander, 57
ancien régime, 81, 85, 91, 92, 93, 103, 105, 167, 181; *see also* monarchy
ancient democracy *see* democracy
anthropology, 82–3, 84, 160–4
anti-austerity movements, 205
antinomies of politics, 4–5, 6, 9, 12, 15, 21, 27, 45, 77, 80–1, 84, 102, 104, 105, 107, 114–15, 116–17, 140, 151, 152, 182, 185–6, 195, 198, 199, 204, 205

anti-politics, 29
Arab Spring, 205
archê, 29, 39, 47–8, 49, 89, 96, 140, 173, 200
   commandment and commencement, 54–8, 71
   democracy's challenge to, 12, 21–2, 41, 45, 46–7, 53, 60–73, 82, 114, 200–2
   logic of, 29, 45, 47, 49, 50, 52, 54–6, 58, 59–60, 61–2, 63, 69–70, 71, 72, 201
   and Plato, 26–7, 28, 32, 41, 45, 46–7, 50–60, 61, 62–3, 65, 66, 71–2, 200–1
   and the police, 50, 126
   Presocratic conception, 57
   and the State, 50, 173
   verification theory, 54–8
   see also Arendt, H.
   see also Rancière, J.
Arendt, H., 6, 14, 20–1, 64, 79, 99, 130, 150, 154, 155, 156, 181, 183
   on the allegory of the cave, 30–3, 54
   on the archê, 45, 46–7, 49, 56–7, 58, 69, 71
   on political freedom, 35
   on political philosophy, 12, 20–1, 30, 33–4, 38–9, 41, 153, 186, 196, 199
   on politics, 5, 20, 30, 34, 35, 37, 38, 40, 58, 199
   on revolution, 56–7
Aristotle, 36, 154, 155
   Constitution of Athens, 1–2, 15, 130–1, 135
'art of government' (Foucault), 123; *see also* Foucault, M.
assembly *see* ecclesia
Athenian democracy, 1–3, 23, 25, 35–7, 66–7
Athenian reforms *see* Cleisthenes
Athens, 1–3, 13, 15, 23, 67, 202

Augustine, 166
authoritarian/authoritarianism, 31, 158, 184
authoritarian State (Abensour) *see* State, the
authority, 4, 5, 15, 19, 24, 25, 27–8, 31, 33–4, 35, 39, 40, 41, 49–50, 51, 59, 62, 72, 81, 83, 85, 92–3, 94, 95, 116, 118, 122, 124, 125, 153, 154, 160, 162–4, 169, 198
autonomy, 29, 72, 178, 185, 196
autonomy of the political, 152, 167, 178

Badiou, A., 143n8
battle of Salamis, 23
being-against *see* democracy
being-together (Arendt), 19, 30, 181
Benjamin, W., 157
Bergson, H., 13, 174
biopower (Foucault) *see* Foucault, M.
bios theorètikos/bios politikos (Arendt), 30
Black Lives Matter, 205
Blanqui, A., 138
Bloch, E., 157
Bodin, J., 95
boule, 2, 63
Buber, M., 157
bureaucracy, 8, 20, 85, 94, 122, 169

capital/capitalism, 6, 7, 15, 55, 79, 101, 115, 132, 168, 177
Castoriadis, C., 5, 27–8, 29–30, 33, 37, 39, 72, 115, 130, 177, 184, 196, 199–200
Chomsky, N., 49–50
Christian State *see* State, the
Christians, 121
citizen(s), 30, 35, 36, 40, 59, 135, 166

city *see* polis
civil society, 120, 168–70, 178
class (economic), 1, 35, 40, 46, 47, 55, 58, 65, 66–8, 134, 137, 139, 155–6, 173, 194; *see also* working class (proletariat)
class struggle, 132, 156
Clastres, P., 88, 151, 168, 174, 183, 205
   on Hobbes, 160–4
   Society Against the State, 82–4, 176
Cleisthenes, 1–2, 66–7
Cleomenes, 2
coercion, 40, 50, 125, 162, 163
Cohn-Bendit, D., 138
colonialism, 6, 72
communism, 176
concept *see* philosophy
'conditions of no-rule' (Arendt), 35
conflict, 4, 8, 9, 11, 38, 80, 92–3, 102, 129, 131, 132, 135, 149, 150, 151, 152, 155–6, 161, 166, 172, 174, 178, 179, 181, 182, 184, 185, 186, 199, 202
constitution(s), 2, 3, 8, 22, 24, 27, 36–7, 39, 41, 61, 73, 170–1, 175–7
constitution of the demos, 175–6
constitution of the social, 166, 170, 172, 204
constitutionalisation (Wolin), 115
contestation, 4, 9, 39, 80, 81, 84, 99, 101–3, 105, 182, 199
contingency of the social, 5, 47, 48, 50, 60, 61, 63–5, 67, 70, 72, 85, 133, 200, 201, 203; *see also* indeterminacy
contract theory, 69, 161, 172
convention, 5, 60, 63, 64, 201
critical political philosophy *see* Abensour, M.

critical theory *see* Frankfurt School
critique, 14–15, 19–22, 78–80,
　87–8, 105, 106, 142, 152–4,
　156, 158, 196, 197, 205
Croce, B., 155

deconstruction, 14
defiance, 1, 2, 4, 5, 9, 80, 81, 84,
　101, 116, 205
Deleuze, G., 67, 86
　on institutions, 183
　on philosophy, 13–14, 78, 79,
　　106, 197, 198
　on State thought, 162–3, 164–5
　on utopia, 158
deliberation (political), 5, 35, 46,
　66, 68, 69, 199
democracy,
　act of a subject, 133, 140, 195,
　　203; *see also* political subject
　　(political body)
　against the archê, 12, 21–2, 41,
　　45, 46–7, 53, 60–73, 82, 114,
　　200–2
　against monarchy (*ancien
　　régime*), 6, 80, 81, 84–5, 92–3,
　　103, 104–5, 175, 181, 198
　against the police, 12, 115,
　　116–17, 118, 130, 133–6,
　　140, 141–2, 202
　against the State, 12, 115,
　　149–50, 151–2, 167, 172–83,
　　184–5, 202
　ancient, 11, 27, 36–7, 48, 78,
　　115, 135, 136, 201, 202
　ancient versus modern, 114–15,
　　135–6, 202
　being-against, 6, 9, 11, 12, 61,
　　71, 81–4, 93, 103–4, 107,
　　114–15, 116, 117, 120, 132,
　　140, 150, 152, 162, 175,
　　185–6, 200, 202, 203; *see also*
　　antinomies of politics
　critical function, 19–20, 41, 197,
　　205
　definition, 84
　denaturing of power, 48, 201
　domesticated, 4, 7, 15, 79–80,
　　89, 94, 99, 104, 198–9
　and emancipation, 2, 4, 6, 8,
　　78, 80, 81, 84, 105, 117,
　　134, 142–3, 150, 151, 153,
　　184, 195, 199
　and institutions, 15–16, 27, 37,
　　61, 82, 182–3, 203–4
　insurgent *see* Abensour, M.
　lack of foundation, 12, 21–2, 26,
　　39, 40, 47, 61, 70, 73, 81, 200,
　　201; *see also* anarchic condition
　legitimacy, 70
　modern, 77, 80, 84–5, 92–3, 103,
　　105, 135–6, 151–2, 175, 202
　new ontology, 39, 93
　as 'political' or 'anarchic'
　　government *see* Rancière, J
　radical, 16, 97
　savage *see* savage democracy
　　(Lefort)
　struggle over language, 7–8
　see also Athenian democracy
　see also power of the people
　　(*kratos* of the demos)
'democratic man' *see* Plato
democratic government, 61, 66
democratic institutions *see*
　democracy
democratic revolution *see*
　Tocqueville, A. de
democratisation, 1, 2–3, 9–10, 15,
　19, 81, 84, 101, 103, 105–6,
　107, 133, 142, 143, 150, 153,
　178, 182, 186, 195, 204
demos, the, 1–2, 5, 9, 16, 24–5,
　27, 32, 40, 46, 53, 60, 62, 66,
　67, 68, 84, 102, 107, 115,
　116, 130, 135, 136, 140, 149,
　151, 153, 154, 166, 170–7,
　178, 179, 180–1, 183, 185,
　195, 201, 202, 203, 204–5
　'the whole demos' (Marx) *see*
　　Marx, K.
　see also political subject

demystification, 78, 106, 197
Descartes, R., 13
devolution, 175
dialectic of emancipation (Abensour), 158
disagreement (Rancière) *see* Rancière, J.
dissensus (Rancière) *see* Rancière, J.
distribution of the sensible, the (Rancière) *see* Rancière, J.
divine right/divine law, 27, 65
doxa, 13, 27, 30, 31–2, 33, 39, 40, 54, 61, 200

ecclesia (assembly), 2, 27
economics, 119, 167
education/pedagogy, 8, 53, 69, 119, 125
emancipation, 4, 8, 10, 12, 19, 79, 80, 117, 132, 134, 142–3, 150, 151, 152, 153, 154, 155, 158, 172, 179, 184, 186, 195, 196, 197, 199, 205
  see also Abensour, M.
  see also Rancière, J.
emancipatory political act *see* savage democracy (Lefort)
Engels, F., 161
English Civil War, 95
epistemology, 13, 32, 33, 85
equality, 13, 19, 24–5, 47, 58, 65, 67–9, 70, 71, 82, 92, 94, 100, 101–2, 117, 132, 133, 134, 136, 137, 140, 141, 142, 166, 173, 186, 197, 201, 202
  anarchic equality, 13, 15, 45, 71, 82, 173, 200, 202
  see also Rancière, J.
état de droit, 92, 105
'ethical life' (Hegel), 168
ethics, 120
event, the, 142–3, 97
exclusion (modes of), 2, 3, 4, 9, 19, 81, 84, 105, 127, 163, 186
exploitation, 11, 154

family, 10, 51, 121, 122, 136, 168–70
Ferguson, A., 95
fetishism, 177
feudalism, 121, 122, 168
Feuerbach, L., 168
Finley, M., 25, 41n2
Forms, the *see* Plato
Foucault, M., 34, 115–16, 128, 132, 141, 186
  on biopower, 122
  on governmentality, 119–24
  on the police, 121–5, 126
  on population, 121, 122, 123
  on the State, 120, 174
Frankfurt School (critical theory), 150, 154, 155, 156
freedom (liberty), 25, 56, 93, 94, 98–9, 151, 153, 156, 157, 179, 183; *see also* political freedom (political liberty)
French Revolution, 3, 12, 78, 90–1, 92, 96, 137, 167, 181, 198
future, 14, 15, 103, 156, 157, 182, 197, 205

Gauchet, M., 151, 185
gender, 134, 138
German revolution, 180
Godwin, W., 174
Gouges, Olympe de, 137–8
government, 7, 8, 9–10, 12, 26, 28, 31, 33, 34, 35, 36–7, 40, 47–50, 53, 55, 57, 58, 59–60, 61, 62, 63–4, 66, 67–8, 69, 70–1, 72, 91, 96, 105, 115, 119–24, 125, 128, 129, 130, 132, 141, 166, 169, 173–4, 184, 186, 196, 198, 199
  'political' or 'anarchic' government *see* democracy
  see also democratic government
  see also Foucault, M.
government of the sensible *see* police, the

governmentality (Foucault) *see* Foucault, M.
Gramsci, A., 129, 165
Gulabi Gang (India), 205

Habermas, J., 130
Harrington, J., 165
Hegel, G. W. F., 122, 149, 162–3, 164, 165, 180, 196
  on popular sovereignty, 95, 170
  on the State, 168–9, 170, 174, 176
hegemony, 15, 31
'here and now' (*hic et nunc*), 10, 11, 79, 87–8, 104, 106, 153, 156, 158, 183, 197, 205
hermeneutics, 11, 87–8
heteronomy, 115, 130, 178
hierarchy/hierarchical, 3, 26, 49, 52–3, 60, 64, 65, 72, 82, 126, 162, 173, 186, 200, 201
Hippias, 1
Hobbes, T., 6, 26, 34, 88, 162, 163, 196
  on democracy, 95
  on human nature, 121, 160
  on the State, 160–1, 169, 176
Holocaust, the, 139
Homer, 57
hope, 14, 103, 157, 197
human(s)/man, 68, 100, 121, 123, 140, 160, 161, 166, 170, 171, 176; *see also* political animal (Aristotle)
'human emancipation' (Marx), 166–7
human rights *see* rights
humanist/humanism, 132, 165, 166
Hume, D., 183
Hungarian revolution, 180

idealism/idealist philosophy, 168, 190n54
identity, 132, 139–40
identity politics, 139
ideology, 87

Idle No More, 205
ignorance/ignorant man, 27, 51, 52, 53, 66
  ignorant schoolmaster (Rancière), 69
immigrants, 205
indeterminacy, 26, 39, 61, 62, 65, 66, 68, 70, 72, 73, 77, 85, 93, 100, 102, 103, 135, 136, 140, 180, 198, 200, 201
Indigenous peoples, 161
inequality, 4, 19, 60, 65, 84, 93, 143, 173, 201
institutions, 3, 7, 15–16, 19, 27, 51, 60, 61, 64, 72, 82, 84, 90, 93, 100, 105, 115, 118, 126, 129, 140, 160, 161, 168, 178, 182–3, 184, 186, 194, 195, 199, 201, 203–4
  democratic *see* democracy
  and laws, 183
insurgent democracy *see* Abensour, M.
interpretation *see* hermeneutics
Iran, 205
Isagoras, 1–2
isonomia, 35

Jacobins, 137
James, H., 194–5
Jew (political name), 138–9
justice, 13, 27, 28, 39, 54, 65, 85, 125, 131, 157, 161

Kant, I., 4, 168
  on aesthetics, 146n54
  on revolution, 110n34
Kantorowicz, E., 92
Keane, J., 48–9, 60, 75n36, 201
king *see* monarchy

La Boétie, É. de, 173
Laclau, E., 9, 68
language, 130–1, 134, 137
  political, 7
  see also logos

law(s), 5, 31, 39, 40, 54, 85, 92, 93, 123, 125, 130, 131, 156, 161, 163, 183, 184, 199; see also rule of law
Lefort, C., 3–4, 6–9, 10, 12, 14, 15, 20, 21, 46, 60, 68, 72, 77–81, 84–94, 96–107, 114, 129, 135–6, 143, 149, 150–1, 152, 154, 155, 156, 165, 167, 170, 175, 180, 183, 184, 195, 197, 198, 200, 202
  on ancient and modern democracy, 135–6
  on Clastres, 84, 163
  on contestation, 38, 81, 84, 99, 101–3, 105–6
  on the democratic form of society, 88, 99–100, 184
  on hermeneutics, 11, 87–8
  on indeterminacy, 3, 68, 73, 77–8, 85, 86, 93, 100, 102, 103, 135, 136, 140, 198, 200
  on Machiavelli, 10, 11, 87, 153, 155–6
  on mastery, 85, 96–7
  on philosophy, 77–8, 197
  on politics, 38, 129
  on rights, 98–101, 140, 163–4
  on the State, 163–4
  on Tocqueville, 81, 90–2, 93–4, 99, 103, 105–6
  see also savage democracy (Lefort)
legislation, 66, 175
Leibniz, G., 13
Lenin, V., 90, 185
Leroux, P., 157
Levinas, E., 157, 173
Levi-Strauss, C., 109n25, 162
liberal democracy, 16, 104
Livy, 137
logos, 128, 130–1, 142
lot (sortition), 62–3, 65, 66

Machiavelli, N., 149, 150, 156, 174, 179, 183–4, 205
  literature critical of, 122–3
  and political critique, 10, 11, 79, 87, 153, 155–6
  on political liberty, 155
  republicanism, 165–6
  see also Abensour, M.
  see also Lefort, C.
  see also 'Machiavellian moment'
'Machiavellian moment' (Pocock), 152, 165–6, 167, 172, 183–4
Madison, J., 95
Marx, K., 6, 7, 20, 79, 99, 139, 149–50, 152, 158, 164–79, 180, 184, 186
  Economic and Philosophic Manuscripts, 167, 168
  materialist conception of history, 156
  Theses on Feuerbach, 14, 154, 197
  on Hegel, 169–72
  on the State, 164–72, 177, 180, 184–5
  on 'the whole demos', 170–1, 172, 173–4, 177
  on 'true' democracy, 149, 152, 165, 166, 171–2, 175, 179, 185; see also Abensour, M.
  see also political alienation
Marxist/Marxism, 20, 85, 94, 106, 132, 154, 165
mastery see Lefort, C.
May '68, 3, 20, 78, 90, 94, 96, 138, 180, 198
means of production, 10, 55
Meier, C., 5, 21, 35–7, 40, 199
mercantilism, 122
Merleau-Ponty, M., 88–9, 183
minority, 11, 84, 102, 135, 139
modern democracy see democracy
modern State see State, the
modes of domination see social domination

monarchy, 6, 45, 46, 59, 72, 80, 92–3, 103, 105, 167, 170–2, 174, 175, 176–7, 184, 194, 198
   constitutional monarchy, 168
morality, 121, 166, 168
More, T., 158, 160; see also utopia
Morris, W., 157
Mouffe, C., 9, 42n18
Muslims, 205

Nancy, J.-L., 72–3
nation state see State, the
natural law, 52, 54
nature, 16, 39, 48, 51, 52–4, 56, 59, 61, 63–5, 66, 72, 101, 121, 199; see also state of nature
neoliberalism, 125
neo-utopianism, 157
new utopian spirit (Abensour) see utopia
Nietzsche, F., 13–14, 78–9, 103, 157, 197, 205
nomos see law

Occupy Wall Street, 205
Odysseus, 57
Old Oligarch, 3
oligarchy, 5, 6, 9, 24, 36, 45, 46, 55, 72, 82
ontology/ontological, 23, 26, 29, 39, 73, 81, 85, 88–9, 92, 93, 105, 136, 155, 174
   closure, 39, 89, 130
opinion see doxa
originary division of the social, 93, 102, 155–6, 179
Other, the (heteron), 139–40

Paris Commune, 167, 180, 184–5
participation/participatory, 4, 9, 12, 15, 19, 23, 35, 36, 63, 80, 103, 131, 151, 159, 166, 195, 199
patriarchy, 6, 72

PCF (French Communist Party), 7
pedagogy see education
people, the see demos, the
people of colour, 116, 134, 135
perception, 116, 127–30, 133, 134, 141, 202, 204
   democratisation of, 133, 142
Pericles, 1
permanent contestation see contestation
phenomenology/phenomenological, 85, 88–9
   political, 34, 38, 199
philosophy, 12, 13–14, 20, 39, 77–80, 106, 152–4, 196–7, 205
   political use, 78–9, 184, 197
   see also political philosophy
phônê, 128, 131
phusis see nature
Plato, 6, 13, 15, 36, 39, 48, 64, 68, 73, 82, 89, 95
   and the archê, 26–7, 28, 29, 32, 41, 45, 46–7, 50–60, 61, 62–3, 65, 66, 71–2, 200–1
   on 'democratic man', 23, 24–5, 26, 28, 53
   and the Forms, 13, 30–1, 32–3, 34, 53–4
   moral psychology, 24–5
   and political philosophy, 12, 20, 21, 22–34, 41, 57, 58, 79, 125, 154, 162, 163, 196
   and politics, 26–7, 28–30, 31–2, 33, 34, 39–40, 41, 54, 125, 196, 200
   see also allegory of the cave (Plato); allegory of the ship (Plato)
pleb (political name), 137
Plutarch, 4
Pocock, J. G. A., 152, 165; see also 'Machiavellian moment'
polemics, 27, 37, 44n47, 71, 79, 129, 178, 195, 196, 199

police, the, 50, 139, 140, 153, 169, 173–4, 186, 204, 205
  democracy's challenge to, 12, 115, 116–17, 118, 130, 133–6, 140, 141–2, 202
  Foucault's concept of, 119, 121–4
  and politics, 117–18, 132, 134–5
  Rancière's concept of, 115–19, 120, 124–30, 141, 143
  as regime of representation/government of the sensible, 116, 127–30, 131, 134, 141, 204
  and saturation, 126–7, 129, 134
polis, 5, 12, 21, 27, 30, 31, 34–8, 39, 40–1, 46, 56, 58, 59, 60–1, 66–7, 71, 72, 130, 199–200, 201
politeia see political community
political agency, 3, 9, 140, 195
political alienation, 149, 168, 177–8, 186, 204
'political' or 'anarchic' government see democracy
political animal (Aristotle), 130
political community, 35, 37, 38, 69, 131, 181
political freedom (political liberty), 35, 154–5, 181, 185; see also Arendt, H.
political names, 136–40
political objectification, 175, 176
political philosophy, 10, 14–15, 39, 41, 78–80, 87–8, 91, 105, 106, 153–4, 196–7, 205
  critical political philosophy see Abensour, M.
  tradition of, 3, 12, 13, 20–1, 26, 29–30, 33, 34, 35, 38, 41, 45–6, 57, 58, 79, 125, 153–4, 160, 162–3, 186, 196, 199
  see also philosophy
political society, 40, 54, 103, 172, 200

political subject (political body), 12, 36, 68, 115, 116–17, 126, 130–40, 171, 173, 181, 186, 195, 202–3, 204
  see also demos, the
  see also Rancière, J.
politicisation, 5, 36, 40, 138, 177, 178, 199, 200
politics, 5, 11, 12, 20–1, 26, 27–8, 29, 30, 32, 33–4, 37–8, 39, 40–1, 47, 54, 56, 58, 59, 60–1, 64–5, 67, 68, 70, 71, 72, 79, 102, 117–18, 129, 130, 131, 132, 133, 135, 153, 155, 166, 172, 173, 178, 179, 184, 186, 199–200, 201, 205
  Greek invention of, 35–7, 40, 199–200
  see also Abensour, M.
  see also Lefort, C.
  see also Rancière, J.
politike techne (Protagoras), 68–9
Polybius, 95
poor, the, 9, 25, 40, 68, 135, 139, 142, 203
Popper, K., 174
popular sovereignty, 95, 170
population, 121, 122, 123
populism, 205
post-Marxist, 7
power, 3, 5, 35, 48, 49, 56, 60, 83, 92, 93, 117, 128, 135, 151, 153, 201
  as an empty place, 135
  power of the people (*kratos* of the demos), 4, 19, 46, 67, 72, 104, 136, 196, 201–2
power relations, 5, 117, 139
praxis (Arendt), 56, 57
Presocratic philosophy, 57
primitive societies see tribal societies
principality, 123, 155
'principle of anarchy' (Schürmann), 97–8, 106, 132, 203

proletarian (political name), 138
Protagoras, 68–9, 71
public health, 120, 121, 122, 123
public sphere/public realm/public space, 30, 34, 35, 56, 129, 135, 150, 152, 179, 181, 185, 202

race/racial inequities, 134, 136
radical democracy *see* democracy
Rancière, J., 5, 6–9, 10, 11, 12, 15–16, 20, 21, 23–9, 32, 33, 38, 39, 40, 45, 46–7, 49–60, 61–73, 79, 80, 86, 100, 101–2, 104, 114–19, 120, 121, 124–43, 149, 150, 152, 153–4, 173–4, 185–6, 195, 196, 201, 202–3, 204, 205
  on the allegory of the ship, 23–9, 32
  on the anarchic title, 47, 61–3, 66, 67, 68, 69–70, 71, 173, 201
  on ancient and modern democracy, 135–6
  on disagreement, 38, 101, 102, 131, 132, 135, 137, 142
  on dissensus, 4, 9, 38, 71, 116, 118, 133, 134, 135, 203
  on the distribution of the sensible, 101, 126–7, 128, 129, 131, 133, 134, 141
  on emancipation, 117, 132, 134, 142–3, 150, 153
  on equality, 65, 67–8, 69, 70, 71, 100, 101–2, 117, 132, 133, 134, 136, 137, 140, 141, 173, 186, 201, 202
  on *logos*, 128, 130–1, 142
  on the police, 12, 50, 115–19, 120, 121, 124–36, 139–43
  on 'political' or 'anarchic' government, 47, 67–8, 69, 70, 132
  on political philosophy, 26–7, 29, 39, 79, 125, 153–4, 186, 196
  on political subjectivation, 12, 68, 115, 116–17, 126, 130–40, 173, 186, 202–3
  on politics, 38, 117–18, 129, 131, 132, 140, 186
  on wrong, 134, 203
'rational State' (Marx), 167
recognition, 137, 139
Reformation, 121
refugees, 205
regime of representation *see* police, the
reification, 175, 177, 204
republic, 125, 137, 155
republicanism/republican tradition, 165–7, 172
revolution, 56–7, 90–1, 94, 181
Rheinische Zeitung, 165, 167
rights, 11, 98–101, 137, 138, 140, 163–4, 197
rights of man, 8,
right-wing nationalism, 205
Rimbaud, A., 131
Rome, 137, 155, 156
Rousseau, J. -J., 14, 150, 170, 172, 176, 181
Rosanvallon, P., 178
rule of law, 8, 16, 51, 105
Rushdie, S., 98
Russian Revolution, 90

savage democracy (Lefort), 3–4, 12, 16, 77, 84–94, 99–107
  Abensour's reading of, 77, 78, 80–1, 84, 86, 87, 96–8, 100, 105, 106, 150, 156, 159, 160, 164, 198
  and democratic revolution, 81, 90–2, 93–4, 99, 103, 105–6
  as emancipatory political act, 4, 78, 81, 96–9, 100, 103, 106
  as essence of democracy, 85–6, 89–90, 106
  as exercise of thought, 78, 80–1, 84–5, 86–7, 103–5, 106–7, 198–9

and insurgent democracy, 180
as 'libertarian idea' of democracy, 84, 96–7
and May '68, 3, 78, 90, 94, 96, 198
and Merleau-Ponty, 88–9
and permanent contestation, 81, 99, 101–3, 105–6
and rights, 99–101
Schmitt, C., 34
Schumpeter, J., 38
Schürmann, R., 97–8, 106; *see also* 'principle of anarchy'
secession of the plebeians, 137
self-determination, 149, 151, 152, 166, 170–1, 176, 181, 185
social, the, 10, 31, 47–8, 53, 55, 59, 64, 65, 66, 71, 72, 102, 103, 116, 117, 124, 128, 130, 140, 141, 142, 155–6, 169–70, 173, 178, 199, 200
and the political, 5, 64–5, 102
see also constitution of the social
see also contingency of the social
social democracy, 16, 104
social domination, 6, 10, 11, 79, 81, 84, 93, 98, 105, 132, 142–3, 153, 154, 155, 205
Socrates, 29
in the *Republic*, 22–3
Solon, 1, 2
sophists, 29
soul, 24–5, 53
sovereignty, 12, 20, 30, 34, 78, 85, 95, 119, 125, 155, 161, 164, 170, 172, 186, 199; *see also* popular sovereignty
Spanish Civil War, 180
Spinoza, B., 50, 151, 166, 171
spontaneity, 2, 80, 90, 94, 96–8, 106, 132, 172, 174, 180, 183, 203

State, the, 7, 9, 10, 12, 15, 20, 34, 78, 79, 82–3, 85, 99, 118, 119–20, 121, 122, 123–4, 125, 142, 153, 160–72, 173–9, 180–2, 183, 184–5, 186, 196, 199, 202, 204–5
absolutist State, 26, 119, 120, 122
abstract State, 165, 173, 175, 177
apparatus, 120, 176, 178
authoritarian State (Abensour), 184
Christian State, 167
democracy's challenge to, 12, 115, 149–50, 151–2, 167, 172–83, 184–5, 202
democratic State, 179
modern State, 168, 171, 184
reduction of see Abensour, M.
State-form, 50, 83, 151, 152, 164, 172, 174–5, 177, 179, 185, 196
see also totalitarian/totalitarianism
state of nature, 88, 161
State thought, 162–3, 164–5, 196
statistics, 122
Strauss, L., 155
subject *see* political subject (political body)
symbolic/symbolic order, the, 77, 85, 88, 90, 92, 99–100, 116, 128, 129, 131, 132, 133, 135, 136, 140, 141, 163, 167, 170, 175, 202
constitution of society, 127–30, 134, 204
Lefort versus Rancière, 129

telos/teleological, 24, 97, 169
theological–political, 167
theology/theological, 166
Thompson, E. P., 101
time, 14, 48, 55, 58, 70, 78, 98, 103, 158, 181–2, 197

timocracy, 24
Tocqueville, A. de, 5–6, 23, 60, 92, 95, 179
   democratic revolution, 81, 90–2, 93–4, 99, 103, 105–6
totalitarian/totalitarianism, 5, 8, 15, 20, 30, 35, 38, 80, 85, 93, 103, 105, 125, 129, 143, 157, 174, 184, 198
   anti-totalitarian, 7
tradition of political philosophy *see* political philosophy
tribal societies, 82–3, 161–2, 163, 183
Trotskyism, 7, 90
'true' democracy *see* Marx, K.
Trump, D., 205
truth, 27, 31, 33, 39, 48, 64, 171, 179, 185, 200
tyranny, 1, 24, 31, 35, 183

untimely, the *see* Nietzsche, F.
utopia, 156–9, 160, 165
   critical function, 157
   and democracy, 159
   new utopian spirit (Abensour), 157–8
   as thinking against, 158–9
   see also Abensour, M.
utopian socialism, 157

vita activa, 166

war, 40, 88, 161–2
'war of position' (Gramsci), 129
Weber, M., 182
Whitman, W., 16
'the whole demos' (Marx) *see* Marx, K.
wild being (Merleau-Ponty) *see* Merleau-Ponty, M.
Wolin, S., 2–3, 36, 175
   fugitive democracy, 3, 115
woman (political name), 137–8
Wood, E., 115
working class (proletariat), 8, 101, 132, 134, 138, 139, 140, 168
wrong (Rancière) *see* Rancière, J.

Yellow Vest protests (France), 205

Žižek, S., 7